STRATEGIC CONTROL

ESTABLISHING MILESTONES FOR LONG-TERM PERFORMANCE

STRATEGIC CONTROL

ESTABLISHING MILESTONES
FOR LONG-TERM PERFORMANCE

MICHAEL GOOLD
WITH
JOHN J. QUINN

The
Economist
Books

INTERNATIONAL MANAGEMENT SERIES

▲
▼▼

Addison-Wesley Publishing Company

Reading, Massachusetts   Menlo Park, California   New York
Don Mills, Ontario   Wokingham, England   Amsterdam   Bonn
Sydney   Singapore   Tokyo   Madrid   San Juan
Paris   Seoul   Milan   Mexico City   Taipei

Ashridge

Library of Congress Cataloging-in-Publication Data

Goold, Michael.
    Strategic control : establishing milestones for long-term
performance / Michael Goold with John J. Quinn.
       p. cm.
    Includes index.
    ISBN 0-201-60899-5
    1. Strategic planning. I. Quinn, John J. II. Title.
HD30.28.G664 1993
658.4'012—dc20   93-4023
                                      CIP

First published in Great Britain by Hutchinson Business
Books Limited, an imprint of Random Century Limited

Jacket design, by One Plus One Studio

1 2 3 4 5 6 7 8 9-MA-96959493
First printing, August 1993

Addison-Wesley books are available at special discounts for
bulk purchases. For more information, please contact:

Special Markets Department
Addison-Wesley Publishing Company
Reading, MA 01867
(617) 944-3700 × 2431

Contents

Acknowledgements

The mission of the Ashridge Strategic Management Centre is "to research the roles of the corporate headquarters and division levels in multi-business companies and to produce results that will improve the strategic management process", and our work on the strategic control process has been a major component of the Centre's research programme since its founding in November 1987. During this time we have received valuable advice and encouragement from the Ashridge Strategic Management Centre's member companies (BOC Group, British Petroleum Co., Courtaulds, Digital Equipment Co., Grand Metropolitan, ICI, Lloyds Bank, Shell International Petroleum Co. and United Biscuits) and, in particular, from their representatives on our Research Committee. We are grateful for their support, without which this work would not have been completed. The contributions of Guy Jillings, Alan Pink and Paul Vaight were specially helpful in shaping our thinking.

We would also like to thank the Boston Consulting Group, who sponsored the research, providing both intellectual and financial assistance to us. Stephen Bungay, David Hall and Barry Jones were particularly active members of the BCG case team on the project. Their ideas and experience have improved the book in many places.

We owe a considerable debt to the companies that agreed to discuss their strategic control processes with us, and particularly to the 18 companies described in Chapters 3 and 4. Without their cooperation, our work would not have been possible.

The final shape and expression of the book benefited greatly from the work of Nancy Jackson, who assisted us with writing up conclusions, and from the advice of Carolyn White at The Economist Books.

At Ashridge, Philip Sadler provided a valuable critique of a first draft of the book, and Andrew Campbell has been closely involved in challenging and refining our conclusions throughout the project. Lastly, we are very grateful to Siân Turner, Juliet Venter and Sally Yeung, who converted illegible drafts into final form, with scarcely a complaint about the innumerable revisions along the way.

CHAPTER 1

STRATEGIC CONTROL:
THE KEY ISSUES

"We spend a lot of time on our budget planning process. But we don't agree specific profit targets or get written reports on whether businesses are meeting their budgets." Any chief executive who made such an assertion would be regarded as eccentric and, probably, incompetent. How could it be worth spending time on preparing a budget if no explicit agreement on profit targets was reached? What value would the budget have if there was no formal monitoring of actual results? Budgetary planning without budgetary control would lack the teeth to make things happen. Yet, in company after company, we find businesses with strategic planning processes that do not lead to any clear agreement on strategic objectives, or to any systematic monitoring of whether the businesses are on track with their strategies. Small wonder, then, if many senior managers complain that strategic planning is a waste of time, and that strategic plans never get implemented.

Research that we have carried out with over 50 companies in the UK, the USA, Europe and Japan has convinced us that, for strategic planning to be worthwhile, companies must establish some form of strategic control process. Strategic control should concentrate on targets that measure strategic progress, just as budgetary control focuses on annual profit targets. The strategic control process should ensure that there is a clear agreement on the strategic targets that businesses are pursuing and a means of monitoring achievements against them. It should also provide incentives for business managers who achieve their targets, and should prompt central intervention where necessary to close gaps between planned and actual results. Without a strategic control process, strategic plans too often remain vague about their specific implications, and even good strategies can too easily be blown off course.

WHY STRATEGIC CONTROL IS NEEDED

Not long ago, the chief executive officer of a large corporation told us a story that captures the fundamental problems associated with a lack of strategic control. Three years earlier, the head of one of his subsidiaries had convinced corporate headquarters that an acquisition should be made. The proposal had been justified on the grounds that it would allow rationalization and cost-savings, and would offset a price war that was expected to break out among competitors in the business. In the event, prices held up better than anticipated, allowing post-acquisition profits to exceed the initial forecasts. Partly as a consequence, however, the subsidiary's management did not push aggressively for rationalization.

After two years, prices finally fell sharply, causing the new acquisition to plunge into losses. A crash programme to implement the original rationalization programme was put in hand, but, against the background of intensified competition and a falling market, it could not be completed soon enough to prevent a severe dent in the published corporate results.

"I really wish I had been able to push the business into rationalization earlier," maintained the chief executive. "But we lacked a specific agreement on how much progress would be made with rationalization by what date. They claimed their strategy was in great shape and, since their profits were ahead of budget, I found it hard to disagree and put pressure on them."

Most companies have made mistakes of this sort at one time or another. Yet even after such experiences, few companies have specified clear strategic goals or objectives;[1] instead they continue to rely on profit objectives as the main basis for control.

Managers of any business, whatever its size, ought to have a clear idea of the objectives by which they will measure strategic progress. But the need for strategic control becomes much more pressing in the setting of a multi-business company. It is inextricably linked with the issue of decentralization.

The essence of decentralization is to locate primary responsibility for proposing strategy and achieving results with the general managers of individual profit centres or businesses, not with central management.[2] The purpose is to ensure that strategies are based on detailed knowledge of specific product-markets, to increase business level "ownership" of strategy, and to reduce the overload on the chief executive and top management team. All this is desirable. But decentralization can work well only if two basic conditions are fulfilled.

1. Central management must be able to determine whether the businesses are succeeding with their strategies. Unless the centre knows when it does need to intervene, decentralization of responsibility

becomes abdication of responsibility. To deal with this problem, Imperial Chemical Industries (ICI) has introduced a much more explicit and structured strategic control process in recent years. As we were told by a senior corporate manager: "It isn't a change in principle from past practice. But, previously, although it was all there, it was in very woolly, motherhood sort of terms. You couldn't look at a business and see if it was really on track or not."

2. Business heads must know what top management will count as good performance. Without clear goals, the whole concept of decentralized responsibility suffers, since the conditions under which a business can expect to operate free from corporate pressures are ill-defined. Central interventions are then liable to be seen as arbitrary and capricious. A typical comment, drawn from an interview with a business manager, was: "It's never really clear what they [the corporate centre] will count as good performance. You have a reasonable idea of it, and one can begin to interpret the feedback. But you don't quite know until you've reached the end of the road whether what you're doing will prove acceptable." Such ambiguity can fatally reduce the motivation of managers and damage the relationship between the businesses and the centre.

Unfortunately few companies yet meet both these conditions satisfactorily, since effective strategic control processes are rare.

STRATEGIC CONTROL AS A BALANCE TO FINANCIAL CONTROL

The importance of the corporate control process has been widely recognized, at least in so far as almost all large companies now have budgetary control systems.[3] For the vast majority of companies, budgetary control is a well-established and understood part of the management process. But budgetary control frequently fails to encompass important strategic objectives. It does not cover non-financial objectives that may be important to achieving secure profitability and competitive strength; it pays no attention to long-term goals and objectives; and it does not deal with a company's progress relative to its competitors. An exclusive focus on financial results and budgets does not encourage managers to invest and build for longer-term competitive advantage, and can therefore cause problems of short termism.

These problems are typified by the sad story of the demise of the British motorcycle industry. For many years, in the 1950s and 1960s, companies such as BSA, Triumph and Norton were profitable motor-cycle producers. Then, in the late 1960s and early 1970s, faced with competitive pressures from Honda, Yamaha and other Japanese producers, the financial performance of the British manufacturers began to decline. By the mid-1970s, the situation had reached crisis proportions, and the Labour government sponsored a rescue plan that involved mergers amongst the producers to rationalize the industry. When this plan ran into difficulties, the Boston Consulting Group was retained by the Secretary of State for Industry to investigate the commercial options open to the industry. BCG's report[4] demonstrated that the competitive situation had worsened so gravely that there were, in effect, no sound commercial strategies available.

At a post-mortem meeting, a senior official at the Department of Industry made a comment that summed up his view of the situation. "Very sad," he said, "it's obviously too late to do anything now. But when could we possibly have known that these problems were building up?" When it was pointed out that the report showed a dramatic decline in market share for the British producers dating back as far as 1960, his response was: "Ah yes. But there was no proper evidence, no sign of any financial problems until much more recently."

It can, of course, be argued that this was simply the naïve view of a civil servant, who knew no better than to rely on published financial information as the key indicator of corporate strategic health. But our research suggests that this sort of view is by no means uncommon – how many senior managers would have adopted a similar attitude?

Many companies take pride in fostering a performance-driven culture that emphasizes profitability as the key goal for business managers. Companies such as BTR and Hanson, both highly successful acquisitive conglomerates, emphasize tight financial control above all else. But too much stress on profits can be damaging. Pilkington, a British company that has always taken a long-term view of R&D and investment, and whose research laboratories were responsible for the development of the float-glass process, fought off a takeover bid from BTR on the grounds that too great an emphasis on short-term profit controls would hurt the company's long-term prospects. Similarly, Cummins Engine maintains that the dip in its profits in recent years reflects long-term investment and pricing decisions, taken in order to protect its market position from attacks by aggressive Japanese competitors.[5] Both companies have complained about the short termism of stock market investors, whose valuations of companies are heavily influenced by current profitability levels.

But it is not only the stock market that is driven by short-term financial results. In an influential *Harvard Business Review* article,[6] Robert Hayes and William Abernathy lay the same charge against many industrial companies.

> "Innovation, the life blood of any vital enterprise, is best encouraged by an environment that does not unduly penalize failure, [but] the predictable result of relying too heavily on short-term financial measures – a sort of managerial remote control – is an environment in which no-one feels he or she can afford … even a momentary drop in the bottom line."

Too much emphasis on budgetary control and short-term profit can therefore disguise strategic problems from senior management and cause business managers to be risk averse and short termist in their decisions. What Hayes and Abernathy call "management by the numbers" encourages pursuit of short-term returns, to the detriment of long-term technical superiority and competitive advantage. What we need are longer-term, non-financial objectives, concerned with underlying competitive success, in addition to financial, budgetary targets. Strategic control is required to balance purely budgetary control.

Many senior managers and strategy experts[7] believe that a combination of strategic and budgetary control is the best, perhaps the only, way to ensure that businesses remain healthy for the long term, while delivering results in the short term. A Courtaulds director stated:

> "It's like playing the piano with both hands. You can get by if you're only playing with the financial control hand and forgetting the strategic control hand. You face a lot of risks if you are dealing only with the strategic control hand and not complementing it with the financial control hand. But for really top performance, you need to play with both hands together."

Strategic control supplements financial control targets with a few key, non-financial criteria of good strategic performance for each business. For example, targets for relative market share or relative product quality, or timetables for strategic action programmes, can help central managers to tell whether businesses are implementing their long-term strategies successfully, and can motivate business unit managers to meet their strategic goals.

Probably the most comprehensive approach to strategic control has been proposed by Peter Lorange,[8] who suggests establishing:

- strategic objectives (the eventual objectives in terms of competitive strategy)
- strategic programmes and milestones (the specific tasks by which the strategic objectives will be accomplished, together with time-tables for their completion)
- strategic budgets (the resources to be spent on strategic pro-grammes).

Performance under each heading must be monitored. The control system must also identify key assumptions on which the strategy is premised, and track any changes to those assumptions and their performance implications. With such a process, strategic control can, in theory, be administered as systematically and tightly as budgetary control.

PROBLEMS IN ESTABLISHING STRATEGIC CONTROL

In practice, strategic control is much more difficult to establish than budgetary control. Three particular problems must be addressed: identifying the right performance measures, determining suitably "stretching" target achievement levels, and deciding how to react to missed targets.

It is seldom easy to identify the right strategic performance measures from the many possible non-financial performance indicators in a business. With budgetary control, it is straightforward to use existing accounting systems to draw up budgets in comparable form for all businesses. There is no similar system for generating non-financial, strategic performance measures, which must therefore be defined separately for each business. The fact that the variables to be measured and the data available are frequently much softer and more subjective[9] complicates the choice of strategic objectives still further. In addition, strategy often focuses on long-term goals, but managers tend not to react strongly to objectives that will be reached only in the distant and uncertain future. Consequently, some writers have argued that long-term goals need to be translated into short-term milestones that provide measures of progress towards eventual goals.[10] But milestones of this sort are not always easy to find.

Determining specific targets for each performance measure is also complex. With budgetary control, it is possible to argue that, since firms are in business to make a profit, maximizing next year's profits must be the ultimate goal. With strategic control, complicated trade-offs between current financial performance and longer-term competitive position, and between different desirable ways of building competitive strength, must be recognized. Precise targets are needed to give substance to the control process, but they cannot be set without a clear insight into the real priorities for the business.

Lastly, the response to missed strategic targets is less straightforward than with budget shortfalls. Failure to hit a strategic milestone may indicate poor implementation of a good strategy. But it may also be caused by factors outside management's control, by a change in the assumptions on which the strategy is premised, or by a shift in competitive strategies that invalidates the original strategy. Corporate management needs to determine whether a missed strategic milestone should lead to a review of the strategy or to pressure for better implementation.[11]

Strategic control is therefore harder than budgetary control, and few companies have yet made much progress in developing their strategic control processes.[12] Thus a survey by Jacques Horovitz of 52 companies in Europe reached the conclusion that: "Analysis of current practices has shown that long-range and in some cases strategic planning exist. However, when one looks at chief executive control, empirical evidence suggests that there is no control system to match such planning."[13] The point was reinforced by Peter Lorange and Declan Murphy, who, drawing on US experience, observed: "The vast majority of companies in our survey sample felt that they were floundering in their attempts to develop serviceable long-range performance criteria for their managers."[14] Michael Goold and Andrew Campbell also found that, amongst 16 British companies that they studied, very few had successfully established a tight strategic control process.[15]

There therefore appears to be a conflict between the evident desirability of a well-developed and clear strategic control process and the practical problems encountered in setting up such a process. To learn more about the ways in which companies have tried to overcome these problems, and about the success of different approaches to the vital subject of strategic control, we undertook the research programme on which this book is based.

RESEARCH PROGRAMME

Over the last two years, we have carried out an extensive programme of interviews concerning strategic control with managers at multiple levels in a number of large companies. (Appendix 1 describes our methodology more fully, and gives background information about the business mix of the main companies covered in the research.) Our research set out to discover what sorts of strategic control processes are found in leading companies and to determine how effective these processes are. We have investigated the precision, explicitness and nature of strategic objectives; the rigour with which objectives are recorded and monitored; and the way in which rewards, sanctions and interventions are tied to achievement of planned objectives. Questions we have addressed include whether it is useful to look at a specific set of indicators of strategic performance; what these indicators should be; how they should be built into the management process; and how they can be used to help the centre and the businesses to work together more effectively. In short, we have attempted to determine what the nature of the strategic control process should be.

OVERVIEW OF CONCLUSIONS

Our research led us to focus on the clarity, explicitness and formality of the strategic control process as a major issue. We found that few companies have a strategic control process that is anything like as formal and explicit as their budgetary control process; most companies adopt a more informal approach. Some companies (such as ICI, Ciba-Geigy and Xerox) however, have successfully introduced more formal strategic control processes in recent years.

We also noted differences in the approach to strategic control adopted by companies with more and less decentralized approaches to strategy formulation. Decentralized companies emphasize a smaller number of key targets in the control process, while more centralized companies track a larger number of control targets.

Chapter 2 lays out the different approaches to strategic control that we encountered, and summarizes their main features for the busy reader. Chapters 3 and 4 provide detailed descriptions of the strategic control processes in 18 large companies and will be of interest to readers who wish to understand more fully the research base on which our findings rest, or to know more about particular companies.

Our work with these companies suggests that more explicit and formal strategic control processes offer a number of advantages.

- They force greater clarity and realism in planning.
- They can encourage higher standards of performance.

- They provide more motivation for business unit managers.
- They permit more timely intervention by corporate management.
- They avoid "back door" financial control.
- They make decentralization work better, by defining responsibilities more clearly.

At the same time, we found evidence of certain problems caused by more formal, explicit strategic control processes. In particular, managers may be less flexible in responding to changing conditions or new opportunities, and the control process itself may add significant cost and bureaucratic delay. Chapter 5 explores these advantages and disadvantages more fully.

As we reviewed the experiences of different companies, we found that in certain situations the advantages of more formal control processes were conclusive, while in others the disadvantages were predominant. We therefore tried to determine what approaches to strategic control work best in different circumstances. The most important influences on the choice of an appropriate strategic control process appear to be:

- The length of time-lags between actions and financial results.
- The nature of the portfolio of which the business is a part; in particular the potential for linkages with other businesses in the portfolio and the diversity of the portfolio.
- The level of risk inherent in the business; in particular the prevalence of "bet your company" investment decisions, the extent of uncertainty, and the speed of change in the business's environment.
- The sources of competitive advantage in the business.

In Chapter 6, we discuss how a company can select an approach to strategic control that fits its particular business circumstances.

The priorities, skills and attitudes of the management team also influence what approach to control will work best. These change gradually in most companies, and are reflected in changes in the strategic control process. In Chapter 7, we trace the ways in which strategic control processes can develop over time in response to shifting management priorities and abilities.

Many companies, we believe, are now reaching the point where they would find it useful to introduce a more formal strategic control process. To help them to think through the implications of doing so, Chapter 8 pulls together our conclusions and recommendations. These can be briefly summarized as follows:

- The corporate centre must take the lead in insisting that clear and explicit strategic objectives are agreed for each business. These objectives should be based upon an analysis of the sources of long-term competitive advantage in the business, and should provide early warning of future problems before financial results turn down.

- Target achievement levels should be proposed by the businesses, but should be stretched by the centre. The targets should be calibrated against the performance of other leading competitors. Any trade-offs between strategic targets and budget targets should be made explicit to avoid incompatibility between budgetary control and strategic control.

- Pressure for managers to deliver on their strategic targets should be provided through regular monitoring of results, linked to personal career progression, salary and bonuses. Top management must also be seen to intervene in businesses that consistently deviate from planned strategic objectives.

- The quality of the strategic control process depends upon the quality of the thinking on which the strategic objectives are based. Companies need to reach a relatively high level of sophistication in their strategic planning before formal strategic control becomes worthwhile.

- Formal and explicit strategic control processes should not become rigid and bureaucratic. Large staffs and lengthy written reports should be avoided, and strategic control should build on existing line management processes.

- The role of the chief executive and top management team is vital in making the strategic control process a success. To add real value, they must have a good understanding of the appropriate strategies and objectives in each of their businesses. This task is hardest in highly diverse companies. Too much diversity is incompatible with good strategic control.

Notes and References

1 The terminology of control can be confusing. Some companies endeavour to make distinctions between objectives, goals and targets. Since such distinctions are often unclear, and the basis for the distinctions differs between companies, we shall use "objectives" and "goals" as equivalent terms to signify what a business is attempting to achieve, while reserving "targets" for the more precise sense of specific, preferably quantifiable, levels of achievement. Thus a business's goal or

objective might be expressed as to increase market share, while its target might be to move from 10% to 15% market share. Objectives will sometimes, but not always, be expressed in specific terms, while targets will always be specific.

2 To simplify the discussion, this book will frequently refer to relationships between the centre and the business as if there were only these two general management levels. Our basic intention is to focus on superior-subordinate relationships at any point in the corporate hierarchy, but with particular reference to relationships between the corporate centre and the major business units. Appendix 2 discusses the roles of different levels more fully.

3 See, for example, P. Armstrong, "The rise of accounting controls in British capitalist enterprises", *Accounting Organizations and Society*, vol. 12, no. 5, 1987, pp. 415-36.

4 See *Strategy Alternatives for the British Motorcycle Industry*, Her Majesty's Stationery Office, London, 1975. As a member of the BCG team, the author of this book became only too aware of the impact of over-reliance on short-term financial performance indicators in this industry.

5 See Anatole Kaletksy, "Strategy before profits", *Financial Times*, October 12, 1989.

6 See R. H. Hayes and W. J. Abernathy, "Managing our way to economic decline", *Harvard Business Review*, Jul-Aug 1980.

7 See K. R. Andrews, *The Concept of Corporate Strategy*, Richard D. Irwin, Homewood, I11., 1980 (original 1971); Robert H. Anthony, *The Management Control Function*, Harvard Business School Press, Boston, 1988; J. Dearden, "The case against ROI control", *Harvard Business Review*, May-Jun 1969, pp. 124-35; P. Lorange, *Corporate Planning: An Executive Viewpoint*, Prentice-Hall, Englewood Cliffs, NJ, 1980; P. Lorange, M. F. Scott Morton and S. Ghoshal, *Strategic Control*, West Publishing Company, St Paul, Minn., 1986; Kenneth A. Merchant, *Rewarding Results: Effectively Motivating Profit Center Managers*, Harvard Business School Press, Boston, 1989; M. D. Richards, *Organizational Goal Structures*, West Publishing Company, St Paul, Minn., 1978; C. H. Roush and B. C. Ball, "Controlling the implementation of strategy", *Managerial Planning*, vol. 29, no. 4, Nov/Dec 1980, pp. 3-12; B. Yavitz and W. H. Newman, *Strategy in Action*, The Free Press, 1982. The Financial Control Research Institute, a gathering of senior managers from the planning and control functions in British industry, has made similar points in *Control Systems for Strategy Enforcement*, 1986.

8 P. Lorange and D. C. Murphy, "Strategy and human resources: concepts and practice", *Human Resource Management*, vol. 22, no. 1/2, 1983, pp. 111-33; P. Lorange, "Monitoring strategic progress and ad hoc strategic modification", in John Grant (ed.), *Strategic Management Horizons*, JAI Press, Greenwich, Conn., 1988.

9 See E. G. Hurst, "Controlling strategic plans", in P. Lorange (ed.), *Implementation of Strategic Planning*, Prentice-Hall, Englewood Cliffs, NJ, 1982, pp. 114-23.

10 For example, H. J. Hrebiniak and W. F. Joyce have argued (*Implementing Strategy*, Macmillan, London, 1984; "The strategic importance of managing myopia", *Sloan Management Review*, Fall 1986) that strategic control will be effective only if it specifies short-term goals whose achievement is essential to the strategy's ultimate success. "To achieve long-term aims, it is necessary to develop operating objectives that purposely translate strategy into manageable short-term pieces for implementation." Hrebiniak and Joyce believe that the way to build constructively on management's natural "myopia" (a focus on short-term rather than long-term goals) is to establish short-term milestones as measures of long-term progress.

11 Some writers argue for a conception of strategic control in which discrepancies between actual and planned outcomes automatically trigger a re-examination of the strategy and its underlying assumptions. See C. Argyris and D. A. Schon, *Organizational Learning: A Theory of Action Perspective*, Addison-Wesley, Reading, Mass., 1978; G. Schreyogg and H. Steinmann, "Strategic control: a new perspective", *Academy of Management Review*, vol. 12, no. 1, 1987, pp. 91-103. Similar points can be made in relation to missed budget targets. But the more complex trade-offs involved in strategic control make the "what if we miss?" problem much harder to deal with.

12 Although there has been a good deal of research on the theory of strategic control, there have been few previous empirical studies of how companies' strategic control processes actually work.

13 J. H. Horovitz, "Strategic control: a new task for top management", *Long Range Planning*, vol. 12; 1979, pp. 2-7.

14 P. Lorange and D. C. Murphy, "Strategy and human resources: concepts and practice", *Human Resource Management*, vol. 22, no. 1/2, 1983, pp. 111-33.

15 Michael Goold and Andrew Campbell, *Strategies and Styles: The Role of the Centre in Managing Diversified Corporations*, Basil Blackwell, Oxford, 1987.

CHAPTER 2

HOW COMPANIES EXERCISE STRATEGIC CONTROL

An important finding from our research was that very few companies have strategic control processes that are nearly as explicit, clear and well developed as their budgetary control processes. This conclusion was reinforced by a mail survey of the 250 largest British companies, in which we asked companies whether they used "explicit strategic object-ives or milestones, which complement financial targets and are used as an integral part of the control process". Only 15 per cent of the respondents claimed to do so.

If so few companies use explicit strategic objectives as part of a formal control process, what approaches to strategic control are being taken, and why? And how do the strategic control processes of those companies that have introduced a more formal and explicit approach work? A major part of our research has been concerned with documenting the way that companies' strategic control processes actually function. This chapter summarizes our findings, which will be illustrated more fully with company case studies in Chapters 3 and 4.

FORMAL STRATEGIC CONTROL PROCESSES

Formal approaches to strategic control are, as yet, relatively uncommon. British Petroleum (BP), Ciba-Geigy, General Electric (during the 1970s), Imperial Chemical Industries (ICI), National Westminster Bank, Pilkington, Rio-Tinto Zinc (RTZ), Shell and Xerox, however, are all companies which believe that a more formal and explicit strategic con-trol process has a vital part to play in the management of large multi-business companies. In particular, a formal strategic control process underlines the importance of strategic targets and action programmes, and clarifies priorities for business managers. This makes strategy imple-mentation more effective, since it is less likely that strategies will be com-promised to achieve short-term budget goals or to protect personal interests or preferences. Other reasons cited for choosing a more formal strategic control process include:

- Explicit objectives make businesses establish clearer plans with a sharper focus on what needs to be achieved (BP, RTZ).
- Strategic milestones make managers think through specifically what they need to do next year to reach their longer-term goals (NatWest, Pilkington).
- The strategic control process allows central management to influence the priorities of businesses (NatWest, RTZ).
- Explicit strategic objectives prevent performance monitoring from focusing too much on the financial goals embodied in the budget, and force "strategic", "real" issues onto the agenda for discussion (ICI, Shell).
- Monitoring of strategic performance can help to provide early warning of emerging problems. For top management this speeds intervention; for business management it is a spur to quicker action to rectify the situation (Ciba-Geigy, Shell).

The advantages and disadvantages, and the nature of formal strategic processes, are described fully in subsequent chapters. Our purpose in this chapter is simply to summarize the main features of such processes in the companies that we have researched.

Periodic strategy reviews

The strategic control process for each business in the corporate portfolio begins with a formal strategy review. Some companies carry out these reviews annually (or biennially); others undertake the reviews less regularly, as needed for each business. In order to provide the basis for a formal strategic control process, these reviews must not only establish broad strategic directions for the business, but also explicitly identify key strategic objectives, by which progress with the strategy can subsequently be measured and monitored. Pilkington's strategic planning process, for example, is specifically designed to ensure that plans include a clear statement of a few key strategic objectives, whose achievement can subsequently be monitored.

The strategic planning process also typically provides a discussion of the general background to the favoured strategy, but, with the exception of Ciba-Geigy, none of the companies we researched made explicit and formally monitored the assumptions on which strategies and objectives were premised. Consequently there tended not to be a formal link between changes in these assumptions and their impact on the agreed strategic objectives. It is understood that changes in background assumptions are important, but most companies seem to prefer a more informal process for tracking their nature and impact.

The quality of thinking behind the strategy reviews, and of the debate between business and corporate management, is a vital influence on the success of the strategic control process. Poor strategic thinking leads to the identification of inappropriate strategic objectives, and therefore undermines any strategic control process. Several companies found that, when they first embarked upon a more formal strategic control process, their businesses' strategic plans were too imprecise to allow objectives to be clearly and explicitly stated.

Selection of strategic objectives
Measures of strategic progress
The strategic objectives, or milestones as they are often called, are intended to represent the best measures of strategic progress in each business. Typically, the objectives include both financial and non-financial measures of performance. At ICI, the head of planning described the company's milestones as "a mixture of quantitative and qualitative markers" against which performance is measured. Examples of strategic objectives include market share in selected segments, new product or process introduction dates, customer satisfaction measures or cost reduction measures. Nearly all companies find the selection of appropriate strategic objectives to be a difficult, though essential, step in the formal strategic control process.

The strategic objectives will generally be different in each business, reflecting its particular strategy and situation. Standard ratios or performance statistics, on the analogy with budget objectives, are not appropriate. Thus, in a research intensive business, success may depend on the R&D pipeline; in a commodity business, on measures of underlying cost competitiveness; and in a niche business, on measures of product quality. If cost position is seen as vital, a strategic objective may be defined that is based on some measure of relative costs (for example, attain costs 10 per cent lower than any other producer), or that will contribute to improving relative costs (for example, introduce new manufacturing process in plant P by time T). However, suitable objectives can be defined only after the key success factors for the strategy have been identified, since they should focus on whatever is most important in implementing the strategy. A common problem with strategic control processes is that the specified objectives are not sufficiently clearly linked to the strategy of the business. In one company, for example, accomplishing an office move on time found its way into the list of milestones, though no one argued that this was essential to the business's strategic success.

Objectives and milestones

Companies' strategic control processes cover time horizons of up to ten years, but most objectives relate to the earlier years. More distant objectives are intrinsically harder to define precisely, and more likely to change as time passes, and so are less valuable in the control process. As a result, strategic control is often concerned with important near-term steps towards long-term goals; hence the common use of the term "milestones". In Shell, we were told that "milestones are not ends in themselves but rather stages that you pass on the way". Some companies, such as Ciba-Geigy and Pilkington, also monitor shifts in longer-term objectives, as a means of checking whether ultimate goals are remaining constant or gradually changing.

Actions and results

Typically, strategic objectives focus primarily on action programmes or projects, and establish specific timetables for their completion. The control process then checks that these action programmes have been implemented as planned. Although some strategic objectives are results oriented (for example, to gain X per cent market share, to raise customer satisfaction scores by Y per cent), most seem to relate more to actions taken than to results achieved, to inputs rather than to outputs. Apparently businesses find it harder to specify measures of strategic results than to define action milestones.

The distinction between actions and results is not clear cut. For example, a milestone to launch a certain product by a given date can be seen as an action, which will have an impact on results in terms of market share, customer satisfaction, profitability and so forth. But it may also be seen as the result of other actions (for example, completion of various steps in the development process, preparation of a launch campaign, signing up of dealers and distributors, and so on). Despite the lack of a clear, principled distinction between actions and results, it is normally possible in practice to see whether a milestone has been set with the intention of ensuring that a given action programme is accomplished, or with the intention of tracking some important outcome measure, while leaving the business free to take whatever actions it sees fit to attain that outcome.[1]

Setting target achievement levels
Precision of targets
All companies that have formal strategic controls try to make targets precise, but none succeed in making them wholly quantitative. Things such as customer service, image or product differentiation are hard to pin down with precise and accurate measures. Trade-offs must then be made between identifying objectives that are important but difficult to measure precisely, and picking parameters that can be readily measured but fail to get to the real heart of the strategy. Targets that cannot be monitored with reasonable objectivity and precision cannot provide clear readings on performance.

Bottom–up proposals
Strategies and objectives are normally proposed on a bottom–up basis. It is up to the business units to propose the strategies to follow, the variables by which to measure progress, and the levels of achievement to be attained. This approach builds on the detailed knowledge of the business managers, and promotes business-level ownership of the strategies and objectives.

Stretching of targets
Typically the centre will accept the performance measures and target achievement levels proposed by the businesses. There appears, in most cases, to be little direct pressure to "stretch" the level of achievement, except through the ultimate sanction of rejecting the strategy as a whole, or through the occasional attempt to compress timetables.

Competitive benchmarks
Very few targets are set relative to the competition. Achievement levels are established in absolute terms (reduce costs by X per cent) rather than competitively (achieve the lowest-cost position in the business). Even financial goals are seldom set in relation to competition (achieve a net margin two points higher than any other competitor, achieve margin growth faster than any other competitor), and stress instead absolute levels of achievement. For non-financial objectives, competitively benchmarked targets are even rarer.

One reason for the lack of competitively benchmarked targets is the difficulty of obtaining the necessary data. However this difficulty is not by any means insurmountable (see the discussion of Xerox and benchmarking in Chapter 3). And, where competitive benchmarks can be set, they are especially valuable, since leading competitors provide an objective standard of best practice, and since targets set relative to competition are less sensitive to uncontrollable changes in industry conditions, which affect all competitors similarly.

Budget targets and strategic targets

Short-term budget targets for profit remain important in all the companies we researched. However, the strategic control process provides a link between strategic plans and budgets. Objectives derived from the strategic plan provide a background to budget negotiations, and allow trade-offs between the strategy and the budget to be raised explicitly. Both Pilkington and RTZ regard the debates that follow as one of the most useful and illuminating aspects of a more formal strategic control process. Strategic milestones may also be included in formal budget or operating plan objectives, giving a non-financial dimension to shorter-term targets. Where operating plan objectives are not clearly linked back to strategic objectives, there is a danger that the operating plans may conflict with the strategy, or may focus on issues that are not vital to the strategy. Inconsistency between strategic milestones and budget targets causes severe tensions and ambiguities for business heads, and damages the credibility of the strategic control process.

Formal monitoring of strategic progress

Companies with formal strategic control processes call for regular reports on progress against strategic objectives. The frequency of monitoring is less than for financial reports, but occurs at least annually. It is generally up to the businesses to prepare and present data on their achievements, although in some cases this function is performed, or guided, by a planning or control staff department. In some companies (for example, ICI and BP), monitoring of strategic results is combined with budget or operating plan monitoring. In others (for example, Ciba-Geigy and Pilkington) it is a separate process. In Ciba-Geigy, for example, strategic control reports are made annually. The reports are typically 2–6 pages long, and concentrate on the key objectives that were agreed at the last strategy review. The questions they cover are whether the critical assumptions behind the strategies are still valid, whether the key strategic programmes are on schedule, and whether the objectives for the longer term are still within reach. On the basis of the report, the corporate executive committee of Ciba-Geigy decides whether it wishes to meet with each business to discuss its progress.

By establishing, documenting and monitoring certain objectives, the company invests those objectives with particular significance. They become the objectives that are seen to matter most, and therefore clarify what the centre regards as the criteria of good performance for the business. This does not mean that information is not gathered on other aspects of performance. Indeed the conscientious CEO or liaison director normally ensures that he is fully briefed on a much wider range of background information than is covered by the formal strategic control reports. But these reports remain the prime focus of attention and the formally agreed basis for deciding whether the business in question is on track with its strategy.

Personal rewards and sanctions

Achievements against strategic objectives are typically not tightly linked to personal career progression, salaries or bonuses. As we were told at ICI: "We don't want to design a noose and ask people to put their heads into it." More indirect links between strategic achievements over a period of time and personal progress are, however, common, and several companies also build a subjective assessment of progress against strategic milestones into their incentive compensation plans. National Westminster Bank and Xerox go further, by incorporating strategic objectives into a formula for calculating personal bonuses (see Appendix 3). Furthermore, the very process of making strategic objectives into formally monitored targets means that there are psychological rewards and penalties associated with attaining (or missing) these targets.

Companies avoid tight links between personal rewards and strategic objectives for a number of reasons. First, strategic control stresses balance between a number of important goals. Trade-offs must be made between these goals, and no one of them is sacrosanct. The larger the number of goals, the more complex the trade-offs, and the harder it is to create tight links in the control process. Secondly, it is recognized that if, for example, competitive conditions change, "good performance" will sometimes require the business to deviate from the pre-set strategic objectives. Finally, strategic objectives are by no means always precise enough to feature in tight, mechanical bonus formulas or appraisal systems. Hence, even if companies do have explicit strategic objectives, they tend to relate bonuses to short-term financial performance, and to use strategic controls mainly for long-term career progression.

Central intervention

Budget shortfalls remain the most important formal triggers for central intervention, but failure to meet strategic objectives is also seen as important. If strategic milestones are missed, the centre is alerted to problems and given legitimacy in intervening. Once there is evidence that a business is failing to achieve its milestones, the centre may press for more information, or for a basic review of strategy, and will be less delegative in its approach to the business. Ultimately, capital investment will be withheld or the management team changed. However, there is more flexibility in the reaction to missed strategic objectives than companies with strict financial controls show towards businesses that miss budgets. This view was well stated at Shell: "Milestones must not be immutable. The dilemma is to get something between fixed goal posts and no goal posts."

INFORMAL STRATEGIC CONTROL PROCESSES

The great majority of companies do not define explicit strategic objectives or milestones that are regularly and formally monitored as part of the ongoing management control process. The absence of such objectives does not, however, necessarily mean that there is no process for identifying strategically important goals or controlling the implementation of strategy. Rather, it can imply that a more informal approach to strategic control has been preferred. Chapter 4 profiles ten companies with approaches to strategic control of this sort. The companies covered are B.A.T, BOC, Bunzl, Courtaulds, Digital, General Electric, Kingfisher, Nestlé, Philips and Toshiba.

The rationale for an informal approach is that setting a small number of specific strategic objectives is hard, and may even be dangerous, since the chosen objectives will at best be only a partial reflection of what needs to be done strategically. More open-ended, informal strategic targets run less risk of unbalancing the business. Formal monitoring then concentrates on the main financial aggregates to avoid getting bogged down in too much detail, allowing regular line management contacts and informal channels to flag up strategic issues of significance. The informal approach also allows for a more flexible response as a business's circumstances change, which is desirable, since strict adherence to objectives set at the beginning of the year could inhibit a necessary change of priorities as the year unfolds.

Other reasons for preferring an informal approach, to be described more fully in subsequent chapters, include:

- A highly structured and formal system of strategic planning and control may introduce undesirable elements of routine and bureaucracy into the strategic decision making process (B.A.T, Bunzl, GE).
- Informal meetings and reviews are vital to achieve the necessary openness of communication and responsiveness of strategy (GE, Nestlé).
- Any finite set of objectives will fail to capture some of the important nuances, especially in the area of people management (Courtaulds). Only a more informal system can encompass many of the things that matter most (Kingfisher, Philips).
- Explicit strategic objectives are difficult to identify and costly to measure, and therefore require too much effort to be worthwhile (BOC, Courtaulds).
- Top management intervention is most valuable when a business is beginning to get "tattered at the edges", a point that may well be reached before specific objectives have been missed. A narrow focus on explicit targets will preclude early intervention in these circumstances (BOC).
- The most important elements of control stem from a corporate culture in which people work together in teams to achieve shared goals. This sort of culture cannot be built through formal control processes (Digital, Toshiba).

Because informal strategic control processes are less systematic and structured, it is intrinsically difficult to generalize about how they work. However, there are certain common characteristics which we will now summarize.

Establishing the criteria of good strategic performance

Although the criteria of good strategic performance are not made formally explicit, the dialogue between the centre and the businesses can still lead to a fairly clear mutual understanding of where the priorities lie.

This understanding emerges from the discussion of prospective plans and past performance. A good example comes from GE: "A business may state that the key to its future is to get delivery cycle times down. This would be noted but not made explicitly into a control measure. Nevertheless, both the business and the centre would expect to see progress against this measure discussed at the next review meeting."

The centre and the businesses can use both formal meetings and informal contacts to express their views, and a shared understanding can develop, even without explicit milestones, provided that the two-way communication is good. There is, however, more flexibility to adjust priorities as circumstances change and to focus on those issues that are currently most important to top management. "Learning to interpret the feedback" becomes a key skill in this context.

Budgets and strategies

Budget targets are formally set and monitored, and are usually accorded high importance. But the budget targets are established in the light of agreed strategy, and a key aim is to maintain strategic strength, not simply to maximize the profit bottom line. Budget discussions can thereby provide a vehicle for communicating strategic priorities and constraints. As we were told at Nestlé:

"You could achieve your monthly budget targets by disturbing the strategy; for example, by repositioning brands or changing media expenditure. But if you did so, it would quickly be noticed by the product group director at the centre. This would not be through the formal control report, but through informal contacts with the country in question."

Performance monitoring

With an informal process, performance monitoring takes place through a variety of means: periodic strategy reviews, operating plan reports, specific investigations or task force reports and, most importantly, regular informal meetings and discussions. Without explicit milestones, there is less formality in the monitoring of strategic progress, and more flexibility in the items that receive the most attention.

Personal rewards and sanctions

In the absence of explicit strategic targets, the control process cannot involve direct or automatic links between strategic achievements and personal careers or compensation. As we have already seen, companies with explicit milestones also avoid tight links of this sort, so that a more indirect, diffuse connection between strategic performance and personal consequences is the norm under both sorts of strategic control. With informal controls, however, business managers may be less certain by what criteria they are being assessed.

Central intervention

Without explicit milestones, intervention from the centre is based on a wider assessment of progress. It therefore runs some risk of being seen as more arbitrary and interfering, but it is also less restricted by pre-speci- fied criteria. Since there are no formal triggers for intervention, the cen- tre needs to find more informal ways of deciding when a business is going off track. A senior corporate manager we met at BOC believes that direct contact with the business is essential for this purpose: "You need a control system, but the really early warnings will never come from the formal control system. They come from your feel for the busi- ness. The touchy-feely things are the ones that you only get to know about by visiting the business and sensing what's going on."

When informal strategic control doesn't work

Given good communications and sensitive handling, an informal approach to strategic control can work well, particularly in certain sorts of business (see Chapter 6). But, while there can be good reasons for adopting a carefully thought through approach to strategic control of this sort, we should note that during our research we also encountered numerous less sophisticated companies, whose informal strategic con- trols follow from a failure to think through what will represent good performance strategically, rather than from a conscious decision to avoid explicit milestones. Here, informal controls lead to confusion and lack of purpose, rather than to flexibility and responsiveness. As one planning director put it to us:

> "People like to avoid being specific. Managers prefer the ants across a sand dune, trial and error approach to strategy. People prefer not having to tell their bosses what they're going to do in case it doesn't happen. You see this between chief executives and their share- holders, and it's no different at lower levels in the organization."

And in another company, we were told: "Our approach to strategic control is basically no more than financial control with strategic excuses."

In these companies, informal strategic controls have been adopted by default. Although companies may choose informal controls for positive reasons, we need to recognize that many companies have fallen into informal controls for less sound reasons.

MANAGEMENT STYLES AND CONTROL APPROACHES

The companies in our research include some whose management style involves a relatively high level of central influence in setting businesses' strategies (so-called Strategic Planning style companies) and others that prefer to leave the initiative in the development of plans to business unit managers (so-called Strategic Control style companies). These two management styles were identified and described by Michael Goold and Andrew Campbell in *Strategies and Styles*.[2] We have found this distinction between management styles useful in examining companies' control practices, and we divide the company descriptions presented in Chapters 3 and 4 into these two categories. To avoid confusion, we shall use upper case letters when discussing the Strategic Control management style ("ICI is a Strategic Control style company"), and lower case letters when speaking more generically of the control process ("ICI's strategic control process is relatively explicit and formal"). Appendix 4 describes the philosophies of the different management styles more fully.

Strategic Control companies (for example, ICI, Courtaulds) tend to monitor a rather smaller number of performance measures than Strategic Planning companies (for example, National Westminster Bank, Shell). Strategic Control companies usually focus on no more than about half a dozen key objectives per business per year, amongst which profit is particularly important, whereas Strategic Planning companies are willing to work with 10–15 objectives. In Strategic Planning companies, objectives tend to be somewhat more detailed and action oriented, and to stress bottom-line profits rather less. However, both Strategic Planning and Strategic Control companies recognize that having a large number of objectives gives a less clear sense of priorities, reduces the motivating power of the objectives, and can lead to interference with the day-to-day responsibilities of a business's management.

In Strategic Planning companies, targets also have a somewhat greater top-down component. Whereas Strategic Control companies leave it almost entirely to the businesses to identify their own objectives and set their own targets, the centre in Strategic Planning companies is more likely to propose both measures and target levels for achievement. Where this happens, as at National Westminster Bank, it allows the centre to introduce an element of stretch into the objectives set.

PERFORMANCE MEASURES AND CONTROL INFORMATION

In examining companies' approaches to strategic control, we have focused on the set of objectives that are recognized by the centre and the businesses to constitute the criteria of good performance. These are the objectives that are emphasized in the formal reporting systems; that receive most attention in discussions between the centre and the business; that provide the main basis for personal rewards and sanctions; and that are seen as the most legitimate triggers for central pressure and intervention if targets are missed. The value of such criteria of good performance is that they clarify the nature of delegated responsibilities. They define the circumstances in which the centre will become concerned about business performance, and hence the space within which business managers are free to operate.

However, in most companies the centre will also inform itself about a much wider range of issues, using informal contacts and sources of information as well as the more formal reporting systems. Top managers may seek information on the performance of other competitors, the attitudes of customers, changes in the market, the technology or the business environment; or they may probe into particular issues within the business. Personal site visits, chance meetings in corridors, items picked up from magazines read on an aeroplane, all supplement periodic budget and strategy reviews as sources of such information.

This wider information base is useful in setting objectives and interpreting results in terms of the more narrowly defined criteria of good performance. It helps central managers to judge what targets are suitably stretching, to decide how to react to deviations from planned objectives, and to determine whether, in exceptional cases, intervention is needed, even if planned objectives are being met. The broader base of information is valuable in allowing the centre to understand its businesses better and to make more informed decisions about them. But it cannot replace the more limited criteria of good performance, which clarify the prime responsibilities of business management.

The controls used by Strategic Planning and Strategic Control companies differ primarily in terms of the criteria of good performance.

Strategic Planning companies tend to place rather less emphasis on profitability and to be concerned with a larger number of objectives in defining the criteria of good performance, whereas Strategic Control companies focus their attention on a smaller number of key objectives, amongst which profitability is particularly important. When it comes to the broader base of control information, the differences between Strategic Planning and Strategic Control companies are less clear cut. Indeed the extent and nature of the background information gathered about businesses vary as much with the personality, interests and energy of the CEO as with the management style. For example, Sir Christopher Hogg at Courtaulds, a prime exponent of Strategic Control, spends a great deal of time gathering a wide range of background information on the performance of his businesses. Several Strategic Planning CEOs, on the other hand, seem more interested in planning than in control, and therefore devote relatively little attention to gathering a wide range of performance information about their businesses. Typically, however, Strategic Planning companies keep track of a wider range of background information than do Strategic Control companies.

The distinction between the criteria of good strategic performance and the broader base of control information is, of course, clearer with formal strategic control processes that define explicit objectives than with informal strategic control processes. Nevertheless, business managers invariably try to identify the key performance measures, the "hot buttons". Even though they recognize that their bosses may wish to discuss a much wider agenda in order to get a feel for progress in a fuller, more holistic sense, business managers' behaviour is most influenced by their perception of what these hot buttons are.

STRATEGIC CONTROL PROCESSES

To summarize, we have observed important differences between companies' strategic control processes along two dimensions:

1. The formality and explicitness of the process.
2. The number of criteria of good strategic performance, and the emphasis placed on profitability. Strategic Control companies usually employ fewer criteria of good performance than Strategic Planning companies, and stress profit more.

Figure 2.1 characterizes the strategic control processes of the companies described in Chapters 3 and 4 in terms of these distinctions. We believe that the framework in Figure 2.1 is useful for classifying strategic control processes. We will return to it in later chapters of this book where we analyse the merits of different approaches to strategic control and their suitability in different company circumstances.

Figure 2.1 **Strategic Control Processes**

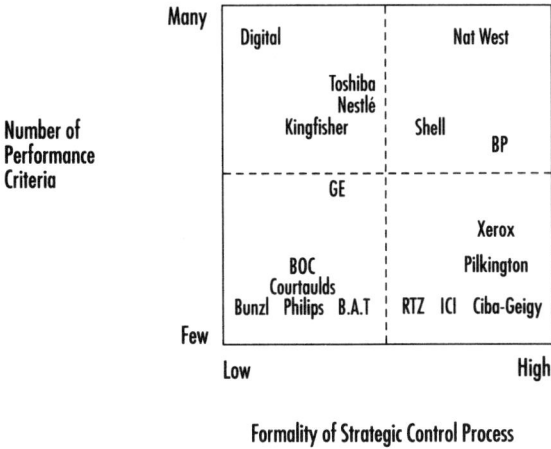

Formality of Strategic Control Process

Notes and References

1 See also K. A. Merchant, *Control in Business Organisations*, Pitman, London, 1985, which uses this distinction.

2 Michael Goold and Andrew Campbell, *Strategies and Styles: The Role of the Centre in Managing Diversified Corporations*, Basil Blackwell, Oxford, 1987.

CHAPTER 3

FORMAL STRATEGIC CONTROL PROCESSES

This chapter describes the control process of nine companies that have relatively formal strategic control processes. Of these companies, we have classified six (ICI, Ciba-Geigy, Pilkington, RTZ, Xerox and the GE of the late 1970s) as followers of the Strategic Control management style and three (Shell, BP and National Westminster Bank) as closer to the Strategic Planning style.

STRATEGIC CONTROL COMPANIES

The philosophy of Strategic Control, as described in Appendix 4, involves delegating a high degree of responsibility for strategy to the business units. The control process then focuses on a few key objectives that represent the criteria of good performance for the businesses. Typically, profitability is one of the most important of these criteria, but there is an attempt to balance the importance of profit controls with other, more strategic objectives. The companies described in this chapter make their strategic objectives an explicit part of the formal control process.

We will begin with a relatively full description of the control process in ICI, and use the other companies to complement or draw contrasts with the situation in ICI. We will cover:

- the objective setting process: budgets and strategic objectives or milestones
- the monitoring process
- rewards, sanctions and corporate level intervention.

Imperial Chemical Industries (ICI)

During the 1980s ICI decentralized responsibility for strategy to the principal executive officers (PEOs) of its main businesses. Twenty-four units, of which 12 are major business groups (for example, Pharmaceuticals, Agrochemicals, Paints, Chemicals & Polymers), report directly to the corporate executive team (main board executive directors).

Within the 12 main business groups there are upwards of 50 strategic business units (SBUs) whose strategies are separately reviewed by the centre. The businesses are responsible for proposing strategies and budgets, and the executive team's primary role is to allocate resources between them in the corporate interest.

The planning process between the businesses and the corporate centre consists of a regular annual budget cycle and a less regular strategy review process. Businesses undertake strategy reviews whenever the executive team feels that there is a need, either because circumstances have changed or because of the passage of time. Typically, each business would have a strategy review every three to five years, but some, such as the Seeds business, where ICI's position changes much more rapidly, are reviewed annually or even more often.

Objective setting: budgets

Each business prepares its budget in the early autumn. The budgets involve detailed planning for one year ahead, and a forecast of a further two years. The submission to the head office, which does not go into extensive line item detail, is first considered in a pre-meeting which involves the chairman of ICI, the liaison director,[1] and the general managers of finance and planning. This meeting sets the agenda for the formal budget review meeting, and the corporate staff are asked to look into any issues arising. The PEO of the division receives a copy of the minutes of the meeting, so that he is forewarned on questions that may come up during his presentation.

During a couple of weeks in November ("hell fortnight") all the ICI businesses present their budgets to the corporate headquarters. On the day before each presentation, the executive team have a half-hour preparatory meeting. The purpose is to refine the agenda and decide on a focus for the discussion. The presentation itself is a 2–3 hour meeting. "It requires considerable self-discipline by board members to make it work. It is necessary to concentrate only on important issues rather than getting into detail," we were told. If any director has a particular concern about the business, he is likely to handle it through an informal visit in the first instance, rather than by raising it at the formal presentation.

Objective setting: strategic milestones

The budget process is well established in the company, but "it had tended to be financially rather than strategically driven, and to focus much more on the first year than the second and third year of the plan." In addition, "there wasn't a sufficiently clear contract as to investment, quality, market share and other strategic achievements." In other words, the budget and the strategy were not sufficiently linked. As a result, ICI decided that each business's strategy review should include the agreement of specific strategic objectives or "milestones", progress toward which could then be monitored. The strategic milestones were intended to complement and balance budgetary objectives.

Since 1986 strategic "milestones" have therefore been introduced into the planning process. The milestones are measurable, preferably quantitative, objectives that indicate progress in implementing an agreed strategy. "They set out what success would really mean for us, strategically." Milestones have, therefore, become an integral part of the strategic planning and control cycle, and strategy reviews now cover: key issues (often identified by the executive team and the central planning department at the initiation of the review); strategies proposed, including action plans and programmes; *and* milestones to measure performance on a year-to-year basis. ICI defines milestones as follows.

> "The milestones cover a ten year period, being more detailed and precise in the early years and less so later on. They are a mixture of quantitative and qualitative critical factors which provide reference points for the annual evaluation of budgets. They also act through time as key markers against which to test whether performance is meeting requirements or significantly and persistently falling short, indicating the need for strategy to be reappraised."[2]

The milestones are proposed by the businesses, after discussion with the corporate planning department, who will suggest the sorts of things that should be covered. Provided the executive team accept the strategy proposed, they will generally accept the milestone measures put forward by the business. But, ultimately, if the executive team are not satisfied with the projected overall performance, they will reject the strategies being put up. "Businesses with unambitious and unexciting strategic plans are told that, if they can't do better than that, they will not find a long term place in the portfolio."

The items monitored as strategic milestones are sometimes financial (for example, cash flow, return on capital employed, profit level, profit growth) and sometimes non-financial (for example, market share, accomplishment of an acquisition, entry to a new territory). Financial milestones concentrate on a few key items only, and look further ahead than the budget. The non-financial milestones measure progress with important non-financial tasks, and attempt to get at the underlying competitive health of the business. Preferably they should be quantitative and precise, but this is not always possible. Typically many more milestone measures are set for years one to three of a strategy than for subsequent years. In year one there may be three to ten milestones for a major business.

To understand how milestones are used, we talked with managers in several businesses. In the Chemicals and Polymers Group, milestones are used both in the dialogue between the corporate centre and the Group, and within the Group. Individual businesses within C & P have discretion on what milestones to propose and on how many to set. "The more you legislate on milestones, the more you just get mechanical thinking." Accordingly, different businesses select different sorts of milestones to reflect their own view of strategic priorities.

The non-financial milestones specified are "deliberately catholic". The sorts of milestones used include:

- volume or capacity achievements in selected product areas
- energy usage
- feedstock mix
- capacity utilization
- timetabled achievement of specified key success factors
- market share in specified regions
- new product or process introduction dates
- technical achievements and timetables
- product quality levels
- safety standards
- plant closure dates
- acquisition, joint venture or collaboration agreement timetables
- objectives concerned with people and organization ("although we have not been too clever in defining these so far").

A business's milestones can also include broad financial parameters for longer-term achievement, and unit cost targets.

Any one business would, of course, not cover all these items. Some businesses have as few as two or three milestones per year, while others set up to ten. But between seven and ten is generally considered the upper limit. "If we have too many milestones, we lose sight of what is really key for the overall strategy."

Non-financial milestones are intended to capture the key "real" factors that must be achieved to allow the strategy to work and to deliver the required longer-term financial performance. In businesses that are exposed to commodity price shifts and to exchange rate volatility, these underlying achievements are seen as important and often more meaningful than short-term profit fluctuations.

In R&D-intensive businesses such as Agrochemicals and Pharmaceuticals, milestones tend to put more stress on research achievements. For example:

- discovery of a lead compound with certain minimum properties by a particular date
- rate of progress through the development process of a new compound
- date of registration of a new compound
- market share penetration at given dates after the launch of a new product.

Research is emphasized because success in new products is so important to realizing the strategic aims of these businesses. But research milestones are often particularly difficult to make "hard" or quantitative; and achievement is less controllable by individual managers, because of the intrinsic uncertainties in the research process. "Several of our milestones are in the lap of the gods," one manager said. There is, however, particular emphasis on the timetable in development, which is more (though not totally) within management control. Research milestones also need to be complemented by commercial milestones. A key benchmark for ICI Pharmaceuticals, for example, has been to achieve a rate of profitability growth faster than the average of the best ten US pharmaceutical companies. (US companies were chosen as the comparison group for reasons of data availability and comparability.)

The nature of milestones reflects a business's strategic priorities. The emphasis may be on growth by acquisition, on new market penetration, on cost reduction and plant rationalization, or on research-based product development. Furthermore, as a business such as the Seeds business moves from its early days towards greater commercial maturity, the emphasis will change. These changing emphases must be reflected in the milestones.

"Milestones are just a way of getting people to be a bit more explicit about their objectives for the business." This reflection, coming from one business manager in the Agrochemicals business, captures much of what the strategic milestone process is about in ICI. Strategic controls and explicit milestones are, in this view, essentially a matter of good housekeeping in the strategic management process. The milestones, however, do also force into the open an agreement between the centre and the businesses on what objectives are most important for each business.

The board does not want a detailed statement of how milestones are going to be achieved; this is left to the business. "We are not trying to get into the innards of a business. We cannot really be aware of what is possible within the businesses." Even the degree of stretch or optimism to build in to the milestones is left largely to the businesses. However, the board and central planning department do provide some check on whether businesses are putting forward milestones that are reasonable, challenging and – as far as possible – measurable.

Monitoring

Monthly and quarterly monitoring of results at the corporate level concentrates on financial performance against budget. The monthly reports are kept to a minimum, focusing only on sales and profit figures for the main businesses. The quarterly reports are somewhat fuller, covering, for example, gross margins, trading profit and major cash items. The executive team meets for approximately two hours to review the quarterly reports, with an emphasis on exceptions and deviations from plan. In general there is no face-to-face meeting with business management to discuss the quarterly results. There is also no reporting on strategic milestones in the quarterly reports. The liaison directors may, however, have informal discussions with their businesses to discover more about their progress. The extent of these informal contacts, and the topics on which they focus, depend on the personal interests of the liaison directors, and the nature of their relationship with the business in question.

The main formal performance review meeting is the annual budget session in November, when the previous year's results are reviewed at the same time as the budget is set for the coming year. Typically the strategic milestones are taken as the first item in the budget review, and set the context for the subsequent discussion of the budget. The corporate planning department provides a briefing on how far milestones have been achieved, and the businesses are encouraged to introduce their budget with a review of progress against the previous year's milestones and a statement of what the budget will do to keep them on course for future years' milestones.

Within business groups, milestone reviews may take place more frequently. Typically C&P review their businesses' milestones at least twice a year in formal meetings and more frequently through informal contacts.

Rewards, sanctions and intervention

In ICI, profit budgets and strategic milestones are intended to represent "contracts" between the centre and the businesses. As such, they represent the primary criteria of good performance. On the other hand, the company has not historically had a culture of tight control with major personal incentives and sanctions directly linked to plan achievements. In this context, milestones are described as "objectives that are supposed to be met in broadly the right area rather than precise targets". They are challenging objectives to which much effort is devoted, not "no excuses" targets with people's jobs on the line.

A divisional PEO summed up the process in this way: "Milestones are a good discipline for the business. It is very helpful to try to quantify objectives, since this forces realism and hard choices. But it's important not to get too focused on the milestones per se, rather than the underlying strategy. Not everything can be captured in specific quantitative milestones. What you need is not too slavish a reading of the runes."

If businesses do miss their milestones, planned capital allocations will be re-examined. Indeed, PEOs must request a review with the executive team as soon as they see themselves encountering circumstances that may require trade-offs between achieving budget targets and strategic milestones. This meeting will consider what corrective action should be taken and whether to modify budgets, capital spending, or strategic goals.

If the problems seem likely to persist, a fundamental review of strategy for the business is likely. The existence of strategic milestones, however, acts as a balance to the emphasis on financial budget targets. For example, in 1988 two major businesses in C & P were off budget. One was also missing its strategic milestones and was pushed into a fundamental review of its whole strategy. The other was on track with its milestones, and received a less unfavourable assessment, with more time given to get the financials to come right.

Simply making the milestones more explicit and visible also creates extra pressure for performance. "In the old days we'd have played around in the lab for ten years before getting anywhere in some new product areas," a business manager observed. "Now a clearer focus on milestones and achievements prevents this." On the other hand, profit still retains high importance. "Delivering profits is what it's all about. If you can do that, you will have a very free hand."

At the personal level, management teams that consistently fail to deliver their agreed budgets and milestones over a 2–3 year period are at risk. The specific role of milestones here is hard to specify. "It's an overall judgement about financial performance, strategic milestones and general management capability. You can never disentangle the sources of dissatisfaction with a business," we were told. A track record of meeting objectives and milestones also counts in the promotion process, especially for business heads, but "they are questions that are around in the debate, rather than a matter of ticking boxes. Basically, you are in a judgement area."

In terms of personal financial compensation, a superior performance rating from the boss may give an individual up to 30 per cent above the salary set for his grade. This rating, however, is subjectively determined. For business heads there is no formula through which budget or milestone achievements are linked to cash bonuses. One corporate manager noted, "ICI tend to fight shy of amazingly mechanical or bureaucratic systems," in part to prevent managers from distorting their strategies to achieve pre-specified goals. "If we were given strong performance-related pay bonuses linked to milestones, it would increase the degree of game playing," a business manager explained.

Review

Perhaps the greatest perceived benefit of the milestone approach in ICI is that, by identifying a small number of key objectives for emphasis, it gives focus and priority to strategy making and control. "This has both danger and value," we were told. "The danger is that the milestones artificially pin down managers on a limited number of issues. The value is that they focus attention on the few really key things underlying the business. If you acknowledge too much complexity, nothing happens." The milestones clarify, for both the centre and the businesses, what matters most. For ICI, there has also been particular value in introducing some non-financial, strategic milestones to prevent the dialogue between the businesses and the centre from becoming dominated by financial results. "Strategy naturally focuses on 1995, finance on 1990; the milestones bring these perspectives closer together."

The majority of ICI's non-financial milestones relate to key action programmes or events. These are linked to the strategy, and therefore test whether implementation is taking place. Many fewer of the milestones, however, relate to results or outcomes, mainly because the businesses find it more difficult to identify suitable non-financial targets of this kind. The ICI milestone process also does not place great emphasis on making explicit the assumptions behind strategies. During the last few years, most of ICI's businesses have been performing well enough to have surpassed their milestones and their financial budget targets. If, in the future, business circumstances become less favourable, and there is more need to deal with businesses that have failed to hit their milestones, a greater focus on results and background assumptions may be needed.

Ciba-Geigy

The giant Swiss chemical and pharmaceutical firm, Ciba-Geigy, is organized into six major divisions and three groups (see Figure 3.1). The distinction between divisions and groups is not clear cut, but in general the groups are somewhat smaller than the divisions and do not have their headquarters based in Basle. In addition to the central functions, divisions and groups shown on the organization chart, Ciba-Geigy has so-called "group companies" in each of the major countries of the world. In principle, however, the corporation sees itself as running global businesses, so the prime line of reporting and responsibility is to the divisions, which in turn report to the executive committee.

Objective setting
Strategic planning starts with a segmentation of the Ciba-Geigy activities into 18 business sectors, each of which may contain several strategic business units (SBUs). Ciba-Geigy defines a business sector as a business with a specific market scope, a defined strategic mission within the corporate portfolio including a bottom-line profit responsibility, and management and resources that are largely independent of other business sectors.

Strategic plans are drawn up for each business sector and discussed with the executive committee. The long-term objectives, key strategies and funds requirements proposed in these plans are based on a comprehensive analysis of such issues as market attractiveness (including size, growth rate, entry barriers, innovation potential), key success factors and instabilities with regard to demand, technology, competition and

Figure 3.1 **Ciba-Geigy Ltd Organization**

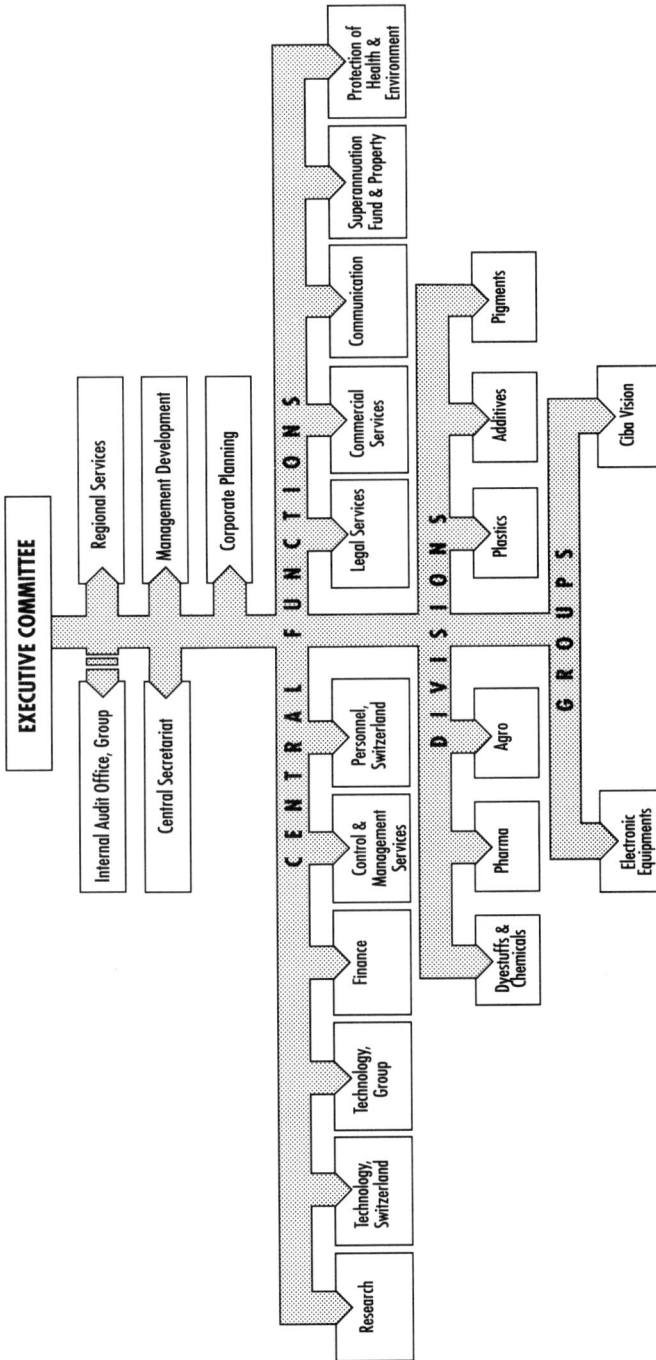

government regulations. Ciba-Geigy's strengths and weaknesses are identified, and provide the basis for the strategies proposed.

The various business sector plans also serve as inputs to a portfolio review at the corporate level. At intervals of 4–5 years, and using a planning horizon of 7–10 years, the corporate prospects for profitability, cash flow, and spread of risks are assessed. Differentiated strategic missions and specific targets are then assigned to the individual business sectors, and resources are allocated to support the missions. Corporate strategies (priorities, diversification policies, structures, etc) are also defined.

Figure 3.2 diagrams the strategic planning and control process in Ciba-Geigy.

Figure 3.2 **Strategic Planning and Control in Ciba-Geigy**

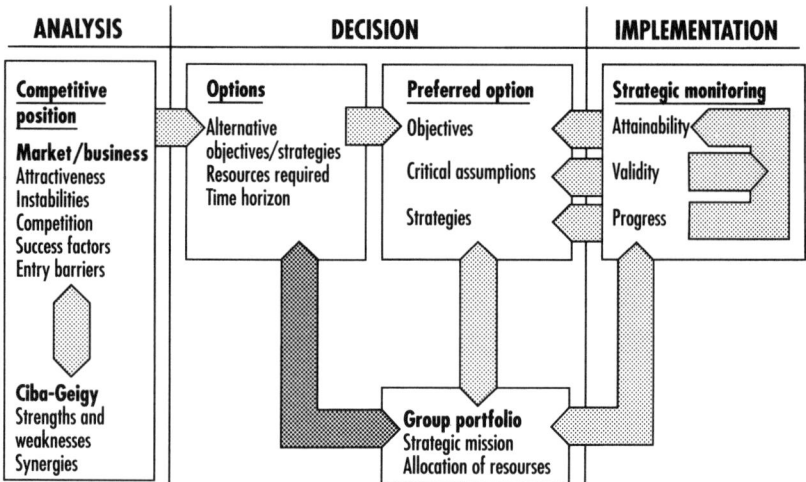

Monitoring

Strategic control is seen by Ciba-Geigy as "the connecting link between strategic planning and its implementation". The plans for each business sector define control parameters, which remain valid until the next strategic plan is drawn up. New strategic plans are made at least every four to five years, in the context of a fresh corporate strategic plan that extends the time horizons of the previous plan, but may be drawn up more frequently in businesses that face rapid change or particularly important strategic issues. For each business sector, the control parameters are monitored in a 2–6 page strategic control statement on long-term objectives, key strategies and projects that are necessary to reach the objectives, and critical business assumptions. The format and topics to cover are laid down by the centre, but the specific objectives and strategies are proposed by the business sector. There is then an iterative process of discussion of the objectives between the business sector and the executive committee, but Ciba-Geigy believes that a fundamentally bottom–up process creates more ownership by the business sector in question. Each business sector defines some 8–20 strategic control parameters, phased over 7–8 years: "It's a constant reminder of the need to deliver and to remember long-term progress in running the business." As such, the strategic controls act as a counterweight to shorter-term budgetary pressures that also exist.

Strategic control reports are made annually. They focus on whether the critical assumptions behind the strategies are still valid, whether the key strategic programmes are on schedule and whether the objectives for the longer term are still within reach. An illustrative and simplified example of a report is shown in Figure 3.3. The report brings out the progress that has been made in terms of the strategic control parameters. It includes figures on the relevant strategic control objectives and, if appropriate, a brief explanation of how they have been achieved. It also gives selected financial data.

The strategic control progress reports, which are made between February and May, also form the background for budgets (due by the end of January). One-year plans must be consistent with strategic objectives, and must take account of progress that is being made.

Rewards, sanctions and intervention

On the basis of the report, the executive committee decides whether it wishes to meet with each business sector. Some, the principal businesses, are seen every year or more frequently; others much less often. If the plan is fully on track there may be no particular communication from the executive committee to the business sector. If there is a minor deviation, the business's liaison director may simply meet with the business to discuss the problem. If the deviation is a major one (or if there is some change in management, or a new portfolio role, or a proposal to go into some new area of business), there will be a full dialogue with the executive committee.

The strategic control process therefore provides a regular formal review of progress against strategic objectives that are, as far as possible,

---

Figure 3.3 **Illustrative Ciba-Geigy Strategic Control Report,** April 1986

Source: Strategic Plan June 1982

Strategic mission: Cash Generator

1.   Longer-term targets (1990)

1.1   To consolidate position as market leader (market share in value X%).

1.2   To achieve a positive funds flow 1983-90 of Y million SFr.

Status 86

> • Market share maintained
> • Funds flow below expectation resulting from price erosion and higher ecology expenses

Outlook

> We anticipate a shortfall in the funds flow of A million SFr. Lower price erosion and productivity improvements will not compensate for additional investments/expenditures in ecology (B million SFr)

2.   Critical assumptions/risks

2.1   Our market potential will increase in volume by X%, in value by Y% p.a.

Status 86/Outlook

> The extremely high demand in 1985 (+Z% in volume terms) will slow down till 1990 (+A% p.a.). The increase in value will stagnate at B% p.a. for a further 2-3 years.

2.2   The share of developing countries of the total market potential will increase from 50 to 60% till 1990.

Status 86/Outlook

> The expected market shift will take place at a lower pace and will have significant effect only after 1990.

3.   Key strategies/projects

3.1   Launch of a second generation of ABC active ingredients by end of 1986

Status 86/Outlook

> Launching delayed by 1½ years for quality reasons (loss in contribution through 1990 X million SFr.)

3.2 To strengthen the quality/price image by TQM measures. Review of the 1984 customer perception by a further audit in 1987.

3.3 Establishment of the new reactor technology in the production sites D + E by the end of 1986 at the latest, in site F till end of 1987.

Status 86/Outlook

> Successful extablishment in site D by end of 1985. For site E the deadline can be met. In site F new investment priorities will cause a delay of presumably one year.

measurable and controllable. It creates pressure on the businesses to propose and take corrective action if important deviations from key objectives are occurring, and it gives the executive committee early warning of problems that might not otherwise surface until later. Significant and persistent deviations lead to revision of the sector plan and of the associated control parameters.

Strategic control objectives are also beginning to be built into formal Management by Objectives (MBO) and personal bonus schemes. A proportion of bonuses for senior managers now depends on personal goals that are related to strategic control objectives. However, the assessment of performance against these objectives is necessarily more subjective and judgemental than with budget objectives. "It is more difficult to use strategic controls as part of an objective bonus formula because, in contrast with budget targets, they are not sufficiently precise yardsticks."

In general, the strategic control process is currently used less as a motivating force for individual managers and more as a means of fine-tuning strategies. "You can't punish people for a mistake in planning, otherwise they'll play games with the strategic process next time round," a corporate manager explained. Thus deviations from the plan may not prompt an immediate change in management or even in strategy, although, in due course, action will be taken. "You care, but you give time for implementation to take place."

Review

Like ICI, Ciba-Geigy sees value in defining explicit strategic control objectives, and in monitoring achievements against them. Other points of similarity concern the need for a bottom–up objective-setting process to gain business ownership of the objectives, and a rejection of tight or mechanical control against strategic objectives.

Ciba-Geigy's monitoring process is somewhat more formal and structured than ICI's. Through its separate annual strategic control report Ciba-Geigy has a more systematic way of monitoring strategic achievements than does ICI, which combines strategic milestone monitoring with the annual budget reviews in a rather more informal manner. Ciba-Geigy also goes further in spelling out strategic control parameters, since it looks for coverage of key assumptions behind strategies, as well as objectives and action programmes.

Ciba-Geigy believes the prime value of the strategic control process is to ensure that strategy is implemented, and to identify situations in which businesses are straying from their targets. Also the strategic control process prevents strategic targets being "reinvented" each year. "The discipline of strategic control is useful. We are not as inflexible as state planning in the Eastern bloc, but it is useful to check back on the previous plan's targets," we were told. And the view from one business, after five years of the strategic control process, was: "We would do a kind of strategic control for ourselves now, even if we didn't have to write a document on it for the centre."

Pilkington

Pilkington has 20 major operating companies engaged principally in producing glass and related products, ranging from flat and safety glass through to electro-optics. The company introduced strategic milestones into its planning and control cycle in 1985, and has developed their use progressively since then.

Objective setting

The planning process begins in March, when planning guidelines are sent out to the operating companies. The guidelines include a description of the planning process, key issues to be addressed by all the operating companies, issues specific to individual operating companies and background environmental assumptions. They indicate the form in which individual strategy reviews should be presented, including three-year profit and loss, balance sheet and cash flow projections. Capital expenditure looks five years ahead. These are guidelines rather than edicts, and the management of the operating companies can vary them in the light of their particular circumstances. "The guidelines are not forced on the operating companies but are offered as assistance," we were told.

In September, the operating companies supply their strategy reviews in brief written form to headquarters. They are produced in consultation with the group planning function, whose six account executives each have responsibility for developing a relationship with a small number of operating companies. The strategy review includes the operating company's commentary on progress towards the milestones agreed in the previous year's strategic review (see below). Group Planning, working together with the finance, technical and personnel functions, consolidates the financial profiles provided by the operating companies and produces a commentary on each of the companies as a basis for individual strategy review discussions. The commentary includes a matrix to show what the operating companies promised to achieve and what was actually achieved (in terms of profits) for any given year. Figure 3.4 illustrates the matrix.

Figure 3.4 **Pilkington Planning Matrix**

Performance for year
(Profit before interest and tax)

		1984	1985	1986	1987	1988	1989	1990	1991
	1984	P	F	F	F				
Year	**1985**	A	P	F	F	F			
Plan	**1986**		A	P	F	F	F		
Made	**1987**			A	P	F	F	F	
	1988				A	P	F	F	F

A = actual performance
P = projection for current year
F = forecast based on current plan

This matrix will have footnotes to explain any major variations from the planning assumptions, including environmental changes (such as exchange rate movements) and structural changes (such as major acquisitions). Its purpose is to straighten "hockey sticks" (unrealistic projections) and to instil realism without making the strategy review a numbers exercise.

For each of the major operating companies, a half-day strategy review meeting is held in October involving the chairman and deputy chairman of the group and the heads of the planning, finance, technical and personnel functions. The operating company is represented by its chief executive and colleagues selected by him. The main board "sponsoring director" will always be present, and other directors may choose to attend.[3] "The strategy review is a once-a-year opportunity for the chairman and the operating company CEO to interface on strategic issues rather than the numbers. There are no minutes of this meeting, just working notes. A little bit of fluidity is a favourable thing to have until the total picture is agreed," we were told.

Following the meetings with individual operating companies, there is a review of headquarters' initiatives. Certain acquisitions, divestments and restructuring projects fall in this category, as may programmes of research, analysis or investment involving several operating companies. The group strategy review is then prepared for consideration by the main board. This is both a corporate and a business strategy document, with four major sections:

1. Objectives, policies, portfolio management, headquarters' initiatives and headquarters' milestones.
2. Corporate strategy towards each operating company, confirming its mission and noting its milestones.
3. Each operating company's strategy in its own theatre of operation.
4. Financial appendices.

In December the main board discusses, modifies and approves the group's strategy. There follows a process of feedback to operating companies and headquarters' departments in which "outline planning consent" is given and milestones are confirmed.

The final stage of the planning cycle is the budgeting round, held between November and March. The operating companies produce detailed budgets for the next year and confirm their financial forecasts for the two years beyond. In strategy terms the budget should be "surprise free", though there may be variations in matters of timing.

Monitoring

An important component of the strategic planning and review process is the use of milestones. Six to ten milestones for each operating company are developed. They are proposed by the operating company, or may be suggested by Group Planning, based on the strategy proposed by the operating company in its September papers. Milestones are discussed and agreed at the October strategy review meeting.

For each of the operating companies, one or two milestones may be identified as needing particular headquarters support. They may become the responsibility of the sponsoring director for that company. The other milestones are the responsibility of the chief executive of the operating company. Typically these will be of the form: complete the construction of plant A to budget; achieve a production cost of £B per tonne; produce the capital case for investment C; maintain market share of product D. "The milestones do not purport to be a complete description of what the business needs to achieve but are a number of issues that the centre and the operating company agree are priorities. They should provide a sensible basis for carrying the business forward."

In addition, some 20–30 milestones relating to group issues are identified. Responsibility for each of them is ascribed to an executive director. Directors' personal milestones are of the form: acquire W; divest X; ameliorate relations with customer Y; establish a presence in country Z.

In the first year after milestones were originally introduced, there was no formal monitoring of progress against them. In some cases, too little progress was achieved. An experiment with frequent reporting proved cumbersome and inconsistent with the group's devolved structure. A successful compromise has been twice-yearly monitoring with higher-frequency attention arising naturally where it is needed. The system is not seen as a tight control process. Its effect is to confirm rather than usurp the authority of the operating company chief executives. "In Pilkington, people are not controlled against milestones but are invited to say how they have progressed towards them."

Rewards and sanctions

Pilkington has established management incentive programmes that link rewards to the achievement of MBO objectives. Business milestones can be embodied in these objectives, provided they are measurable. There are, however, also softer, less measurable milestones which are viewed as equally important but which, because they cannot be objectively and unambiguously measured, are not considered suitable for inclusion in an incentives programme. These milestones are an important supplement to the more mechanistic targets within a manager's reward package.

Review

The Pilkington planning cycle is typical of many formal corporate planning processes. For reasons that are similar to those cited by both ICI and Ciba-Geigy, Pilkington has found it an advantage to have formal strategic controls, using explicit milestones. The action orientation of milestones is similar to ICI's, as is the flexible link to personal reward. Distinctive features of the Pilkington strategic control process are the "anti-hockey stick" matrix, and the relatively frequent monitoring of progress against milestones. Pilkington also sets strategic milestones for the corporate level in addition to the business level.

Within the company it is felt that milestones have led to clearer communication and more forceful implementation of strategy. As one operating company chief executive maintained: "Milestones are not a burden, but an aid to involving people and moving things forward. Strategic controls were forced on us by circumstances, not by fashion."

RTZ

RTZ's business portfolio has become less diverse in recent years, and now concentrates on mining, minerals and certain industrial businesses. The management and strategy of the operating divisions and subsidiaries (for example, RTZ Pillar) is very much a decentralized responsibility, with the centre acting as "the ultimate banker and shareholder". "Their main job is to ensure that we are doing a good job," said one operating group chief executive (see Appendix 2 for further discussion of the structure of the company, and the role and management style of different levels in RTZ).

Since 1985 a corporate strategic planning process has been in use. Each subsidiary conducts a "strategy dialogue" with the centre, at least once every two years and sometimes more frequently, particularly if the business is growing rapidly or facing a swiftly changing environment. The strategies agreed in these dialogues form the context for the annual planning process, which identifies both financial objectives and "key management objectives" (strategic objectives).

RTZ believes that no single system of planning and control is appropriate for all their different businesses. So, in the annual plans, RTZ is looking for the subsidiaries to identify their own key management objectives. There should be fewer than ten such objectives, "or they are not really key objectives". Objectives may be set, for example, in terms of market share or the making of specific acquisitions, but "it's no good if they can't be phrased sufficiently precisely to be able to see if they have been, in fact, achieved". Each year's plan now reports on progress against last year's key objectives. The system is a comparatively new one; businesses were first asked to submit key objectives in 1986 but not required to report on achievement against those objectives until 1987. There is a similar but less formal process for identifying key objectives in the biennial strategy plan.

RTZ tends to give different signals on the balance between financial and strategic objectives to different subsidiaries. In some cases the emphasis is more financial, in others the intention is to push strategy more. The balance depends in part on the nature of the business: for example, in commodity businesses it may be difficult for management to control profitability, and therefore the emphasis will fall more on relative competitive cost performance. But RTZ also compensates for the natural inclinations of the manager running the business. Hence, if a subsidiary managing director is very growth oriented by nature, the centre emphasizes performance against financial objectives. By contrast, new strategies and ideas will be stressed if the MD has done well in the past in achieving planned financial objectives, but there is some question about long-term development.

Key strategic objectives tend to be less precise than financial objectives, but, as one manager observed,

"it may be desirable that strategic controls should remain less precise than financial controls. If, for example, making an acquisition is a key objective, there is some danger that the subsidiary will go for an acquisition which in the event is not a good one, just in order to achieve the objective. And it can be very hard to pre-specify the criteria by which an acquisition should be judged as good or bad before the particular candidate has been identified."

In other words, RTZ believes that it is not easy to specify in advance what will be a "good" strategy for a particular business, so that there needs to be some flexibility to allow the strategy to evolve with circumstances.

Compensation and rewards have not yet been formally linked to key objectives, although this may come in time. However, RTZ feels that key strategic objectives are unlikely to become as pressing as financial controls. "The strategic objectives are less precise, and in any case you can seldom manage to hit all of them. Occasionally you come up against a wall and it's no good trying to go through it."

Since a formal strategic control process has only recently been introduced in RTZ, it is not yet as fully developed as at ICI, Ciba-Geigy or Pilkington. But the basic motivation and process are similar. Also RTZ's use of strategic controls to steer different managers according to their natural dispositions is an interesting and potentially valuable way of using the process.

Xerox Corporation

Xerox Corporation has two principal businesses: Business Products and Systems (BP&S), the company's original business, which accounts for about two-thirds of the company's sales; and Financial Services, accounting for about one-third of sales. The two businesses produce approximately equal profits. The Financial Services business is carried out almost entirely in North America, but BP&S is a genuinely worldwide operation, with Rank Xerox covering Europe, Africa, the Middle East and the Indian subcontinent, Fuji Xerox responsible for Japan and the Far East, and the Xerox Corporation itself handling the Americas. Our research has focused on strategic control in BP&S and, within BP&S, especially on Rank Xerox.

In the early 1980s Xerox faced problems. It had lost its position as the unchallenged leader in the increasingly competitive photocopier market. The company recognized that it could no longer continue with its traditional, engineering-driven approach to strategy but would need to become more customer-oriented. This move to a customer-led strategy became the dominant theme for the whole of BP&S. One major initiative was the Leadership through Quality programme, introduced in 1983, which has since provided the constant backcloth to the company's strategic planning. Besides providing this central strategic thrust of quality, the company has also suggested the tools by which this strategy should be implemented (for example, benchmarking – see pages 56-57).

Within the overall corporate themes of customer service and quality, the development of detailed strategies is a decentralized, bottom–up process. Primary responsibility for strategy development rests with product-oriented SBUs for product planning and design, and with regional companies for marketing, selling and servicing. The regional companies (for example, Rank Xerox) in turn work through national operating companies (for example, Rank Xerox (UK)). Overlaying this business structure, a functional structure is responsible for developing functional strategies.

Objective setting

The SBU, regional and operating company management within BP&S have, then, an overall strategic framework within which to develop their medium-term and annual operating plans. They know the central issues they have to address (customer satisfaction and quality) and the means by which they are expected to tackle them. This strategic framework is balanced by a profit requirement, set in terms of return on assets.

The SBUs are required to produce five-year strategic plans and present them to the corporate centre in the form of a structured, four-page Business Resource Management Statement (BRMS). A corporate manager explained: "Through this format we have tried to focus the discussions with the top management on strategic issues, not on the day-to-day management of SBUs. What is important is the paring down of information to the absolute essence and its structuring so that corporate management can concentrate on the essence of the strategic issues."

The operating companies, however, are not asked to produce plans for a period longer than three years. "Product development involves long lead times and requires the commitment of substantial resources, so they have to take a longer view. For us, however, the market is changing too fast for long-range planning. We manage the long term through the short term."

Although the centre in Xerox tries to ensure that customer service and quality are stressed in strategy development, it does not generally agree specific targets at the business level nor does it monitor progress against such targets. Thus the centre will want to know, for example, that a benchmarking programme is in place but will not generally concern itself with what is being benchmarked or the specific action programmes emerging from the benchmarking. "There is discretion for the individual to discuss whatever he has been doing in the benchmarking area, and the purpose is simply to show there is a benchmarking process in place and that some use is being made of it," we were told. However, the centre does monitor certain targets: profit, return on assets, customer satisfaction and market share.

The achievement of profit targets is seen as a necessary condition for good performance, but it is not sufficient. How profit is achieved is equally important. The customer satisfaction rating, in particular, is also regarded as a necessary condition for good performance.

Customer satisfaction is seen as key to Xerox's future profitability for several reasons. First, the technologies involved in Xerox's products

BENCHMARKING IN XEROX

Xerox's benchmarking system attempts to improve performance by comparing some aspect of the business with the best practice established elsewhere. The process has six phases: Planning, Data Collection, Analysis, Integration, Action and Maturity.

The **Planning** phase addresses a number of questions:

- What will be benchmarked? It may be some aspect of a production process (such as cost or production speed), a service (customer response time) or a product (reliability).
- Who is the best competitor? When it comes to benchmarking, the concept of "competitor" is very broadly understood and could include some other unit in Xerox, or a direct competitor such as Kodak or Canon, or an organization in a totally different market but with a related problem (Rank Xerox compared itself with Procter & Gamble when looking at distribution).[4]
- How will the data be collected? The methods used for measuring competitive performance or collecting the necessary data will depend on the nature of the problem and the availability of information. Examples include scanning published statistics, the direct exchange of information between "competitors", and the use of consultants to gather the information.

Having decided what data to collect and how to collect them, the **Data Collection** phase is conceptually straightforward, though it may be technically difficult. Xerox has found that, once the subject of the benchmarking exercise has been clearly defined, it is almost always possible to gather adequate data on competitive performance, provided sufficient effort is made to do so.

The **Analysis** phase establishes the extent to which the competition is better than the Xerox unit doing the benchmarking, the reasons why and the lessons to be learned by Xerox. Comparative measurement of performance is important in benchmarking, but is only the first step. More important is to understand how a competitor achieves a superior performance. Then superior practices can be adapted to the Xerox organization. The idea is not just to know that there is a difference but to learn how that difference has been achieved.

In the **Integration** phase, the lessons learnt in the Analysis phase are used to establish goals and strategies to improve current practice. But, before this is done, management must accept the benchmark results and analysis and commit itself to develop action plans based on the benchmarking exercise.

In the **Action** phase, these strategies are implemented, and progress is monitored.

Finally, in the **Maturity** phase, Xerox should be the leading company as measured by the benchmarked parameter. Benchmarking remains an integral part of the management process.

A good example of benchmarking was a study into the management of equipment pools (for sale or rental). The study was sponsored by Rank Xerox and also involved seven other comparable companies (multinationals with European headquarters). Each supplied consultants with data on its performance and processes, which were reported to the other firms on an anonymous basis. As a result, Rank Xerox introduced changes that led to substantially reduced equipment holdings and improved customer satisfaction (quicker delivery, fewer out-of-stocks, etc).

A second example comes from Rank Xerox in France. The company, wanting to improve its return on assets, did a benchmarking exercise on the turnover of assets. It benchmarked itself against other office equipment companies and also appliance companies seen as having similar operations. The leading "competitor" on this measure was found to be Sony, and the exercise enabled Rank Xerox France to improve its performance greatly.

Other examples include the French company's use of a survey to check its own efficiency in handling telephone enquiries from customers, and studies by Rank Xerox (UK) on software marketing practices, cost base, management of key accounts, and indirect sales channels.

The techniques of benchmarking are fully documented in internal Xerox handbooks, and there is a centrally coordinated benchmarking network to assist operating units in setting up and carrying out benchmarking exercises. Although the idea of benchmarking is not unique to Xerox, the company has made an unusually strong commitment to the practice.

(transporting paper and powders) are inherently difficult to make reliable, so customer service is important. Second, because technological innovations are quickly imitated by competitors, it is seldom possible to maintain competitive advantage based on technical features, so customer service is the best basis for differentiation. Third, the market is now dominated by replacement purchases, making customer loyalty important. Finally, the market is increasingly being defined as document management rather than the supply of machines, and the customer is looking for solutions to problems rather than just pieces of hardware. Understanding the customer's business needs thus becomes an important aspect of a service approach. Although each business needs to develop action plans to improve customer satisfaction, it is recognized that the specific actions required may differ depending on the market and competitive conditions prevailing in any given geographic region.

This approach to strategic objectives between the centre and the regional companies is duplicated within the businesses in their relationship to the operating companies. Thus, Rank Xerox (UK), the operating company handling Rank Xerox's business in the United Kingdom, will have to demonstrate to Rank Xerox that it has programmes in place for customer satisfaction, benchmarking, and so on. It will not normally have to agree specific targets in these areas at the planning stage, but may do so for programmes of particular significance.

As part of its internal strategic control processes, Rank Xerox (UK) has also developed a set of strategic indicators (such as penetration of strategic accounts, skills profile of its employees, and corporate image). These are used for target setting and control, but are not a requirement of the regional or corporate centre.

Monitoring

In BP&S, the businesses submit monthly and quarterly operating reports together with twice-yearly reports on progress against the three-year plan. More frequent reviews of specific problem areas may be initiated by either the business or the centre. There is also regular informal reporting between the general manager of a business and the centre. The managing director of Rank Xerox, for example, has monthly, one-to-one meetings with the general managers of the national companies.

Because of the matrix structure of BP&S, plans cover three dimensions: the business, the regions and the functions. The monitoring of functional performance appears to be the most detailed. The functional staff in the operating companies have strong communication lines with regional and corporate functional management, who will test the functional plans at the centre. This ensures a consistency in planning throughout the company.

Rewards, sanctions and intervention

Managers within BP&S receive financial incentives based on three main criteria:

- profitability (return on assets)
- customer satisfaction
- market share.

A complex formula is used to relate these criteria, with different weighting factors depending on the manager's responsibilities.

Customer satisfaction is measured by survey. Each operating company commissions an external agency to survey users of Xerox and competitors' equipment. "This is the most important of all benchmarking exercises and must lead to action plans," we were told. The survey is carried out quarterly in the major markets and once or twice a year in the smaller markets.

When customer satisfaction targets were first introduced into Xerox, each national company developed its own measure of customer satisfaction. However, as customer satisfaction became one of the bases for financial rewards, some standardization was brought in, and all companies now have to include three questions in their survey:

- Are you satisfied with Xerox (or Rank Xerox, Fuji Xerox)?
- Would you recommend Xerox to a friend?
- Would you deal again with Xerox?

Managers are rewarded on the basis of the customer satisfaction survey to ensure that they do not cut corners in trying to maximize short-term profitability to the detriment of the company's long-term performance.

The measure of market share used for assessing performance and reward is the improvement in market share in specific product sectors (for example, low-volume copiers or high-speed electronic printing). The product sectors included will be chosen to reflect the business's strategy.

If managers meet these three performance criteria (return on assets, customer satisfaction and improved market share) without fulfilling specific actions detailed in the functional strategies, they will still receive their bonus. That is, the reward system is results-based rather than action-based. ("Good performance is recognized as good performance.") However, as one manager put it, "Competition is now so great that it would be criminal for a general manager to reduce investment in maintenance and customer service." And, since actions are monitored through the annual review of functional strategies, it is unlikely that any manager could ignore the functional strategies for long. Because plans are updated annually "the centre in BP&S is quick to spot anyone 'dressing the books' and sacrificing long-term plans for short-term performance."

As well as a bonus system tightly related to measurable performance criteria, the company also operates a Management by Objectives scheme related to "softer" objectives, which can influence a person's grade, career progression and development. Furthermore, to supplement financial rewards, Xerox is also trying to develop a "culture of recognition" including thanks, public recognition of performance, and so on.

Review

In Xerox the corporate centre exerts its influence by defining the strategic thrust of the company (Leadership through Quality), the measure of its achievement (customer satisfaction) and the tools by which the strategy is to be implemented (for example, benchmarking). But it leaves the businesses to determine the specific content of their strategies and to monitor detailed implementation. BP&S is, of course, somewhat closer to its SBUs and operating companies than the corporate centre, in both planning and control. It operates a relatively formal strategic control process, using a small number of explicit performance measures, which are more directly linked to a compensation bonus formula than in companies such as ICI and Ciba-Geigy. Xerox's use of a formal competitive benchmarking process as a background to target setting is also a distinctive feature of the company's planning and control process.

Through this approach to strategic planning and control Xerox has arrested its competitive decline in the photocopier business, and achieved substantial performance improvements in numerous areas. It is widely recognized in the company that the use of benchmarking and of measurable strategic performance criteria has been important to these achievements.

General Electric

A final example of a Strategic Control company using explicit strategic milestones as part of their control process is General Electric (GE) – but the GE of the late 1970s and early 1980s, rather than the GE of today. It is worth taking this look back into history, both because GE was probably the pioneer of the Strategic Control style and brought it to a high degree of sophistication, and because it is necessary to understand GE's past to grasp the rationale behind its current management style, which we will describe more fully in Chapter 4.[5]

By 1980, GE had become a vast and highly diversified company, with total sales of nearly $25 billion. Its chairman and CEO, Reginald Jones, believed that the only way to run the company was through extensive decentralization, knitted together by a corporate strategic planning process. At this time the company had five levels of general management: the department, the division, the group, the sector and the corporate office (see Figure 3.5 on pages 62–63). Overlaid on this line management structure was a separate structure for the purposes of strategic planning. The strategic structure focused on some 40 strategic business units, which could be located at the department, division or group levels, and which could cut across line management structures. This system enabled GE to plan strategically for businesses that did not necessarily coincide with the operating line management structures. SBUs could be defined not in terms of the existing power structure, but in terms of the major sources of competitive advantage. (The criterion was that an SBU should be able to "stand alone as a viable and completely successful independent company, within its own market or market segment".)

Objective setting
Strategic plans were prepared annually for each SBU and for each sector. These plans were reviewed at various levels in the structure and ultimately by corporate management. After a series of discussions, agreement on each SBU's strategy was reached, including initial capital budgets and net income targets for the coming year. A more detailed budgeting process then ensued. The budget was expected to include a specific line item for expenses associated with carrying out agreed strategic programmes. This practice was intended to prevent managers down the line from achieving their net income figures by "eating their seed corn". These programmes were thus akin to many of ICI's strategic milestones. SBU budgets were broken down into department budgets,

Operational
Organization
Levels

Figure 3.5 **Partial Representation of GE's 1980 Organization Structur**

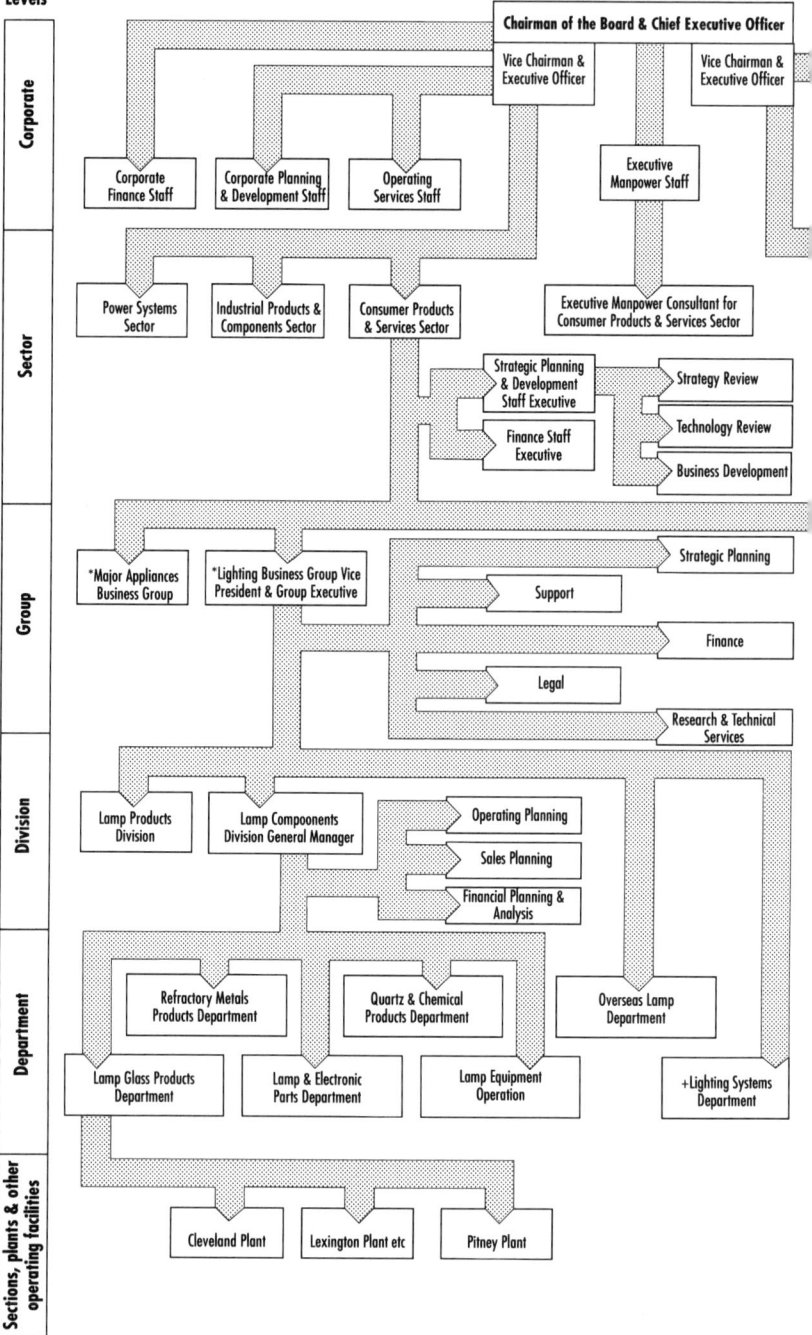

Corporate

Sector

Group

Division

Department

Sections, plants & other operating facilities

Chairman of the Board & Chief Executive Officer

Vice Chairman & Executive Officer

Vice Chairman & Executive Officer

Corporate Finance Staff

Corporate Planning & Development Staff

Operating Services Staff

Executive Manpower Staff

Power Systems Sector

Industrial Products & Components Sector

Consumer Products & Services Sector

Executive Manpower Consultant for Consumer Products & Services Sector

Strategic Planning & Development Staff Executive

Strategy Review

Finance Staff Executive

Technology Review

Business Development

*Major Appliances Business Group

*Lighting Business Group Vice President & Group Executive

Strategic Planning

Support

Finance

Legal

Research & Technical Services

Lamp Products Division

Lamp Compoonents Division General Manager

Operating Planning

Sales Planning

Financial Planning & Analysis

Refractory Metals Products Department

Quartz & Chemical Products Department

Overseas Lamp Department

Lamp Glass Products Department

Lamp & Electronic Parts Department

Lamp Equipment Operation

+Lighting Systems Department

Cleveland Plant

Lexington Plant etc

Pitney Plant

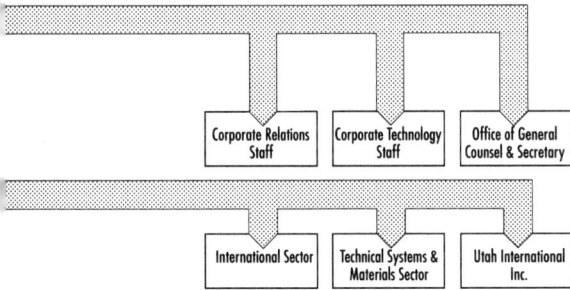

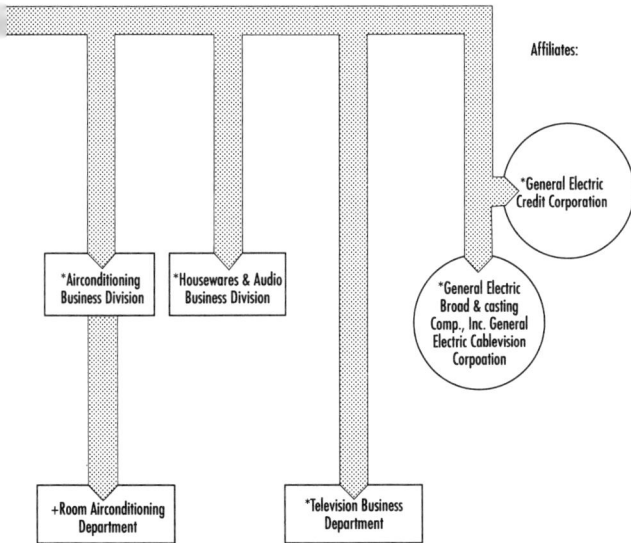

**Strategic
Planning Process
Levels**

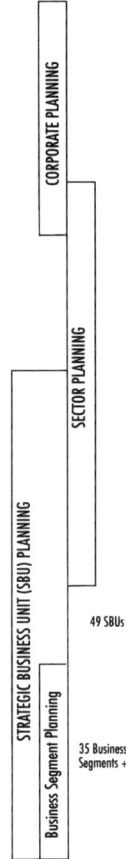

Corporate Relations Staff

Corporate Technology Staff

Office of General Counsel & Secretary

International Sector

Technical Systems & Materials Sector

Utah International Inc.

Affiliates:

*General Electric Credit Corporation

*Airconditioning Business Division

*Housewares & Audio Business Division

*General Electric Broad & casting Comp., Inc. General Electric Cablevision Corpoation

+Room Airconditioning Department

*Television Business Department

CORPORATE PLANNING

SECTOR PLANNING

STRATEGIC BUSINESS UNIT (SBU) PLANNING

Business Segment Planning

49 SBUs

35 Business Segments +

+: Business segments
*: Strategic business units (SBU's)

with responsibility for implementation located in the regular operating hierarchy rather than the "strategic" SBU structure.

Monitoring

A standardized monthly reporting format was used to monitor results. The focus, especially for corporate management, was on the major financial aggregates, with discretion on how these targets were achieved left to the line manager responsible. Space was, however, provided in the reporting format for each unit to report on key non-financial measurements that the general manager in charge felt were relevant. A brief strategic commentary was also given.

Rewards and sanctions

SBU managers each developed a set of explicit financial and non-financial objectives (known as a performance screen) on which they believed they should be evaluated. The objectives (which were related to the strategy and the budget for the unit) might cover financial targets such as net income, return on investment, cash flow and operating margin; and also actions (such as "increase market share by X per cent", "maintain cost leadership", "develop a total quality programme") that would provide future benefits for GE. After discussion with the manager, the sector head would assign relative weights to each measure, depending on their importance for the strategy of the business. A manager's results achieved versus the performance screen were then used as inputs to salary reviews and incentive compensation decisions.

Review

By the late 1970s, GE had in place a sophisticated process for determining strategic objectives for each of its many businesses, and for making them an explicit part of the monitoring and evaluation process. The formal linkage between strategic planning, budgets, the control process, and personal evaluation and incentive schemes went further in GE than in any of the other companies described in this chapter.

Eventually, as we shall see in Chapter 4, this formal process became overly bureaucratic and was dismantled. But, although much of the formal structure of planning and control has now been abandoned, GE still adheres to the principle of the centre agreeing strategic objectives with each business, and then finding means of checking that the strategy is being successfully implemented.

STRATEGIC PLANNING COMPANIES

The corporate level in Strategic Planning companies wishes to be somewhat closer to their businesses than is typical in Strategic Control companies. Strategy formulation is more of a joint activity between the centre and the businesses, and the centre normally monitors results more closely than in Strategic Control companies. Consequently control can encompass a wider range of objectives. Because the principle of decentralized responsibility for strategy is stressed less than in Strategic Control companies, there is rather less need for a few clear measures of overall performance. Nevertheless certain targets represent the key criteria of good performance. We will describe three companies (Shell, BP and National Westminster Bank) that try to identify such targets and to make them into explicit and formal strategic control objectives.

Shell

In the Royal Dutch/Shell Group (henceforth referred to as Shell) strategy development and implementation are primarily the responsibilities of operational company management, but the central office exerts a strong influence on the process. To understand how the process works it is necessary first to understand the structure of the company and its managerial culture.

In Shell the basic business unit is the operating company, such as Shell Chimie (the chemicals company in France) and Shell UK Oil (the downstream oil company in the UK). These operating companies are supported by a number of central service companies based in London and The Hague, representing three dimensions of the group: business sectors, regions and functions (Figure 3.6 on page 66). The regions represent the shareholders in the group: they appoint the senior management of the operating companies, arrange annual planning and appraisal meetings, and agree budgets and plans. The business sectors provide technical and commercial advice to the operating companies, orchestrate international trading, coordinate major investments, and guide the international aspects of strategy. The functions are either corporate activities (such as finance) or central services (such as research).

Line management in the operating companies reports up through the region, sometimes by way of a national company (see Figure 3.7 on page 67). However, the operating companies must also coordinate with and use the resources of the business sector and appropriate functions. The functional structure is reproduced within the sectors and the operating companies; for example, there are planning functions within Shell International Chemicals Company (the business sector) and within Shell Chimie.

Within this three-dimensional structure, many people have an interest in any major decision, and the Shell approach is to gain agreement from all parties before acting. One manager explained: "Although the sector is not responsible for producing the operating company plans, it has to approve them if they are to get budgetary support. The region must also give its approval. A plan, therefore, needs three 'yeses' if it is to get approval. Shell is the leading consensus-hunting organization in the western world."

Or, as another manager put it, "Nobody says 'yes' or 'no', but lack of support in the appropriate places can kill a project."

Figure 3.6 **Shell's Organization Structure**

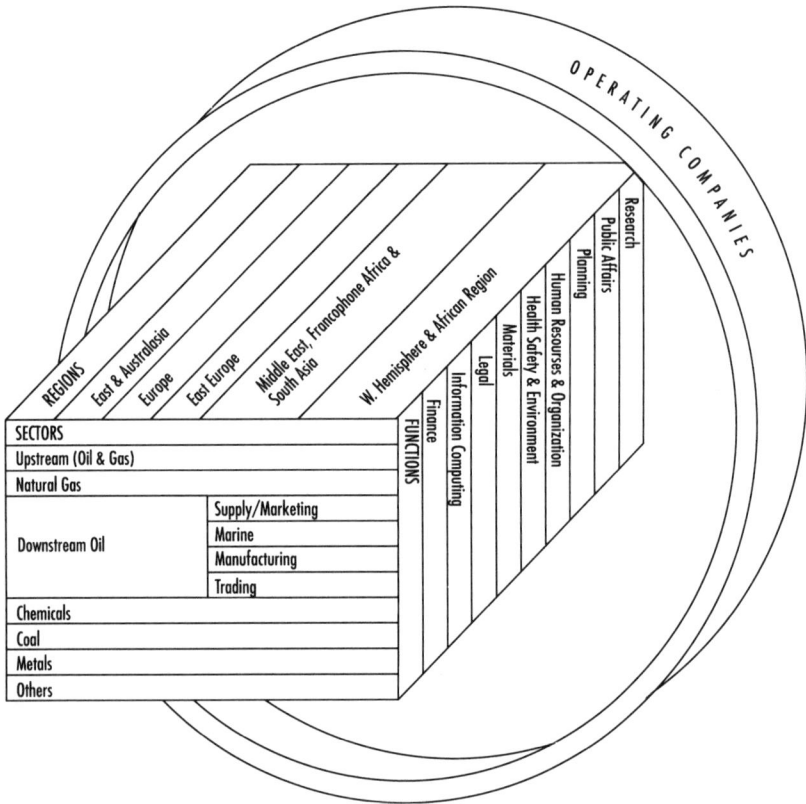

Shell's structure and culture are seen as having both advantages and disadvantages. "The structure through which decisions evolve is complex. It means we miss the worst mistakes but are sometimes slow in reacting to opportunities such as acquisitions."

Objective setting: strategies and budgets

Each Shell operating company is responsible for generating company strategies, business plans and budgets, though it is expected to seek assistance from the central offices as appropriate. Strategic reviews of the larger operating companies are conducted in the spring. The operating company makes a presentation to the region, describing its previous year's performance and any proposals to modify strategy. The sector and functional service companies provide inputs to this review in the form of commentaries on the operating company's performance. The meetings are not rubber stamping exercises but are expected to be surprise free, as the operating company should keep the service companies informed of its thinking on an ongoing basis. The time frame for strategy varies between companies but will typically cover 10–20 years.

The starting points for the strategic review are the operating company's existing strategy and the sector strategy. Strategies also take account of the economic and environmental scenarios developed by Group Planning.

Figure 3.7 **Reporting Routes in Shell**

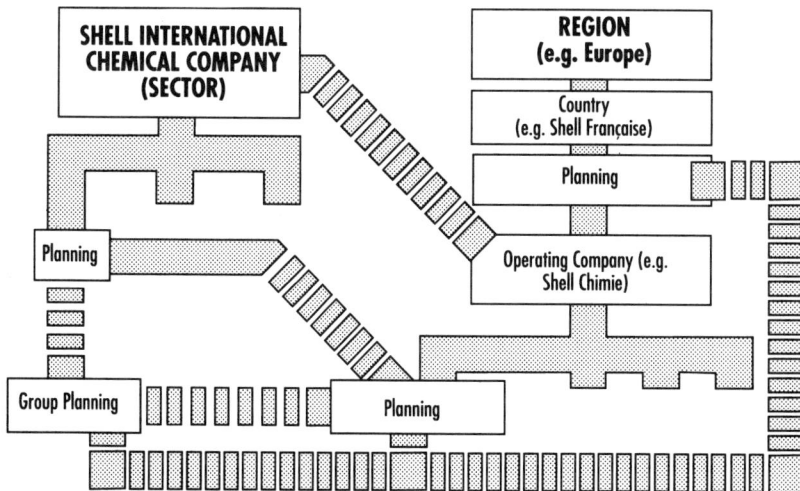

The sector strategy is built up from the strategies of the operating companies. The role of the sector is to ensure a coherent and comprehensive international strategy, avoiding unhelpful duplication between the operating companies. Working with the key operating companies it develops strategies that cut across national boundaries; for example, a strategy for exploration and production of oil in the Far East or a total detergent business strategy. The sector then works with the operating companies to draw up an implementation plan.

The sector strategies have until recently been reviewed every two years, but are now revised on an as-necessary basis. Sector coordinators[6] present the sector strategy to their peers (some of the other coordinators plus some managing directors) to outline the sector thinking and seek their advice. Then presentations are made to the full committee of managing directors, and subsequently to the members of the boards of the parent companies, which lead to the endorsement of some specific, clear, if qualitative targets. After each of these stages feedback is given to the principal operating companies.

The sector cannot impose strategy nor can it act independently to implement strategy. But it can prevent the implementation of operating company strategy, as its approval is generally required for any major investment and for the allocation of R&D resources. Thus, for example, if Shell needed to make one major investment in ethylene capacity and two operating companies were bidding for it, the sector would work to gain consensus on which was the better option (considering both financial and strategic criteria), and would be in a position to block progress on the alternative.

The sector can also suggest strategic initiatives, but will need to sell them to operating companies if they are to be implemented. The involvement of the sector in the development of strategy varies among businesses. In Upstream Oil and Gas, the operating companies rely on a fairly small number of highly skilled technical staff based in The Hague to develop strategy in terms of whether and where to drill. The operating company's role is to manage the project, acquire licences, communicate with governments, and so on. In contrast, Downstream Oil operates in practically every country in the world, each of which has its particular market structure in terms of size, products and competition. As a result the sector has far less to contribute to operating company strategy.

Following agreement on strategy, the operating companies present their five-year business plans to the regional management each autumn.

This document, termed the country plan, is an indication of how the strategy is to be realized and covers both qualitative and quantitative issues. The financial numbers, however, are generally taken as a reference case, accompanied by sensitivities, rather than a forecast. The first year of the business plan includes an outline budget for the following year. This is generally refined and firmed up in January or February.

Objective setting: milestones
In the Chemicals sector, the strategic planning process is taken through to the agreement of specific strategic milestones. Thus, the national companies are encouraged to include within the chemicals section of the country plan a statement of strategic milestones: key events by which strategic progress can be monitored. Although the milestones cover the five years of the plan, they concentrate on the earlier years, especially year one.

A strategic milestone, as the term is used within the Chemicals sector of Shell, is not an objective in itself but rather an event that has to occur if a strategic objective is to be attained. As mentioned in Chapter 2, we were told that: "Milestones are not ends in themselves but rather stages that you pass on the way." Thus, for example, if the objective was to introduce a new product, the milestones, each with an associated timing, might include assembling a project management team, establishing an R&D programme, gaining capital expenditure approval, and so on.

Although the centre wishes to see a wider use of strategic milestones, the culture in Shell does not allow them to be imposed on the operating companies. The role of the centre is rather to develop methodologies for identifying and monitoring milestones and to advocate their use.

Monitoring
The prime responsibility for monitoring progress against milestones lies with the operating company management, who are expected to flag a missed milestone. "You have got to trust people. You cannot spend all your life monitoring things," a corporate manager explained.

Progress against milestones is also formally reported by the operating company to the regional coordinator at its appraisal review meeting in the spring. At this meeting the business sector service company may also comment on the company's strategic progress. Where a milestone relates to a multi-country project, the sector is responsible for monitoring progress.

Milestones were introduced to provide a stronger focus on the implementation of strategy. "We felt that there had been a lack of attention to the implementation of strategy. The strategic drive got dissipated because of a lack of discipline in implementation, a lack of milestones. Strategies were put forward without a clear plan for their implementation, nor any system of measuring progress in implementation."

Milestones, then, provide the basis for monitoring progress on strategy. But they are viewed by the central offices primarily as a way of tracking the implementation of strategy and of triggering strategic reviews rather than as a measure of managerial performance. "Milestones are points consistent with the formulated strategy. If they are not achieved that is an indication that the strategy should be revisited."

If a strategic milestone is not reached by the planned date, it prompts questions such as:

- Is the strategy still valid?
- Are sufficient resources being devoted to the strategy?
- Are the milestones realistic?
- Are the timescales for the milestones realistic?

Since considerable effort goes into the development of strategies, people are reluctant to change them. As one manager put it, "If the strategy to get market share requires a new technology by year N but R&D say they cannot deliver by then, do you abandon the strategy or defer the deadline? People tend to duck the issue of changing strategy if a milestone is not met."

Rewards, sanctions and intervention

Traditionally, the managerial reward system in Shell companies has been based on career progress, status among one's peers and access to capital for investment. However, some companies are now introducing an element of performance-related pay. Each manager's job is assigned a market-assessed level of reward, and the manager can earn 90–120 per cent of that level, depending on performance in the job. The appraisal process is quite formal and includes both operational and strategic performance criteria. The process is, however, somewhat subjective and not formula-based.

The company also employs a system termed Currently Estimated Potential (CEP) for planning the careers of its managers. This system is strongly linked to a manager's ability to perform strategically. Shell wants to ensure that managers who might be expected to reach the most senior posts are moved through the company quickly, giving them increasing responsibility and broad experience of the company's activities and businesses. CEP therefore is an estimation of the level individual managers are expected to reach, and their career will be planned on that basis. Managers normally know their own CEP, but not those of others, except for their subordinates.

A CEP is not set in tablets of stone. After the annual performance appraisal, a manager's boss may recommend a change in the CEP, which will be considered by the management of the parent function or sector for senior managers in Shell headquarters. Decisions about changes in CEP pay particular attention to the ability to act strategically (that is, to display "helicopter quality", as it is termed in Shell). There is less interest in the ability to deliver in the short term, but short-term performance against financial and strategic milestones will generally be a necessary condition for a manager to get his boss's recommendation for an improved CEP in the first place.

Milestones in Shell Chemicals UK
The operating companies that have made the greatest use of explicit milestones have been those in the Chemicals sector. In our research we have considered in some detail the example of Shell Chemicals UK (SCUK).

The structure of SCUK is shown in Figure 3.8. In addition to the

Figure 3.8 **Structure of SCUK**

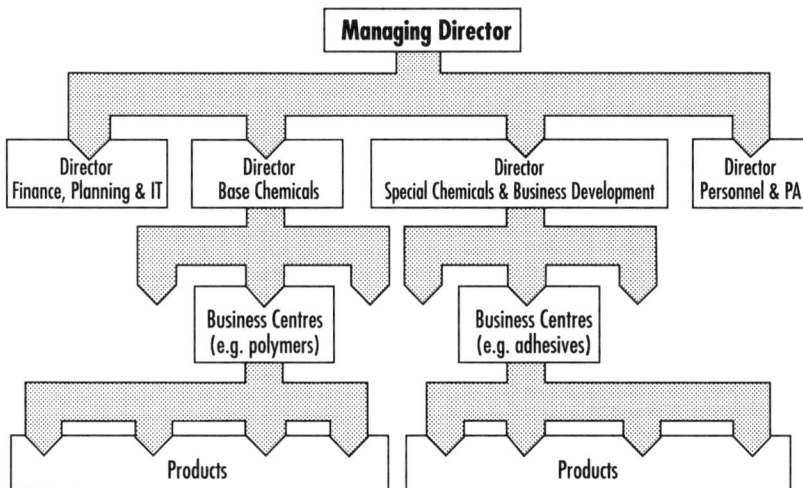

functional directors, directors responsible for two main business streams – base chemicals and special chemicals – report to the managing director. Each of these business streams has a number of business centres, each with its own general manager. For example, the base chemicals business includes a polymer business centre, and the special chemicals business includes an adhesives business centre. In turn, each of these business centres is organized on a product line basis.

Most milestones are generated at the business centre level. Business centre managers have considerable freedom to propose their own milestones, which are then agreed with the senior management. This process engenders a sense of ownership that is seen as important. "If people don't have a lot of scope to set their own milestones they become very evasive," we were told.

In addition to these business centre milestones, each business stream and each corporate function has its own distinct milestones, and there will be some milestones that relate to the overall business. There is no pre-set norm for the number of milestones, but each business centre, business stream and function could expect to have about three in the five-year business plan, giving a total of 30–40. Of these, about 10, including the overall business milestones, would be highlighted to the regional management as SCUK's milestones.

Examples of milestones for each level might be as follows:

Business centre: Enhance the capacity of plant X by N% by 1990.

Base chemicals: Secure long term contract with customer Y by 1991.

Finance function: Complete installation of new system by 1990.

SCUK: Integrate acquisition Z by 1992.

Although Shell regards milestones as "signposts rather than objectives", at the operating company level they tend to become embodied in the objectives set for managers. In SCUK the major milestones set for the company will form the basis for some of the managing director's objectives. The MD will also have a range of financial and operating objectives. These objectives are "cascaded down" through all levels of the organization. Having agreed objectives with the regional coordinator, the managing director of SCUK presents them to the management team and invites them to propose their own objectives, designed to support the managing director's objectives. When these have been agreed, the senior managers will in turn present their objectives to their own managers and invite them to suggest a set of objectives. Eventually, in theory, everyone has a set of objectives consistent with and supportive of the operating company's objectives, including the strategic milestones. Individuals' objectives are then expressed as targets, which will usually be quantified, and deadlines will be set. These targets are translated into a set of agreed tasks. The targets and tasks form the base data for appraisal under the company's MBO scheme. Despite the view of the centre that strategic milestones should be used as indicators of strategic progress rather than of individual managerial performance, in practice they do tend, therefore, to become indirect measures of individual performance.

Milestones were seen by the SCUK senior management to be of value in several ways. First, milestones avoid "second guessing". "Without milestones there was a tendency for managers to second guess their superior's objectives in the light of environmental changes. Milestones provide a framework that forces discussion of the issues."

The milestones also link the strategic planning process and people's actions. Since people focus on what is measured, explicit milestones create more effort in implementing strategy.

"Without milestones the planning process became detached from the business. People lacked ownership of the plans and could not see how their personal performance was related to the plans.

"The major benefit of milestones is that over 90 per cent of people in the organization are personally involved in the direction of the business. This leads to greater interest, improved motivation and a sensible consideration of priorities."

On the other hand, there is concern that the costs of operating the milestone system (for example, detailed regular monitoring) should not outweigh the benefits. "Milestones are an essential part of strategic management, but I'm scared to death by the potential for bureaucracy and costs." A further concern is that excessive focus on milestones might distort business decision making and lead to misdirection of effort, particularly in unstable market conditions.

Review

The strategic control process in Shell reflects the Strategic Planning style of the company. Milestones go into rather more detail on the action programmes and projects through which strategy will be implemented than is typical in Strategic Control companies, and they are intended, in the first instance, to check whether a strategy is on track rather than to provide a basis for evaluating individual managers' performance. Explicit strategic milestones are not defined everywhere within Shell, and there is recognition of other, more qualitative factors in judging strategic progress. Nevertheless, the additional motivation and discipline provided by the definition of strategic milestones is seen as valuable by those parts of the company that have set up a more formal strategic control process.

BP

In *Strategies and Styles,* BP was described as a Strategic Planning company, for several reasons. First, the top corporate management were directly involved in the strategic decisions of the main business streams; major exploration investments, refinery capacity rationalization, re-branding of retail outlets were all decisions where the influence of the corporate executive directors was strong. Secondly, there was an extensive planning process and large corporate staff, with detailed reviews of strategies and plans at a number of levels. Thirdly, in the oil business time scales and risks are such that tight short-term control is infeasible, and objectives need to look towards long-term results. For these reasons BP has been a less detached corporate parent than Strategic Control companies such as ICI and Courtaulds.

But, if the BP centre has been more involved than in Strategic Control companies, it has also been much less involved than companies such as NatWest or Digital. The philosophy of the management team under Sir Peter Walters stressed increased devolution of responsibility to business streams and sharper control processes. And the very size (sales of £25,922 million in 1988) and geographical diversity of the company made some measure of decentralization inevitable. Even the business stream headquarters, such as BP Oil International, attempted to decentralize responsibility to individual country managers, and to avoid excessive coordination and directiveness by the business stream headquarters. The recent changes to BP's corporate structure and management processes introduced under Bob Horton, the company's new chairman, took place after our research was completed, but seem likely to reinforce the decentralization theme.

During our research BP was, in fact, mid-way between Strategic Planning and Strategic Control – although the corporate centre relative to the business streams was, of course, closer to Strategic Control and the business streams relative to the business units were closer to Strategic Planning. We will describe the control process at both these levels.[7]

Objective setting at the corporate level

BP has a three-phase formal planning process: strategic plans, development plans and operating plans. Each business stream draws up a strategic plan on approximately a two-yearly cycle. The strategic plans look towards the ten-year time horizon and beyond. They concentrate on how BP can establish positions of sustainable competitive advantage, and avoid detailed numerical forecasts. At the completion of the strategy review, the centre issues guidelines to the business stream concerning its broad portfolio role and objectives. The development plans are prepared annually, and include a medium-term (five-year) projection, which is intended to be consistent with the strategy. The operating plan covers the annual budget and also associated non-financial objectives.

In terms of control, the operating plan is the basis for each business's contract with the centre. The non-financial objectives in the operating plan, which are termed "milestones" by BP, are important for strategic control. The initiative lies with the businesses to propose milestones as part of their operating plan. These milestones for reporting to the centre will typically be a subset of those that the business stream itself reviews internally, which in turn are a subset of the milestones reviewed by individual business units. Thus the business stream may report on 8–10 key milestones to the centre, may look at 20–30 milestones internally, and may consist of half a dozen business units, each with 10 milestones of its own. At lower levels, the milestones tend to become more detailed and specific.

The milestones tend to stress physical targets or events: do X by Y date is a typical form. In principle they are expected to define the actions needed to achieve progress in terms of the key success factors identified in the strategy review. Examples, each with a target date, include: integrating an acquisition; implementing a reorganization; bringing on stream a new computer system. Milestones are easier to set in project based businesses, such as Exploration, than in market oriented businesses, such as Downstream Oil. Where strategy consists of a series of major project investments, the milestones can concentrate on the key physical measures that determine the progress and value of the project (for example, level of reserves, development timetables, cost per barrel discovered and produced).

The milestones proposed by the business are reviewed and agreed by the Corporate Control Department (CCL). Normally this agreement is routine, but occasionally CCL will reject a milestone that it feels is too nebulous or fuzzy. ("You have got to be able to fail and know that you've failed.") But some objectives are hard to convert into precise and measurable milestones. ("One of the business streams has differentiation as a key strategic thrust. How do you set mathematical and measurable milestones to check progress with that?") CCL will also hold discussions with Corporate Planning (CTP), who administer the strategic planning process, about the milestones being proposed in the operating plans. The business stream boards also review and agree the milestones proposed by the business.

Monitoring at the corporate level

The centre monitors business stream performance through regular monthly and quarterly review reports, and through the membership of main board executive directors on business stream boards. The monthly performance reviews are primarily financial in nature, but the quarterly reviews also report on progress with non-financial milestones and major projects. The commentary, which concentrates on deviations from plan, discusses both past performance and implications for the near-term future. The quarterly reviews are prepared by CCL, though the businesses receive copies and can comment on what CCL has produced. There is a balance between discussion of financial and non-financial targets, but "a tendency to make financial targets more important because they are a simpler shorthand, especially in businesses away from the oil core which we don't know so well". The reviews are discussed at the main board, but the businesses will be represented only through the executive directors who sit on their boards.

The second means of corporate monitoring is less formal, and relies on the fact that a BP main board executive director is non-executive chairman of each business stream board. In addition one or two other main board directors or senior corporate executives sit as non-executive members of each of these business boards. The boards meet every two months, which, together with much more frequent informal contact, allows the corporate representatives to follow progress in the business stream.

Rewards, sanctions and intervention at the corporate level

Milestone achievements are an important part of business performance assessment, and balance the financial criteria in the operating plans.

Nevertheless it is acknowledged that ultimately the most important objectives are always the financial targets on funds flow and profitability. "They are ends in themselves, and therefore take precedence over strategic milestones. Even if the milestone is missed, there is always a chance to reset the tiller and hit it later, whereas if a financial target is missed then that is a failure in itself."

Reaction to missed targets and milestones depends very much on circumstances. Because of the volatility of oil prices a number of business targets have been missed, but it is hard to determine whether a given deviation was controllable by management or not. Furthermore, personal responsibilities are difficult to establish, given the long time scales in the business and the shared responsibilities in BP's matrix structure. Despite a desire to tighten control, BP feels the need for some flexibility in reacting to results. Managers are always given an opportunity to explain their failures. One observed, "I doubt whether there has ever been a missed objective in BP that has led to 'the last cheque'." On the other hand, "professionalism and people's commitment to doing their job do make milestones matter", and "resource allocation to a business, and individuals' careers, are damaged based on objectives being missed over a period of time". Some formal links between milestone achievements and cash compensation are also currently being introduced.

Strategic control at the business stream level

It is interesting to contrast the corporate approach to planning and control with practice at the business stream level. There are many similarities, but also some differences. We will focus this discussion mainly on BP Oil International (BPOI).

BPOI has a complex matrix structure with nine business development units (for example Refining, Retailing, Lubricants, Aviation) responsible for strategic development in their areas and more than 50 national companies responsible for operations.

The basic planning cycle of strategic plan – development plan – operating plan is identical to the corporate cycle, with BPOI's plans feeding into the corporate process. Milestones also play an important role in the operating plan cycle within BPOI. "We now put almost as much emphasis on milestone measures as on shorter-term financial targets in BPOI," one manager explained.

The milestone concept has been in use for three or four years in

BPOI. Within BPOI, as at the interface with corporate headquarters, milestones tend to concentrate on key action programmes (for example, arranging an asset swap, establishing a certain number of automobile maintenance centres, implementing a programme to improve image). Action milestones are often easier to monitor than output milestones. ("You can see what has been spent to create the new image; but what result this has had is much harder to measure.") Also, milestones of performance relative to competitors are hard to set, since so many of the competitors are integrated operators who do not report results for their separate businesses in the oil sector. At the business level within BPOI, milestones become more specific and detailed. But even at this level, some managers fear that the few chosen milestones can be "a very crude shorthand", failing to reflect the realities of the marketplace.

Typically a business may have three or four relatively hard and measurable milestones and an equal number of softer ones ("increase marketing effectiveness", "raise quality").

"As a strategy becomes clearer, so the milestones get more precise. In the first instance you may have a milestone to complete a strategic review by a given date; once achieved, this might lead to a second milestone of drawing up a specific plan by a certain date; and once the plan is decided, this might lead to a number of specific action milestones to implement the plan. Thus there could be an issue about refinery capacity in Europe; the first stage might be to get in place a strategy to deal with it, leading through to a plan to reduce capacity, and subsequent implementation milestones concerned with particular refineries."

Milestones for businesses also emerge in response to questions from the centre or from BPOI.

BPOI can obviously be rather closer to its businesses than can the corporate centre. For example, more milestones are established and monitored within BPOI than are reported to the centre. In the last couple of years, however, the number of milestones for each business has been reduced. "One of the hardest problems has been establishing a manageable number of milestones," we were told. "You need to identify the things that matter most for each manager, and stop short of long lists of 40 or 50 objectives. You have to concentrate on a small number of them to mean much." BPOI's more detailed knowledge of its businesses also makes it easier to "stretch" milestones proposed by the businesses, "often through setting a tighter timetable, rather than demanding a higher performance level, since so many milestones are yes/no events rather than more/less targets."

The monitoring cycle is similar to the corporate level's, with formal quarterly reports prepared by BPOI's control department on milestone performance. However, the planning and control functions are combined in one department in BPOI, an arrangement that is felt to improve communication and integrate longer-term strategic plans better with short-term control. ("Putting planning and control together is a natural combination. Control is really just seeing that the plans have been implemented, and milestones are just a way of reminding people to try to be objective.") Day-to-day line management contact within BPOI supplements the more formal quarterly reports with frequent informal updates on progress.

Within BPOI milestone achievements matter for personal rewards and promotions. But they are not supposed to dominate the thinking and actions of individual managers. ("If there is too much pressure, it prevents people down the line from coming up with good new ideas. We want the business manager to be open about the status of his strategy and whether it needs to be changed, rather than going all out simply to meet the milestones for their own sake.") Milestone achievements are part of a wider, overall judgement.

Review

The BP strategic control process is structured and formal, calling for clear definition of milestones and quarterly reporting of results. This frequency of reporting on milestones is unusual, and reflects the integration of the milestones into the operating planning cycle. Separate departments – Planning and Control – administer the strategic planning and the strategic control process, although within BPOI these two departments have been integrated to improve liaison. The milestones tend to concentrate on key action programmes, and are more detailed at lower levels in the company.

For both the centre and the businesses, the key value of the milestones is in creating a focus on certain important non-financial issues. ("They focus the dialogue through the year.") For the business, they also make for a clearer dialogue with the centre and a greater degree of mutual commitment. As one manager explained, "The milestone process fosters understanding at the next level up. It forces them to focus on important strategic items. Milestones are also useful in making clearer to the centre what resources we have to command in order for our strategies to work." Milestones have clarified the relationships between levels, and made decentralization work better in BP.

National Westminster Bank

The National Westminster Bank (NatWest) is moving from a more hands-on, centralized style of management towards the Strategic Planning style. The company has recently reorganized into the structure shown in Figure 3.9. There are three main businesses – UK Financial Services, International Businesses, and Corporate and Institutional Banking – together with a number of central functions and support services. The reorganization has grouped similar businesses together to provide a more strategic structure.

Although the bank operates in a variety of product markets, it is a more homogeneous business than most of the other companies in our study. Furthermore, most of the senior management have long experience with the bank, and a detailed knowledge of its operations. Historically, therefore, the centre has been able and willing to be closely involved in running the main businesses. In particular, the Chief Executive's Office, advised by the Business Development Division (now included in Group Strategy and Communications), has until recently had almost complete responsibility for strategic planning in the bank, including the development of strategic plans for the businesses. Although the centre continues to provide planning guidelines and set broad strategic objectives, the growing complexity and internationalization of the bank's markets have made it increasingly difficult for the centre to participate in developing detailed strategies. A larger strategic role has fallen to the businesses, a trend assisted by the corporate reorganization.

Objective setting

The planning approach within NatWest is based on a five-year corporate plan (revised annually) and a one-year operational plan. The strategic framework for the bank is developed by a central strategy committee comprising the Chief Executive's Office plus the chief executives of the businesses.

For the businesses themselves, the planning process begins with the establishment by the Chief Executive's Office of group targets and objectives, both financial (for example, return on capital, cost/income ratio) and commercial (what businesses does the bank want to be in?).

Figure 3.9 National Westminster Bank Structure

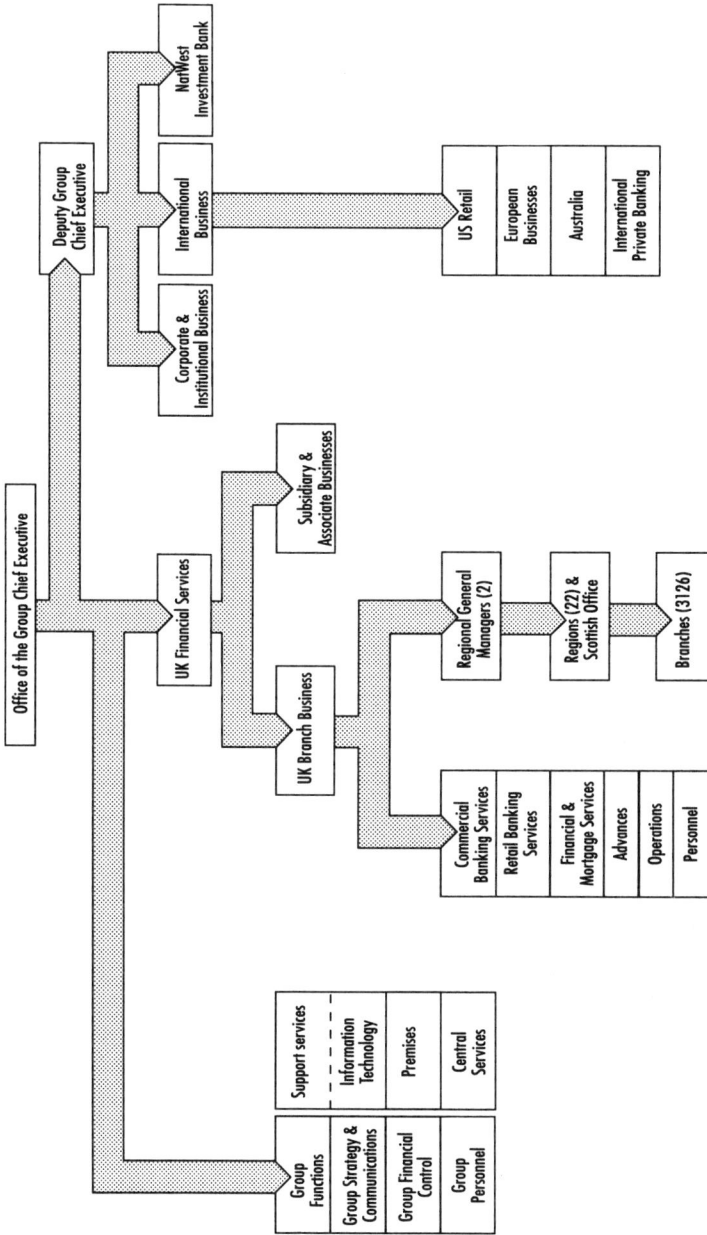

Office of the Group Chief Executive

Deputy Group Chief Executive

NatWest Investment Bank

International Business

Corporate & Institutional Business

US Retail
European Businesses
Australia
International Private Banking

UK Financial Services

Subsidiary & Associate Businesses

UK Branch Business

Regional General Managers (2)

Regions (22) & Scottish Office

Branches (3126)

Commercial Banking Services
Retail Banking Services
Financial & Mortgage Services
Advances
Operations
Personnel

Support services
Information Technology
Premises
Central Services

Group Functions
Group Strategy & Communications
Group Financial Control
Group Personnel

Next, given the existing strategies and historical performance of the businesses, the centre estimates what each business, through the organic growth of its current activities, should be able to contribute to the bank's total targets over the period of the corporate plan, but with particular emphasis on the first year. This view is communicated to the businesses as an indication of what the bank expects of them. The centre also provides a set of planning assumptions, covering things such as economic forecasts and exchange rate projections.

With this information, and based on their current strategies, the businesses work up operational plans and budgets on a product-by-product and segment-by-segment basis. They also carry out analyses on pricing policy, cost savings, and so on. The businesses then estimate the profit they can deliver, and a dialogue with the centre ensues. If the gap between the requirements of the centre and what a business believes it can deliver with its current strategy is unbridgeable, the strategy and planning assumptions are reconsidered. Eventually, agreement is reached on what each business can deliver, including a set of targets against which performance can be judged.

The final stage in the planning process is to consider the development of the businesses through non-organic growth (new directions, acquisitions) and new approaches to performing the bank's activities. This task, once the preserve of the Chief Executive's Office, is increasingly becoming the responsibility of the businesses themselves. Thus, for example, the UK branch business is developing its own strategies on delivery systems (for example, telephone banking, through-the-wall banking terminals).

Although the businesses now have a greater role in developing their own strategies, the centre retains overall control and guides the corporate development of the bank. "Throughout the planning process, we check the aspirations of the business sectors to ensure that the allocation of capital is the best for the bank as a whole. The important thing is that the business sector strategy is not incompatible with the corporate strategy."

As well as five-year profit targets, the corporate plan also contains intermediate targets for the businesses, the achievement of which is seen as necessary if the strategy is to be successfully implemented. "The ultimate targets for the business are in terms of financial performance over five years, but shorter-term targets must be set and achieved which underpin the achievement of the five-year financial targets."

Thus, for example, one business manager has a mix of targets; about half are profit related, about a quarter are market share and sales related, and the rest involve solving specific problems.

Inherent conflict is deliberately built in to the targets set for the businesses. "It is important to have counterbalancing goals to avoid extreme action. For example, in NatWest great emphasis is placed on the quality of accounts. Therefore, it is insufficient to target just the volume of business, there must also be a contribution target."

The targets agreed by a business are also designed to avoid undue emphasis on the short term. The centre and the businesses discuss the factors affecting the long term profitability of the bank and set certain targets accordingly. Thus, for example, the domestic banking business will agree targets in terms of the share of the market for young people in higher education. Although such business makes little contribution in the short term, it is seen as very important in the long run, given the traditional loyalty people have to their first bank. Or the Corporate and Institutional Banking business, given the five-year target of "remaining a leading international finance house to major corporations worldwide", will include operational targets in terms of asset base and pricing that might adversely affect profitability in the short term. This target-setting process is cascaded down throughout the bank so that all managerial levels have a consistent set of targets designed to ensure the health of the bank in both the short and the long run.

Senior managers within a business are also set individual milestones: short-term achievements designed to ensure progress towards strategically important objectives. To give an example, Corporate and Institutional Banking is responsible for financing management buyouts. If, in some particular country, NatWest has not been involved in such deals, the local management might be set the milestone "negotiate six buyout deals this year".

Each manager would expect to have no more than five or six milestones, though this can give a total of several hundred within a business. About six of these are identified as having a major impact on the group as a whole and are monitored centrally by the group Chief Executive's Office as priority milestones for the business.

Monitoring

NatWest uses an annual performance review process to test whether the remaining four years of the planning cycle are robust. Each business prepares a review of its performance in the previous year, and Group

Financial Control and Group Strategy analyse actual performance against the plan, paying special attention to the milestones for the business, to judge whether the business strategy is still achievable or should be reconsidered. "Part of Group Strategy's role is to go into partnership with the businesses to discuss how they can achieve their plans. Planning should not be seen as a 'police force' but as being on the side of the businesses as well as the group."

This analysis provides the basis for briefing the group chief executive before a discussion with the sector chief of the business on the strategy for the business. In this meeting any modifications to the strategy and the key objectives for the business are agreed.

Throughout the year performance is monitored and reviewed, both centrally and within the businesses. Group Financial Control monitors the numbers through the standard reporting systems of the bank. "This implicitly monitors business performance in that, say, market share targets will be expressed financially. For example, if the target is 5% of a £20 million market this will be expressed as a sales target of £1 million."

In addition, progress on major strategic initiatives and against business milestones is explicitly monitored by Group Strategy. But the centre cannot monitor all strategic initiatives in detail. Accordingly, we were told, "the centre only really monitors major programmes in detail and relies on monitoring financial indicators to ensure that the business in general is on course." More routine initiatives will be monitored internally within a business and reported to the sector chief of the business.

Rewards, sanctions and intervention
The traditional incentive for bank staff to perform has been promotion and career progression. Since "most people view a job in NatWest as a job for life", their interests have been thought to coincide with the best long-term interest of the bank. Furthermore, "so many of the people involved have been with the bank for so long there is a strong sense of teamwork and a lot of consensus on where the long term interest of the bank lies," we were told. Yet, with rapid changes in the bank's external environment, it is becoming more difficult to maintain this consensus.

The bank has recently introduced a formula-based, performance-related pay scheme for its managers. The scheme is linked to the financial and non-financial targets and milestones agreed by managers and is quite tightly applied. Several factors have emerged as important for such a reward scheme to be successful.

First, the performance measures and targets must be appropriate to the person's job. ("An account executive would be rewarded almost entirely on his ability to get good-quality business, whereas a business sector manager would also be measured on more strategic metrics.") Second, managers must "own" the goals. ("It is important to get commitment at the front end to an agreed strategy so that the business management see the strategy as achievable and not imposed.") Third, "people must only be judged on things they have some control over".

Given that the strategy is accepted by the business management, "the bank is not relaxed about taking excuses for failure", we were told. Allowances are made, however, for factors outside the control of the business management and targets may be flexed in response to unanticipated environmental changes. Targets are not adjusted subjectively, in response to special pleading, but in a formal, systematic reassessment. Thus, for example, if there is a sharp increase in interest rates, the sales target for mortgages may be reduced across the board. Competitively set targets, such as market share of new mortgage business, would not be modified, as the competition would be faced with the same environmental changes. As one manager observed: "Previously, managers could provide pretty loose explanations for missing targets. Now sympathy is out; precision is in."

Managers who achieve their targets can earn bonuses of up to 20 per cent of salary. This possibility has clearly changed behaviour in the bank, with the negotiations on targets being taken much more seriously. As one manager put it, "People used to accept targets 'on the nod'. Now they look very carefully at the targets being asked for."

NatWest does not focus on one or two simple measures of performance but rather attempts to balance several, possibly conflicting, measures. Accordingly, we were told, "it is inevitable that targets will be missed in a few areas. The reaction to missing targets depends on which targets and by how much." Where important targets within the business management's control are not met, the intervention of senior management may well result. "If a miss is due to management problems then one or two areas may be accepted. But misses in several areas may lead to a manager being moved."

Review

NatWest has gone further than most other companies towards introducing a formal system of strategic control with tight links to personal rewards. The system involves the explicit articulation of the measures required to achieve strategic objectives, which then become the criteria of good performance for the business managers concerned. These measures are followed through in considerable detail. Managers' rewards are systematically linked to the measures as part of a performance related pay structure.

Several factors have facilitated the introduction of formal strategic controls within the bank. First, the homogeneity of the bank's activities enables the centre to have more detailed knowledge of the company's businesses than is generally the case. Second, the bank's markets, although uncertain (because of fluctuating exchange rates, interest rates, etc.) are relatively predictable, so that targets can be systematically recalculated if the environment changes. Third, central management in the bank have been able to develop quite detailed models of its businesses and identify the key long term success factors, which have been used as a basis for setting strategic objectives and targets. Since the strategic control system has only recently been introduced into the bank, it is, however, too early to evaluate its success in improving performance.

Notes and References

1 The liaison director, sometimes called the "godfather", is a main board executive director who acts as a contact point on the executive team for the business. Liaison directors are not line responsible for the results of the business and remain primarily corporate players, but they are closer to their businesses than to other businesses in the portfolio, meeting more frequently with the management, receiving fuller information on them, and acting as a prime communication link between the business and the executive team. This liaison director role has been adopted in an increasing number of companies.

2 Alan I.H. Pink, "Strategic leadership through corporate planning at ICI", *Long Range Planning,* vol. 21, no. 1, 1988, pp. 18-25.

3 Pilkington also has a "godfather" system, with liaison directors for each operating company on the main board.

4 See Francis Tucker, Seymour Zivan and Robert Camp, "How to measure yourself against the best", *Harvard Business Review,* Jan-Feb 1987.

5 GE's management systems in the late 1970s and early 1980s are well documented, in "General Electric Company: Background note on management systems 1981", in R.F. Vancil, *Implementing Strategy: The Role of Top Management;* Division of Research, Harvard Business School Press, Boston, 1982. For a further discussion

of the historical development of GE's approach to planning and control, see Chapter 7.

6 Within the Shell central offices, the senior manager responsible for each business sector or service function is termed a coordinator (there is, for example, a chemicals coordinator). These coordinators are responsible to a member of the committee of managing directors (CMD). Each managing director will generally have a regional, sectoral and functional responsibility. Above the CMD is the ultimate level of consultation within the company, the Shell Conference, which includes all current and past members of the CMD plus non-executive directors from the two parent companies, Royal Dutch Petroleum Company and Shell Transport and Trading Company plc.

7 This description refers to the period before the changes introduced by Bob Horton in early 1990.

CHAPTER 4

INFORMAL STRATEGIC CONTROL PROCESSES

The great majority of companies do not define and monitor explicit strategic milestones as part of the formal management control process. In this chapter we will discuss ten companies that use a more informal process to track strategic progress. As in Chapter 3, we will begin with companies that pursue a Strategic Control style (GE, B.A.T, BOC, Bunzl, Courtaulds, Philips) and move on to those that are closer to a Strategic Planning style (Digital, Kingfisher, Nestlé, Toshiba).

STRATEGIC CONTROL COMPANIES

In many Strategic Control companies, the formal control process focuses on financial results and does not include explicit strategic objectives or milestones. Control reports, however, typically introduce financial data with a "strategic commentary" – a brief narrative that sets the financial results in a broader context. These formal reviews are supplemented by a variety of more informal contacts between the businesses and the centre. The criteria of good strategic performance emerge from the dialogue, both formal and informal, between the centre and the businesses, and from the feedback and rewards provided to the business managers.

We will describe the approaches to control currently adopted by GE and B.A.T Industries quite fully. These case studies will be supplemented with briefer descriptions of BOC, Bunzl, Courtaulds and Philips, which bring out particular points of interest.[1]

General Electric (GE)

In Chapter 3, we described the GE of the late 1970s and early 1980s as a classic example of a Strategic Control company using explicit strategic milestones as part of the control process. Since that time, under the influence of Jack Welch, chairman of GE since 1981, the company has altered its management style dramatically.

The change in style has two major components. First, the corporate centre has become closer to the individual businesses, in part through the process that GE calls "de-layering". Previously (as described in Chapter 3) there were over 40 separate SBUs, grouped together into divisions, which in turn reported to sectors, with the six sectors eventually reporting to the Chief Executive's Office.[2] Now, partly through portfolio rationalization and partly through reorganization, the number of SBUs has been reduced to 14, all of which report to the Chief Executive's Office directly (see Figure 4.1 on pages 90-91). Although GE remains highly diverse, this restructuring allows the centre to get more involved in dialogue with the businesses on important aspects of strategy. "We are very close; much closer to the businesses than in most other companies. Strategically, Jack Welch has made GE a less decentralized company. If there is disagreement on a strategic objective, then he will pursue it until agreement is reached."

On the other hand, the businesses are left free to decide how to achieve strategic objectives, and the centre tries to avoid interfering or dictating to business heads. Although SBUs are encouraged to share ideas and work together where possible (see our description of the Corporate Executive Committee below), the centre will, for example, very seldom insist that an SBU buy from an in-house supplier rather than a third party.

De-layering has increased reporting spans, a change that Welch sees as supporting the non-interference principle: "I have a theory that over-extended leaders – over-extended by the number of people reporting to them – end up being clearly the best leaders. Why? Because they don't have time to meddle, and because they create under them people who by necessity have to take on more responsibility."[3] With the centre closer to the major strategic issues, but still supportive of decentralization, GE has moved from a classic Strategic Control style to the border between Strategic Control and Strategic Planning.

The second shift in style has involved a reduction in the amount of formal, structured planning and control, and an increase in more informal, ongoing dialogue. In particular, there is less reliance on formally recorded agreements and objectives. "There is now a minimum of formal documentation before and after meetings. We intend that there should be a rolling agenda, that everyone should be clear about their respective responsibilities, and that they should not have time to waste in writing down formal descriptions of these responsibilities." Evidently

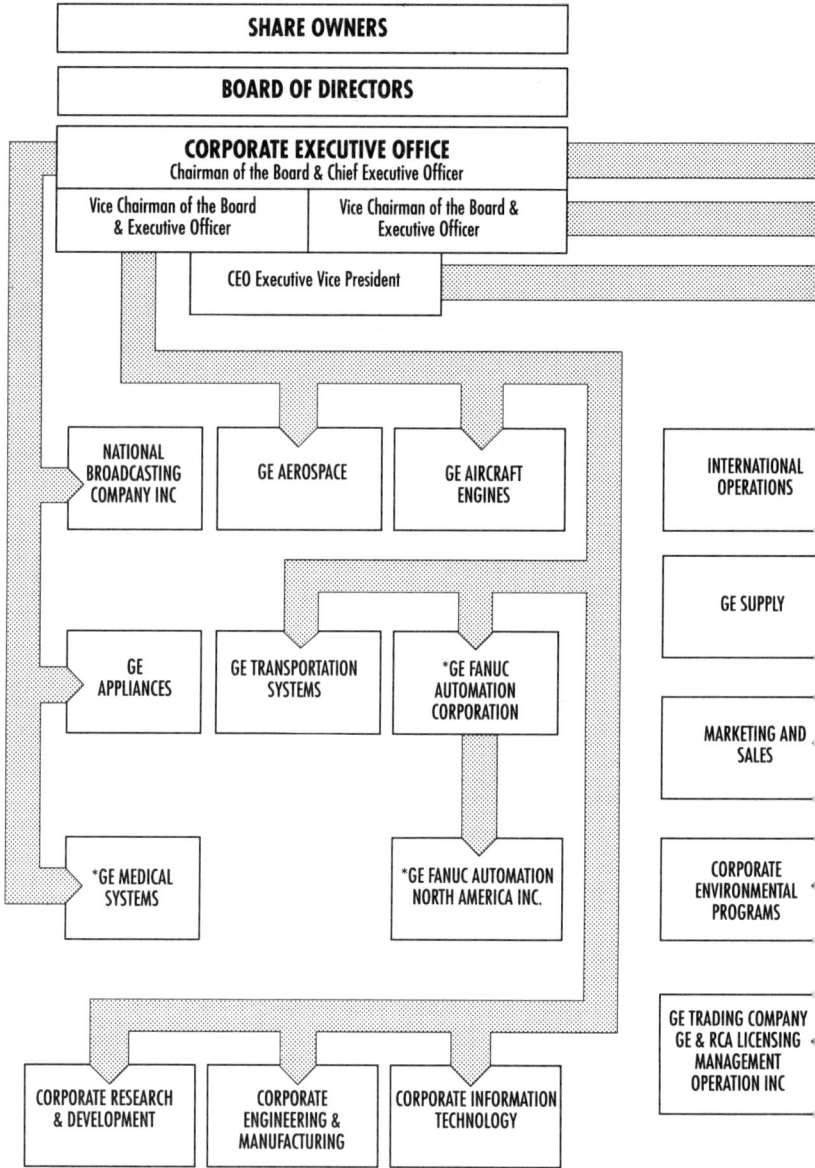

SHARE OWNERS

BOARD OF DIRECTORS

CORPORATE EXECUTIVE OFFICE
Chairman of the Board & Chief Executive Officer

Vice Chairman of the Board & Executive Officer	Vice Chairman of the Board & Executive Officer

CEO Executive Vice President

| NATIONAL BROADCASTING COMPANY INC | GE AEROSPACE | GE AIRCRAFT ENGINES | INTERNATIONAL OPERATIONS |

| GE APPLIANCES | GE TRANSPORTATION SYSTEMS | *GE FANUC AUTOMATION CORPORATION | GE SUPPLY |

MARKETING AND SALES

| *GE MEDICAL SYSTEMS | *GE FANUC AUTOMATION NORTH AMERICA INC. | CORPORATE ENVIRONMENTAL PROGRAMS |

| CORPORATE RESEARCH & DEVELOPMENT | CORPORATE ENGINEERING & MANUFACTURING | CORPORATE INFORMATION TECHNOLOGY |

GE TRADING COMPANY
GE & RCA LICENSING MANAGEMENT OPERATION INC

*50/50 joint venture with GE and Fanuc

Figure 4.1 **General Electric Company Organization Chart** (January 3, 1989)

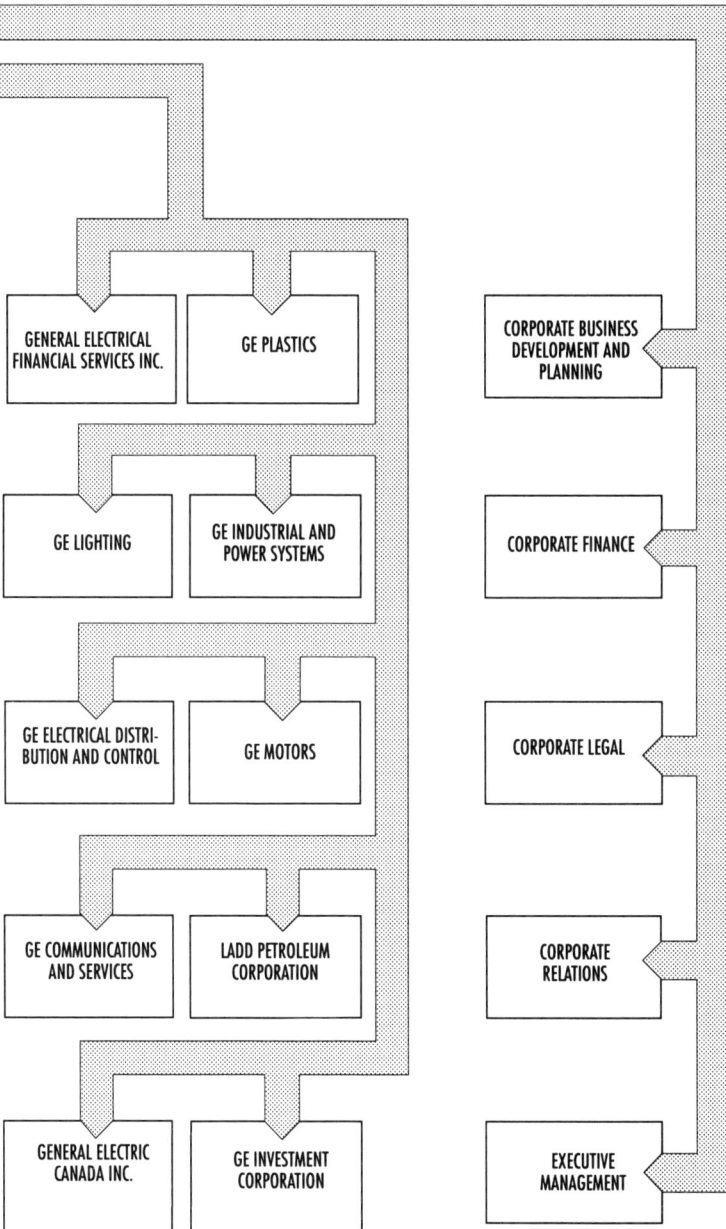

GE has moved away from a belief in the value of a formal control process with explicitly documented objectives.

We will explore the nature of and rationale for these changes more fully in Chapter 7. Here, we will concentrate on how GE's current planning and control process works, as an example of an informal strategic control process that no longer uses explicit milestones.

Strategy reviews

"We have moved away from periodic major data dumps towards more frequent, incremental discussions and decisions," a GE corporate executive told us. In the early 1980s formal annual strategy reviews were discontinued, and the main dialogue on strategy between the centre and the businesses was shifted on to a series of more informal, ad hoc meetings that took place from time to time throughout the year. Some of these meetings would involve full-day reviews of the strategies of major businesses, scheduled well in advance, with appropriate supporting analysis expected ("We go in the night before, have drinks and dinner with a group, then we spend 12 or 14 hours the next day in small groups talking about their business"). Other meetings would have a more limited agenda, with a focus on specific issues. ("We are going for constant communication without it being a burden, a richer appreciation of the strategy and the resources required to implement it in each area than any formal review can give you.")

But, in addition to the frequent, informal, decision-oriented meetings, GE has now reintroduced a once-a-year strategy review in July. This review is less formal than previously, typically involving only a 10–20 page document. But it is an opportunity to put down on paper the framework within which the through-the-year discussions are taking place. The centre can also get an overview of strategic developments in each of its businesses, and can identify issues that require attention.

Budgets / operating plans

The budget process within GE remains formal, structured and important. "The budget, the net income figure, is the most important control system; it is still seen as a sacrosanct commitment," we were told. But the net income figure is set with the strategic issues clearly in mind. Budget presentations begin with a review of last year's financials, go on to a discussion of the overall strategy and development of the business, which then leads in to a projection of financial targets for the coming year and identification of major issues. The budget will also identify large programme expenditures of a strategic nature separately; for example, a major project or engineering development, or a major new marketing initiative. Perhaps significantly, the term "operating plan" was adopted in place of "budget" in 1987. In preparing for operating plan reviews, the businesses are expected to assemble extensive supporting analysis of their strategic positions as a justification for the numbers proposed. Budgets that show a level of profitability that is too high strategically are as likely to be rejected as those that show low returns.

It is possible to revise a budget if circumstances in a business change. Indeed, business heads are encouraged to come in as soon as they are sure there is a possibility of not hitting their budget. If, for example, the market grows slower than expected, or if prices are pushed down by competitive activity, so that profit expectations must be reduced, the centre prefers to know as soon as possible rather than at the last moment.

Lack of explicit strategic objectives

Strategic measures of performance, however, are not made explicitly into controls. We gave an example in Chapter 2 concerning a business which stated in its strategy review that the key to its future was to get delivery cycle times down. "This would be noted, but not made explicitly into a control measure. Nevertheless, both the business and the centre would expect to see progress against this measure reported at the next review meeting."

GE's move away from explicit written-down controls seems to reflect a new emphasis on speed, responsiveness and insight. "In the 1970s we had financial measures and strategic measures and financial analysis and strategic analysis, and we lost focus on the issue of insight," we were told. "If you're looking for more speed and more responsiveness, that requires more trust. This means that formal, written-down objectives are less essential." Moving away from explicit objectives and milestones does not imply that businesses no longer need to have clear goals; the question is simply whether it is necessary to write them down in a formal and structured fashion.

It may appear that GE's celebrated goal of being number one or two in all its businesses amounts to an explicit milestone. "We will run only businesses that are number one or number two in their global markets – or, in the case of services, that have a substantial position," states Welch in the 1988 Annual Report. This principle has been behind many of

GE's divestments and closures in recent years, including the disposal of the GE/RCA television business to Thomson of France. As such, it seems to be an important – and explicit – strategic control objective. But, within GE, this objective is seen as a broad and simple means of getting at competitive leadership and sustained competitive advantage, which is what GE is really looking for. "The number one or two criterion is not slavishly interpreted," one manager told us. Thus it embodies a shared understanding of what GE is trying to achieve rather than a specific and precise target against which to measure business performance.

Monitoring

The businesses meet frequently with the Chief Executive's Office: in November for the operating plan review, in July for the strategy review, and approximately twice a year, usually in April and October, for operating reviews with the business's individual liaison member in the Chief Executive's Office. There is also an annual review of management development and personnel with the Chief Executive's Office for each business. These are on top of the ongoing informal series of meetings and contacts around specific decisions and issues. "Someone from the Chief Executive's Office will usually call me at least once a week," said one business head.[4] Performance thus is closely monitored, particularly in terms of major strategic programmes and operating plan commitments, although the emphasis is on the informal updates.

In addition, the Corporate Executive Committee (the CEC), which consists of the Chief Executive's Office and the heads of the major businesses and functions, meets for one and a half days each quarter. At these meetings the business heads each make a brief presentation (15–20 minutes), covering their performance against operating plan and any other issues they wish to share with the CEC. "The real motivation in GE is peer pressure when you get up in the CEC and have to present your numbers against operating plans. You don't want to be in a position where you have to show a shortfall, particularly if it's because of mistakes that you've made personally." Reporting packages have been slimmed down for monthly results, and control now concentrates on these quarterly reviews.

Rewards, sanctions and intervention

In keeping with the other management systems, management appraisal and compensation processes have become less formally structured. All officers of the company must now submit an individual "performance screen" to their bosses, which reflect their self-appraisal of the previous year's performance. The performance screen tends to begin with a review of how the individual has performed against his operating plan in the previous year, with a fairly quantitative emphasis on financial numbers. This is particularly true for the business heads. They must also include some discussion of more qualitative factors. In the typical performance screen there will be 10–20 individual items besides the operating plan statistics which are reported.

No standard format has been established for the performance screen, and managers each decide what topics should be covered. There is no specific link to the strategy of the businesses for which they are responsible, but "inevitably, it's one of the things that gets discussed". Topics also emerge from the regular meetings between a business head and the Chief Executive's Office during the year.

The Chief Executive's Office will then respond with its own assessment of how the individual has performed during the year. This assessment is expressed entirely in the Chief Executive's Office's own words (i.e. it is not a checklist of predefined categories).

Bonuses are an important component of salary for the top level of management in GE. In recent years they have represented more than 50 per cent of total compensation. But there is no objective method or formula for calculating individual bonuses. Rather they are based upon the performance screens and the Chief Executive's Office's view of how well each individual has done.

If things start to go wrong with a business's strategy, the Chief Executive's Office's reaction depends on the cause of the problem. "If Welch feels that the decisions made were taken on the basis of the best available data and analysis, he is apt to be fairly forgiving and to share the responsibility with us. But if he feels that the data we presented were wrong or distorted or myopic, then we take the brunt of criticism."

Decisions about when a business is going off track are complex. They are based not simply on failing to hit budget or any other simple control measures, but on a broader judgement.

"It's a matter of collective judgement. We don't have a formal early warning system. Rather, the whole philosophy is attuned to anticipation – management judgement should spot the problem before any early warning system. If a margin decline was the first signal that a business was in trouble, heads would roll. If you see it in the financial numbers, then it's too late. The time to intervene is when a business begins to lose the strategic initiative."

Readiness for early intervention requires that the Chief Executive's Office stays on top of the strategies of the businesses and depends, again, on the regular, ongoing dialogue that takes place.

Review

In recent years GE has dismantled much of the formal bureaucracy of planning and control. The move to a more informal strategic control process is intended to allow for a faster and more flexible response to the strategic opportunities the company faces, and to reduce the time and effort devoted to formal meetings and reports. Strategic objectives remain important but are set and monitored as part of an ongoing, informal dialogue between the businesses and the centre. In the words of one member of the GE corporate staff, this evolution has left a management system with "very simple processes, but so simple that they're sophisticated".

B.A.T Industries

At the time when we studied the strategic control process in B.A.T Industries, the group had four main areas of activity: Tobacco, Paper and Pulp, Retail and Financial Services (which the group entered in 1984). The group operates worldwide; its organization is shown in Figure 4.2. The operations were generally wholly owned, apart from Imasco where B.A.T has a 40 per cent shareholding, Souza Cruz (75 per cent owned) and V.G. Instruments Plc (69 per cent owned).

The corporate centre receives plans and budgets from each of the operations shown in the boxes of Figure 4.2. Several of these units (for example, BATUS) are multi-business organizations in their own right.

Planning process and objective setting

During B.A.T's annual planning cycle, the centre reviews the budgets, operating plans and strategies for each of the operating units. These reviews are part of an integrated system of planning, monitoring and control, which includes quarterly reports reviewing progress against the agreed budgets and plans. The budgets, plans and quarterly progress reports are presented to the board of B.A.T Industries, and detailed reviews are carried out before the board meetings by the Chairman's Policy Committee (CPC), consisting of the chairman and two other senior directors.

Figure 4.2 **B.A.T Industries Group Organization** (1989)

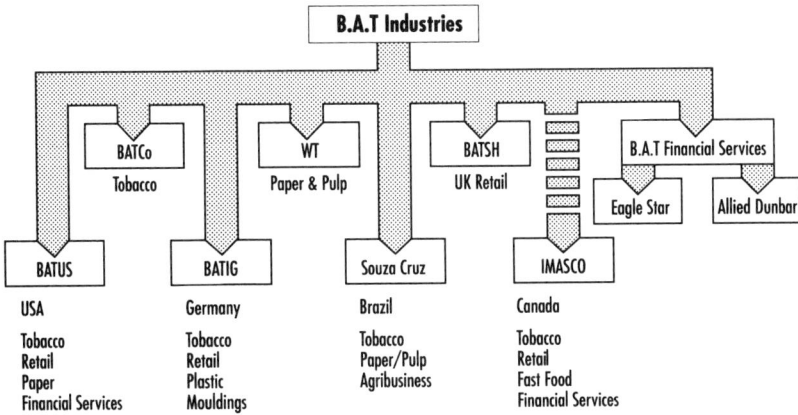

The cycle starts with a board review of the objectives and strategies for B.A.T Industries. Then guidelines are agreed, summarizing the contribution each operation is expected to make to achieving the overall objectives for the group as a whole. The guidelines cover both the expected financial performance and the strategies that have been agreed. They also cover the agreed strategies for positioning the operation to achieve continuing good performance in the longer term. For example, Wiggins Teape had a mandate to concentrate on the pulp, paper and paper merchanting business within Europe; its financial targets focused on return on assets, cash dividends to the parent company and its debt/equity ratio for financing its operations (the three key financial measures for all B.A.T companies); and its strategic issues concerned plans for growth in higher added value segments of the business. Occasionally the strategic issues include specific targets or objectives, but normally they are more broadly stated.

Although revised guidelines are agreed each year, they are often similar to the guidelines issued in the previous year and usually represent an updating of a previously agreed strategy rather than a radical change in direction.

The guidelines are used as the terms of reference for the medium-term operating plans. These plans contain fairly detailed financial numbers looking out over three to five years, and the first year of the plan is the budget. In addition, the plan documents include commentary on recent results and on the key actions and assumptions underlying planned improvements. The commentary is expected to include analysis of competitive positions and of other key issues determining the projected levels of performance. These issues will differ depending on the business. For example, market share and brand positioning are especially relevant for Tobacco, capacity utilization and investment in new capacity are more prominent in the Paper businesses, while rates of growth in premium income and underwriting performance will be discussed in Financial Services. The plans identify major action programmes on whose success future results will depend, and also the key issues and uncertainties facing the business. There is considerable informal discussion between the centre and the operations during the preparation of the plans, and the corporate staff also briefs the CPC before the formal review on consistency with the guidelines and on issues arising from the plans.

At the reviews, the CPC discusses the plans with the chief executive of the operation concerned; together they identify strategic actions that are critical to the success of the plan, whose implementation will be monitored. They also identify and agree strategic issues that must be resolved during the year. These issues are summarized in the minutes of the review meeting, and become an agenda for further review meetings during the course of the year, when each of the issues is considered in more depth. Examples of topics for strategic reviews might be a particular business that is underperforming and needs turning around; the plans for the launch of a major new brand with associated heavy expenditure; or acquisition plans. It is up to the operation to propose a timetable for presenting the results of these reviews to the CPC during the year.

The nature and extent of strategic issue reviews in each operation vary from year to year. Until 1986, all operations prepared a comprehensive strategy review every year. However, this process became repetitive, and the current arrangement of a relatively brief 3–5 year plan, supplemented with specific issue reviews, is intended to give greater focus to B.A.T's planning.

Planning in B.A.T Industries is a continuous process, and a consolidation and review of the operating plans and of the key strategic issues provide the basis for the next review of the objectives and strategies for the group. The next planning cycle then begins with updated guidelines feeding into the next year's review of the plans for the operations.

In addition to the guidelines to the operations, B.A.T Industries' own strategy review identifies corporate issues important to the group itself.

These are resolved through project teams at the centre, which are generally set up:

1. To cover issues within one of the major activity areas (Tobacco, Financial Services, Paper and Pulp or Retail) but involving more than one operation; or
2. To pursue projects where the main initiative needs to come from the centre (for example, the initial entry to Financial Services, the divestment of a major business, a proposed major reorganization, etc).

Strategic control

B.A.T exercises strategic control in five ways in conjunction with this planning process (Figure 4.3). First, there is the formal quarterly performance review of each operation by the CPC and board. This looks at performance against plan, but tends to focus largely on financial achievements. A narrative around the numbers allows the CPC to get into strategic issues as well, but no explicit strategic milestones are included in the quarterly reviews. As a result, it might be argued that these formal reviews have only a limited impact as a means of exercising strategic control.

Greater strategic control is exercised through frequent informal contacts between members of the CPC and the business heads, supplemented (for business heads who are not themselves members of the B.A.T Industries board) by contacts with a nominated board member with responsibility for the operation concerned. These discussions go beyond the formal reporting processes and create a more rounded picture for the centre of how well each business is performing strategically. They also

Figure 4.3 **B.A.T Industries Planning Cycle and Strategic Controls**

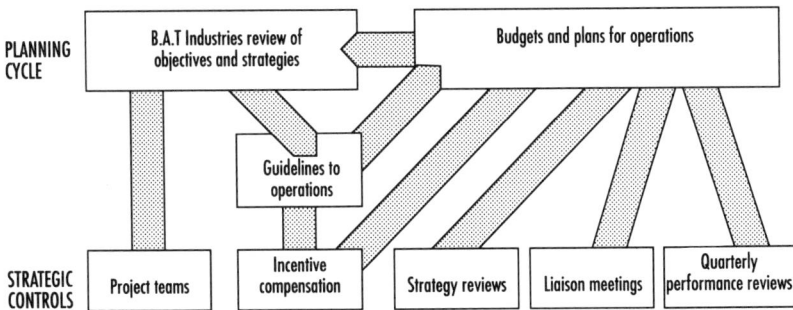

provide feedback to the business on how well the centre thinks it is doing, and on what the centre believes should be at the top of the business's agenda. The minutes of the CPC reviews of the business's plans are often used as an agenda for pursuing the key strategic issues identified as critical to the success of the agreed plan.

A third, more formal means for reviewing progress on the formulation and implementation of strategy involves the agreed programme of strategy reviews carried out through the year. By focusing on specific major issues, these reviews allow the CPC and the operation to examine major problems and opportunities in depth, to determine the optimum strategic positioning for the business, and to agree on appropriate action plans for any repositioning that is required.

The incentive compensation plan for the boards of the operations is a fourth aspect of strategic control. Both financial performance and the achievement of defined strategic objectives are included as criteria used in determining the compensation package for board members of the operations. The criteria are agreed between the CPC and the head of the operation against the background of the guidelines and the plans and budgets that have been prepared. Wherever possible, the objectives are expressed quantitatively. This is comparatively easy for financial objectives, but strategic objectives often relate to whether a given task has been completed or not, so that a judgement must be made about whether a given strategic priority has been met. This, and the need to strike a balance between achievements across the fairly large number of objectives established, means that there is always an element of subjective judgement in the CPC's overall assessment of the operation's performance. The formula is not mechanical, and B.A.T attempts to give managers time to achieve their objectives.

The fifth form of strategic control is applied within the centre, through the project teams pursuing issues that can be dealt with only by B.A.T Industries itself. These projects are subjected to tight review processes, and progress towards resolving the issues that have been identified is taken into account in determining the compensation of the central staff.

Review

B.A.T Industries is highly diverse, in terms of both business spread and geography. Furthermore, the CPC believes that the operations should drive the strategies in their own business areas. A hands-on style of corporate management is therefore neither feasible nor desirable, and the management style stresses decentralization. Control, however, is seen as important: "The essential added-value from being part of B.A.T comes from having better control systems than the business would have otherwise had, and from the disciplines of having to report on performance." This view is supported at the business level:

"We have made great changes in the business in the last five or ten years. I don't think we should have been as successful in doing so without B.A.T's pressure on us. They have continuously pressed us to divest the less successful and more peripheral businesses, and they have sharpened our minds about this, by applying tight financial constraints and insisting that if we wish to have investment money, we must finance it out of our own cash flow."

B.A.T's control process attempts to combine financial and strategic goals. The financial component is strong, featuring prominently in the guidelines for the businesses and in incentive compensation, and dominating the formal quarterly performance reviews. This emphasis has been important in improving the results of the company and in eliminating areas of low performance. Through the planning process and through informal discussions a more strategic view is introduced, although strategic objectives are less precisely specified than financial objectives. Strategic progress is monitored through various processes, both formal and informal, but the approach is less structured than with financial control.

The control process has therefore evolved to strike a balance between financial control and strategic control, between financial performance pressure and "encouragement to businesses to identify the optimum strategies for business renewal". B.A.T recognizes that the size and diversity of the company make this a formidable task, but feels that it is moving in the right direction. "Considerable progress has been made in developing a planning system which is structured to enable the corporate centre to apply a system of strategic controls. However, there is still some way to go before we can be fully satisfied that we are implementing these controls effectively."

As in GE, B.A.T has tried to keep the bureaucracy of planning and control from crowding out real consideration of important issues. The extent and depth of informal contact between the businesses and the centre is somewhat less in B.A.T, and there is somewhat more structure to the dialogue (for example, plan review minutes as an agenda to guide the discussions). However, the flexibility that comes from combining formal and informal elements of financial and strategic control is seen by B.A.T as a good basis for the future development of the group, and is expected to be as applicable to the restructured group in the 1990s as it was previously.[5]

BOC

BOC has altered its planning and control processes during the 1980s. Previously, central management were concerned with detailed monitoring of specific line items in the budgetary process and also called for annual strategic plans. Now budgets focus more on bottom-line profit targets, and the annual strategic planning process has been dismantled, with regular corporate reviews of businesses' strategies a thing of the past. Since the Gases business is capital intensive, capital expenditure project reviews provide fairly frequent occasions for strategy discussions in this area of the company. But it is only if the corporate executive committee calls for an ISR (Intensive Strategy Review) that there is a close examination of the overall strategy of a business.

During an ISR the centre can become deeply involved in the strategies of a business under review.[6] But ISRs are relatively rare (no more than one to two are carried out each year), and most businesses go for long periods without such a review. This approach avoids the routine of strategy planning, but means that there are no regular formal opportunities for establishing or reviewing specific strategic objectives or milestones between the centre and the businesses. Instead, the broad long-term strategic direction is expected to hold good until a fresh ISR is undertaken. ("We don't identify strategic milestones for a business. To do that, we would need to have in place a regular strategic planning process.") The capital expenditure reviews and the budget process establish more specific goals for the businesses and, together with other more informal contacts, help to inform the centre about strategic progress and to identify situations in which an ISR may soon be needed.

While performance against budget is monitored through a monthly reporting package, with somewhat more detail and commentary provided at each quarterly report, the main formal performance review takes place at the annual budget session. This is a full face-to-face review of each business's performance against budget, in a half-day session that is intended to cover both operating and more strategic issues. The budget sessions allow wide-ranging debate, and, since there are no pre-set "strategic" targets as such, the discussion of strategic performance can delve into any matters that top management sees as priority issues. As with B.A.T, these more formal control processes are supplemented by less structured discussions between members of the executive committee and business heads.

In addition, the corporate strategy staff carry out a "top–down" annual appraisal of each business's performance against its key competitors; this assessment is primarily used in calibrating business performance for the senior management Incentive Compensation Plan. BOC's Incentive Compensation Plan resembles B.A.T's. Business heads agree a set of goals with the executive committee, and there is an approximate 50:50 weighting between financial and non-financial objectives. The non-financial objectives are various, including operating goals, personal goals and more strategic goals. These non-financial goals "provide a steer in terms of where managers should place their effort, but are often not expressed in terms which are precisely measurable. The assessment of non-financial performance therefore tends to be more subjective."

BOC's reasons for avoiding a formal strategic control process with explicit milestones stress the need to avoid bureaucracy, and to allow for a more sensitive and flexible approach to performance appraisal. This attitude was common to several companies with more informal strategic control processes. As one corporate vice president (already cited in Chapter 2), put it: "You need a control system, but the really early warnings will never come from the formal control system. They come from your feel for the business. The touchy-feely things are the ones that you only get to know about by visiting the business and sensing what's going on."

BOC also sees considerable difficulty in establishing precise strategic goals. For example, we were told, "The Gases business is very sensitive to changes in the health of the economies in which we operate. You can't control results too tightly if they are essentially dependent on things that management cannot influence. We have a goal to be a leader in terms of plant building technology, but it is very unclear what precise measures we could use to establish our competitive position here."

Like GE and B.A.T, BOC favours an approach to strategic control that is less formal and explicit – and therefore potentially more flexible and more readily implemented.

Bunzl

Bunzl became very much more diverse during the 1980s.[7] By early 1989, it had 16 business units, operating in fine paper, paper merchanting, industrial paper, plastics, and electrical and building materials distribution. The company has grown by acquisition, attracting a number of small entrepreneurial companies into the group. This process of growth has called for a more informal planning and control system. One manager explained, "Part of the attractiveness of Bunzl to these entrepreneurs was that we are a federation in which they would not be subjected to extensive bureaucratic management techniques. A more formal approach would have always been hitting up against companies working together in an informal federation."

Strategic planning, in particular, has downplayed detailed numbers, and has concentrated on ideas. Businesses are not required to lay down precise strategic objectives for the strategy planning process. Accordingly there is no formal system for looking at whether strategic plans are being implemented or not, although the planning department does provide a brief on the operating plans, which will indicate whether the resources are being put into strategic programmes that have been previously agreed. Strategic control is therefore exercised by the corporate management team tracking strategy implementation through the year on a more informal basis. There is also the opportunity at each year's planning round for a general dialogue with the businesses on progress. "So far we have resisted formal systems of monitoring strategy. They are too mechanistic and too interfering. The emphasis is more on educating managers to think strategically than on holding them to precise targets; they should have some flexibility to modify their strategy as they go along."

Bunzl believes that, given the sorts of businesses and managers in the company, this approach creates a better commercial dialogue with the businesses, and avoids "game playing" to achieve specific objectives. But it accepts that there is some uncertainty for business managers about exactly what will be interpreted as good strategic performance.

Courtaulds

Courtaulds is a classic Strategic Control company, with a strong commitment to decentralized responsibility for strategic thinking. Annual budgets are prepared, but they are set within the context of a strategic planning process. The intention is to encourage business managers to think strategically, but to establish budget and cash flow goals that can provide the basis for tight control. The strategic control process then depends on financial results, interpreted against a broader background of strategic progress.

Chris Hogg, the chairman and chief executive officer, believes that, ideally, specific strategic objectives should be set for each business, as part of the control process – "as long as the objectives are not set in aspic". But there is a general view in the company that identifying strategic milestones, particularly for measures of competitive position, is extremely difficult in Courtaulds' businesses. In the plastic film business, for example, relative competitive cost position is seen as the key strategic target. But so much work is needed to assess relative cost positions that it has not been feasible to adopt this target as an ongoing control objective. Instead it is investigated in periodic, major exercises, for example in connection with a proposal for a substantial capital investment. There is a concern that, unless the objectives they incorporate are well founded, ongoing strategic control systems will be more damaging than helpful.

To get meaningful strategic milestones accepted as part of the management process, a major effort is necessary to convince managers that they should invest time and effort in defining them correctly. "It is immensely difficult to get people to change the way that they think about their businesses and to incorporate meaningful and specific strategic objectives in their plans," we were told. As another senior manager commented: "If you give people sophisticated systems before they see the need for them, they won't use them."

Monthly (and more detailed quarterly) budget reviews are the main focus for monitoring performance. The concentration on these reviews reflects Courtaulds' considerable commitment to financial objectives, but the liaison director responsible for each business will also try to get beyond financial results to operating and strategic performance. Courtaulds believes that tangible and objective control processes must be supported by a variety of softer, more people-oriented judgements. Therefore formal monitoring systems and processes are de-emphasized. Instead, informal "chats" play a vital role in keeping corporate management informed about the strategic health of the businesses in the group, and in communicating priorities to business heads. "We manage through people rather than through formal systems."

Informal control processes are, therefore, seen as ultimately more valuable than more formal objective setting and monitoring. In principle, Courtaulds would like to see its informal strategic controls enhanced by explicit milestones and objectives, but the practical costs and difficulties of such an approach have so far dissuaded it from moving in this direction.

Philips

Philips is amongst the most diverse companies that we have researched. It has eight product divisions (PDs), including Lighting, Consumer Electronics and Components, and over 60 national sales organisations (NOs). In 1989, the company's total sales were Dfl 56 billion.

The corporate role in such a company is complicated, with many different areas of functional and geographic concern to take into account. One symptom of the range of issues in which the centre takes an interest is the fact that, until recently, there were 34 different staff departments at the head office in Eindhoven.

The Philips strategic planning cycle is shown in Figure 4.4. Most national sales organizations prepare three–five year plans between January and March, and review their plans with the General Management Committee (GMC) in April or May. The product divisions work on their strategies during the summer and review them with the GMC in October or November. These reviews include four-year financial projections and a strategic commentary. In the second half of the year, the NOs work on detailed budget figures for review with the PDs in the autumn and consolidation into a corporate budget in December.

During the year there is a monthly reporting package on performance against budget, which gives fairly detailed financial information and some non-financial data on items such as market share. Heads of the PDs who are not themselves members of the GMC will meet informally with their GMC contacts to discuss these results, but there is normally no formal reaction from the board as a whole to the PD, unless major deviations from plan are emerging. PD management, however, will review the monthly results thoroughly with their representatives in each NO.

Given the size and diversity of Philips, the corporate centre is inevitably somewhat distant in its planning and control role. This tendency is compounded by the recent enhancement of the role of PDs. Historically, power and responsibility were shared between the PDs and the NO. Now the GMC has encouraged the PDs to play the leading role strategically and has de-emphasized the role of the corporate centre as ultimate arbiter between PD and NO. The control process is putting

Figure 4.4 **Philips' Review Planning Calendar**

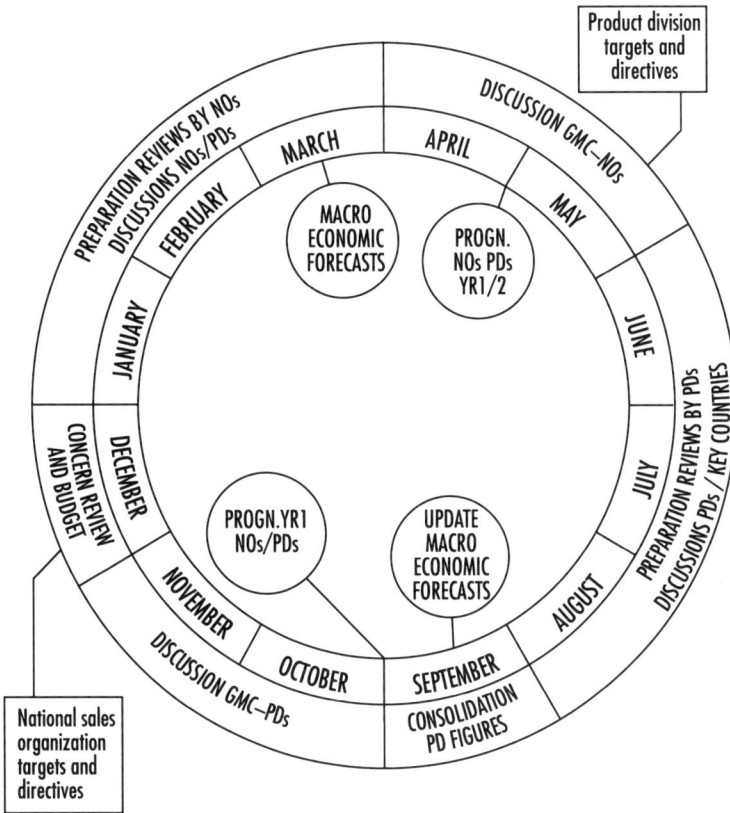

greater emphasis on financial results, and moving away from a more diffuse set of performance measures. In the past, responsibility was always shared between the heads of the commercial and technical functions in each country, and profit was seen as only one amongst several important goals (such as technical progress, social responsibility, market positioning). ("Profit was a condition, not an aim.") Now there is a clearer identification of individual profit responsibilities, and a sharper focus on profitability as the key objective. But the intrinsic overlaps and linkages between the different PDs and between PDs and NOs still make clear personal accountability problematic, and the emphasis on profitability is set within a broader concern for strategic and competitive developments. Many managers feel that no checklist of key objectives can capture everything that is important for a business's long-term success.

Therefore, although the direction of movement is towards clearer and tighter control targets, the complexity of Philips' businesses and organization have so far prevented this development from leading to a more explicit and formal set of strategic control measures.

STRATEGIC PLANNING COMPANIES

We turn now to four companies that use informal strategic controls within a Strategic Planning style. In comparison with Strategic Control companies, the centre in these companies works more closely with the businesses, exerting more influence on plans and tracking progress on a wider range of issues and objectives. Explicit strategic milestones are not defined, but there is extensive discussion about what will count as good performance and close monitoring of results that are achieved.

Our main example will be Digital, but we shall also provide shorter profiles of Kingfisher, Nestlé and Toshiba, which each illustrate interesting aspects of informal strategic control processes.

Digital Equipment Corporation (Digital)

Digital is one of the world's leading suppliers of computer systems. It initially built its position in the market through its strength in minicomputers and, more recently, in networked systems. Product development and manufacturing are either carried out in or controlled from the USA, although recently some small-scale, locally managed engineering has been introduced to customize products in response to local demand. The national companies, such as Digital Equipment Company UK, have acted essentially as distributors with responsibility for marketing and selling the corporate product.

Historically, Digital has been an engineering-driven company, and its vision has been embodied in the product. The corporate strategy has stressed technical superiority and innovation. This strategy was supported by effective national sales forces, but the national companies were not really independent businesses with separate strategies. In this respect Digital was unlike most of the other companies included in this study. Accordingly, strategic controls were less appropriate and the corporation focused on control of operational parameters, and on the profit performance that resulted.

Today, however, the nature of the demand for computer systems is changing. Digital's major customers no longer want simply to buy computers; instead they want solutions to business problems. Hardware, whilst still important, is becoming something of a commodity. The added value now lies increasingly in providing a total system comprising hardware, software and support including consultancy and training.

This systems approach requires an understanding of the customer's needs, based on a knowledge of their business, which is quite different from the more opportunistic selling approach traditionally employed by Digital. The corporation has had to develop marketing strategies for responding to these changes; in the main, these strategies are formulated at the level of the national company.

Planning processes

Digital's executive committee consists of the chief executive, one so-called "in-house" vice president (covering research, product development and operations), one "out-house" vice president (covering sales and marketing), plus representatives of Finance and Human Resources and a "Minister without Portfolio". The executive committee has broad responsibility for "articulating a strategic envelope for the company". Its concerns include such questions as: "What sorts of products should we be in? What sorts of markets should we be in? How should we design our products? How do we get good managers into the company? How do we allocate resources overall to different programmes? What sort of performance goals should we have?" The executive committee meets weekly and also spends up to two or three days a month at off-site meetings to discuss strategic issues.

Below the executive committee are the group vice presidents responsible for the "major dimensions" of the company including, for example, components, systems, applications, distribution channels, industry sectors and geographic areas. The group vice presidents work through a small number of committees to address specific areas of strategy and ensure that "there is good knowledge at senior levels of management in the company of major decisions and trade-offs being made".

The centre, then, is in a position to influence the strategic direction of the company, but does not get involved in the development of detailed marketing strategies for its subsidiaries. Rather, the corporation expects the subsidiaries to develop marketing strategies appropriate to their individual markets, broadly in line with corporate thinking. The management of the UK subsidiary approves of this approach: "The corporation should tell the national companies to take a strategic approach but not what approach."

The corporation assists the planning process for marketing strategy in four ways. First, by defining an overall mission or strategy, it provides the subsidiaries with a touchstone for local market strategy development. Second, by continued product development and technical excellence, it allows the subsidiaries to pursue marketing strategies, confident in the knowledge that appropriate corporate products will be available to allow the strategies to be implemented. Third, by encouraging the flow of information between subsidiaries, it spreads strategically important developments through the world. (For example, value-added networks were first developed by Digital UK before being taken up by the corporate centre and driven through the rest of the corporation.) Fourth, with functional staff in the subsidiaries reporting to corporate functional management as well as local management, it promotes functional excellence.

Digital's development of "strategic accounts" illustrates how a strategic approach may be diffused through the company from the centre. Historically, the company reacted to the market in an opportunistic fashion and owed its success to strong tactical management.[8] As market conditions changed and a systems approach became more important, however, national companies began to identify industry sectors that seemed likely to provide long term profits (based on growth, competitive strengths, and so on) and within such sectors to target "strategic accounts" – customers that could have a leverage on the sector as a whole. Although traditional, more opportunistic selling remains important, Digital's strategy is now to drive the growth of the business through these strategic accounts.

In adopting the strategic account concept corporately, Digital has identified sectors it suggests the subsidiaries should focus on. But subsidiaries in individual countries may emphasize or de-emphasize sectors on the basis of local circumstances. (For example, the corporation has suggested the travel and leisure industry as a strategic sector, but local management in the UK has judged that this industry should not be allocated any extra resources or special attention.[9])

However, strategic accounts are increasingly transcending the company's geographical divisions. Each strategic account is hosted by a region[10] (a subdivision of a national subsidiary), but will need to be resourced from many regions, perhaps from many countries. Thus, for example, one of the UK's four regions hosts the British Telecom account, but all the regions must support the account locally. On a wider scale, accounts such as Ford and BP are now managed globally. In particular, a growing number of accounts is being handled on a European basis, a trend that is expected to intensify following the completion of the single European market in 1992.

Monitoring
The centre exerts a great deal of strategic influence in Digital but does not, as we have seen, get involved with the generation or approval of detailed marketing strategies. Given that the national subsidiaries have been primarily distributors, marketing and selling the corporate product without a significant need to develop marketing strategies, the formal controls exerted on the subsidiaries by the centre were principally concerned with volumes, margins and associated operational parameters such as headcounts and inventories. "The company is at its strongest in reacting to budgetary factors. When it comes to limiting headcounts or reallocating resources we can turn on a pin-head." This emphasis on operating controls is reminiscent of major retailers we have studied such as Sainsbury's and Argyll, whose approach to strategy is also largely centralized.

Although the subsidiaries include strategic considerations in the plans submitted to the corporation, providing the operating plan and budget are met there will be little formal questioning of any failure to achieve strategic development. One business manager remarked: "The plans I present to the centre do include non-budgetary objectives such as market share but if they are missed there is no comeback providing I make my budget. If I make my budget I'm a hero."

Operating performance is monitored systematically and frequently. For example, sales volumes are monitored weekly. But this short-term focus is increasingly seen by the management of the subsidiaries as inappropriate, given the company's more strategic approach to the market. "This sort of monitoring was appropriate to Digital as a distributor, but is inconsistent with a major project approach. This is an example of the company having to come to terms with market changes."

In addition to these formal operating controls there is a strong and pervasive informal control process within Digital, stemming from the company's view of the way organizations should work. A corporate manager explained: "We at the centre need to be very close to the action, so that we can know at the end of the day whose views are most reliable and whose performance is most effective." Digital's product line is based on a philosophy of non-hierarchical networks, and the company's own organization reflects the same principle. Extensive and intensive communication is encouraged. In particular, the company maintains a network employing electronic mail and related technologies that allows all managers to be well informed of developments throughout Digital. The centre uses its involvement in the network to influence strategy in the company.

Rewards, sanctions and intervention

Staff in Digital are rewarded through salary reviews and, for managers, stock options. A salary band, based on market assessments, is defined for each job, and a person's point within that band is based on their performance, as evaluated by their functional and line managers.

Although performance does affect salary and stock options, there is a strongly held view among Digital management that the more important sources of motivation are recognition of achievement, peer pressure and the social environment. Thus, although formal monetary incentives and sanctions are somewhat limited within Digital, informal controls are seen as very strong. The various dimensions of the company have to work together, and there is great emphasis on team building. "Each individual belongs to a number of teams and the team is the key organizational unit within Digital. There is a lot of loyalty and commitment to the team and its success."

Because the team is, in large part, the unit of performance evaluation, there is considerable peer pressure within teams to ensure performance. ("If one person in a team fails, the whole team fails.") Within such a structure, authority is based not on hierarchy but on knowledge and performance.

"Position-based or hierarchical authority receives low attention within Digital. More important is control over budgetary resources which gives budget authority. But most important of all needs to be knowledge-based authority; that is to say, the basis on which negotiations between different dimensions are settled should be according to the level of knowledge and the knowledge contribution from each side."

Control within the company then is less a top–down process and more a matter of whether others within the company will recognize someone's knowledge-based contribution. "The main sanction on somebody who fails to deliver on his commitment is that people will not do deals with him in the future and will not trust his knowledge-based influence."

The tasks faced by teams may be strategic as well as operational, so this process of team building and peer pressure provides the basis for strategic control within the company.

Digital UK

A billion dollar company in its own right, Digital UK, is the largest national subsidiary outside the United States. It reports into the centre via Digital's European headquarters (EHQ), based in Geneva.

Given the corporate drive to develop a more customer-oriented market strategy, Digital UK has spent the last five years developing a strategic planning process that includes a vision (of the long term), three-year business plans and annual budgets. These elements are supported by an organization plan that specifically considers human resources, real estate and information systems (see Figure 4.5).

The strategic planning process then concentrates on linking these separate plans. Thus, for example, the vision and the business plans are

Figure 4.5 **Planning Processes in Digital UK**

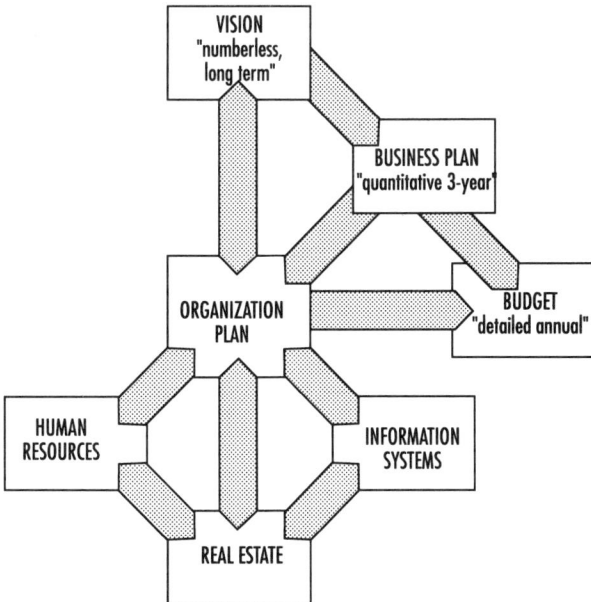

linked through a strategic marketing plan, and the business plan and the human resources plan through a capability plan. As an example of the links between the specific plans, the business plan and the vision, the need to obtain suitable real estate is a major pressure on the company to undertake long term thinking. "The company is currently adding 1,000 people a year and there is a five-year lead time on accommodation. It is the real estate people who are asking, 'How many people will we be employing in five years' time? Where and how will they be working?' This forces strategic considerations of where the revenues will be coming from."

These linking plans focus on managing change, by designing change programmes and allocating resources to these programmes. "There are four or five change programmes designed to get the company where it wants to be. A percentage of the budget is set aside for this before the routine budget-making."

Each change programme is sponsored by a board member and involves people from many functions (see Figure 4.6). "Programmes are task-oriented, typically using multi-functional teams. A programme will move through all stages from concept to implementation, with different functions being important at different times as the programme develops. That is, the programme has both strategic and operational elements."

Digital UK has been in the vanguard in introducing a strategic marketing approach within the corporation. It has taken a leading role in the introduction and development of electronic data interchange (EDI)

Figure 4.6 **Change Programmes**

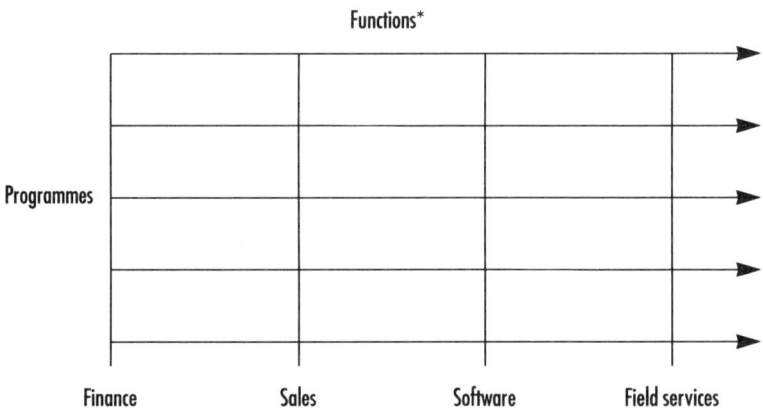

Functions*

Programmes

Finance   Sales   Software   Field services

* There are 18 functions in Digital

products and value-added networks (VANs). Digital UK has also established a Strategic Accounts Office to provide a coordinating role across the four regions in the UK. There is an account team and manager for each strategic account, who are evaluated not just by sales and profit figures but also by more strategic measures such as the quality of the account plan and the number of meetings between the top management of Digital and the top management of the customer. The goals set and the performance measures used will change as the account develops. Thus, given that a strategic account has been identified and an account team set up, typical goals might be:

Year 1   Get the managing director of Digital UK introduced to the managing director of the strategic customer (for example, get the customer's MD to attend a Digital-sponsored event such as the Royal Ballet)

Year 2   Get a policy decision out of the customer (for example, that they will invite Digital to tender for contracts)

Year 3   Sales targets per salesperson

Then, as business starts to flow, more traditional targets of volume and margins become more important.

In Digital UK, progress on strategic goals is monitored continuously by the Director of Marketing Strategy. If goals are not being met a number of reactions are possible: reassessing the goals or even the strategy; sending another message to the field emphasizing the importance of the strategy; providing additional resources centrally, and so on. One manager explained: "This is viewed as a monitoring rather than a control process. Monitoring has the same 'watchdog' connotations as 'control' but the tolerance levels are different. In Digital, people think of control as referring to financial control where there is less tolerance."

Recognition has grown that there is a trade-off between current performance and strategy. "If the company is not hitting the financial numbers, strategy is now less likely to go out the door," we were told. On the other hand, "It is still the case that if a manager is making the numbers there is a tendency not to interfere."

Review

Strategically, Digital Equipment Corporation has historically been a centralized, engineering-driven company. The subsidiary companies worldwide have acted as distributors of corporate product. However, within the computer industry, product differentiation and added value are currently moving away from hardware and towards the provision of software and support systems. As a result, strategic planning within Digital is shifting from the central engineering division to the geographically dispersed marketing companies, reacting to the particular needs of their individual market places.

In response to these market changes, Digital is modifying its planning and control structures, moving from a hands-on centralized style to a more decentralized Strategic Planning style. Its formal corporate control processes continue to focus on short-term volumes and margins, even though such controls seem inconsistent with a longer-term view of the business. But it is argued within Digital that the very strong corporate culture, the good communications between the subsidiaries and the centre, the emphasis placed on teams and peer pressure, and the recognition given to achievement allow the centre to track strategic progress and motivate managers to meet strategic goals without the need for a more formal strategic control process.

Kingfisher

"Kingfisher," says Geoff Mulcahy, the company's chairman and chief executive, "is the first genuinely diversified retailer in the UK." Its separate businesses are: Woolworths, the UK high street chain that was the original core of the company; B&Q, the out of town do-it-yourself chain; Comet, the discount electricals multiple; Superdrug; and Charlie Brown's Autocentres. There is also a newly established property division, Chartwell Land, to manage the group's retail properties.

Kingfisher espouses a philosophy of decentralization to the managements of the individual chains, but the centre nevertheless does get involved. "In theory, we [the centre] can concentrate on making sure that the broad retailing concepts in each chain are correct. In practice, however, we tend to get drawn into all the major decisions, and some of the more detailed ones too."

This involvement is partly a matter of personal preference. Mulcahy maintains that he prefers active intervention to simply monitoring the performance of stable, profitable businesses. ("We like sorting things out. We are basically not interested in stable situations. Our skill is building bigger and better, or sorting out troubled situations.") But it also reflects a view that in retailing the corporate centre can and should work closely with the business heads to develop and control strategy. "Most good retailers are good operators. Competitive advantage, though, is not a term people think about. We can bring some conceptual thinking while they are on top of the detail. We work through dialogue and persuasion with the businesses."

Much of this dialogue is informal, and until recently Kingfisher had little by way of a formal planning process. Now there is a planning cycle, which focuses on key issues and objectives that the centre suggests for each business.

Budgeted financial objectives are agreed as a result of the plan reviews, as are a number of action programmes – around 10–20 for each business. The action programmes might concern things such as store development, market share, the launch and penetration of a credit card, private label products in the overall sales mix, and a variety of other tasks. These action programmes tend not to involve precise and measurable objectives.

"You can have precise budget numbers because they are built up from detailed accounting numbers. But strategic goals, such as store development, are much easier to fudge. The operating company can always keep up with the target rate of store development if they are willing to downgrade the quality of sites they accept, and it is much harder for the centre to tell whether this is being done. Precise strategic targets are not helpful because they are fudgeable."

A fairly large number of action objectives for each business is also seen as preferable to a focus on fewer objectives. "Any business is a system. So a focus on any one variable may lead to pushing the system out of equilibrium. The great virtue of the P&L bottom line is that it is a measure of total system performance, whereas other individual objectives are partial in their impact."

Kingfisher believes that the operating company should be allowed to balance a variety of strategic objectives in the way that it thinks is best, rather than asked to focus heavily on one or two of these objectives.

The chief executive and the head of each operating company meet monthly to review the financial results for the previous month and any issues arising. There is no formal monitoring of achievements against strategic objectives as such, but the central team uses a variety of means to keep informed of progress in most areas. They receive copies of board papers and other management reports from the operating companies, keep up to date on developments in the retail sectors in question, and visit regularly with the companies to get a first-hand feel for developments. "Retailers do not respond well to formal control processes.

There are therefore very few memoranda and reports flowing around this company during the year. Instead we get together regularly with the businesses and talk about how things are going."

This approach also allows the centre to shift its attention to the issues that it currently believes are most important for the operating company. Intervention from the centre is triggered by deviations from budgets and by "a broader sense of dissatisfaction with the way the business is progressing", as well as by lack of progress with strategic objectives.

Incentive compensation is geared around financial results rather than strategic milestones, but career progress (and job security) depend at least as much on success in following through the strategy.

There is some similarity between the GE of Jack Welch and the Kingfisher of Geoff Mulcahy. Both CEOs shy away from formal and explicit strategic milestones, preferring to work closely and directly with the business heads to follow the progress that is being made on issues they regard as strategically significant.

Nestlé

Nestlé is another company that believes in decentralization, but it is rather more involved in planning and control than Strategic Control companies are.

The Nestlé planning, budgeting and reporting cycle is described in Figure 4.7. The cycle begins in January with top–down instructions from the centre to the country markets for the next planning cycle. The countries then work up three-year long-term plans (LTPs). All countries prepare an LTP each year, although in many cases it is just an update on a plan that has been previously agreed.

The LTP is the vehicle for discussion of strategic issues. The countries make proposals covering issues such as brand positioning, media spending and capital investment, as well as financial projections. In the period April–June these proposals are extensively reviewed and discussed by regional and product group staff at the centre, and must ultimately be approved by the Nestlé executive committee.[11] After the LTP has been agreed, there is an investment and revenue budget process in the second half of the year.

The executive committee receives monthly reports on the top 20 country markets, which focus on the main financial budget targets, and do not include specific strategic objectives or milestones. But the monthly formal control reports are supplemented by frequent contacts and visits between the centre and the countries. A Nestlé manager, already quoted in Chapter 2, described the system as follows:

"You could achieve your monthly budget targets by disturbing the strategy; for example, by repositioning brands or changing media expenditure. But if you did so, it would quickly be noticed by the product group director at the centre. This would not be through the formal control report, but through informal contacts with the country in question. Generally, though, country managers understand that if they want to make changes in strategy, these must be discussed and agreed through the LTP process rather than being unilateral decisions."

The Nestlé view is that corporate management can identify strategic progress better through close informal working relationships with business heads than through monitoring explicit strategic milestones.

It follows that corporate management, regional management, product group management and country management must all be involved in

Figure 4.7 **Nestlé's Planning, Budget and Reporting Cycle**

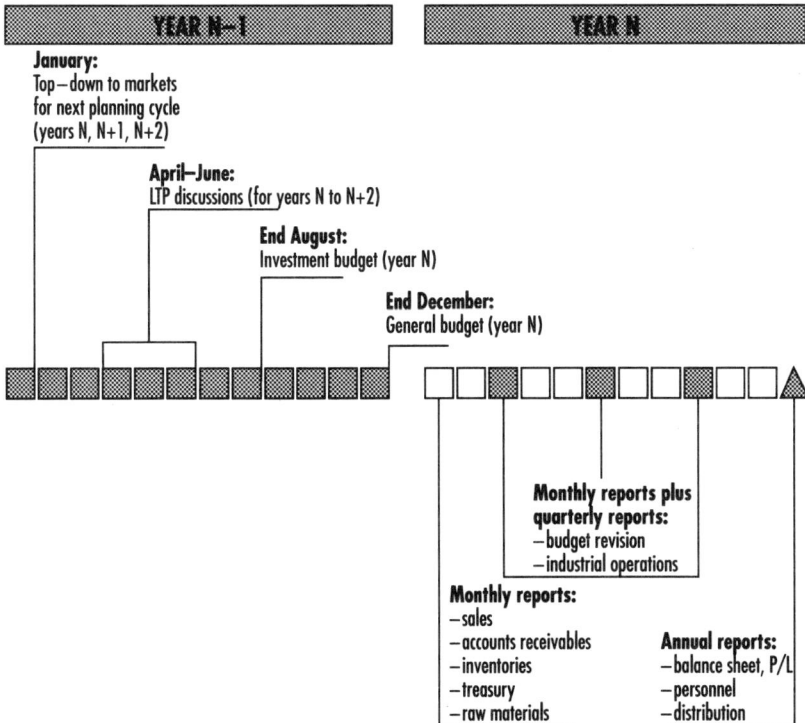

setting strategy, and must have direct knowledge of how the business is developing, gained through visits to the countries in question and detailed discussions of how different product groups are doing.

Nestlé believes that this system of checks and balances at the strategic level, together with decentralization of operations to country managers, works well in the sort of mature, consumer markets that make up most of Nestlé's portfolio. But "in faster changing markets, you have to delegate more to country managers, so that they can respond more quickly to changes in demand," we were told.

Incentive compensation does not play an important role in motivation in Nestlé. "Motivation comes more from peer pressure and pride in performance." So, again, there is less need for explicit strategic milestones in this context. We were also told that Nestlé accepts that "I was wrong" is a useful observation to make from time to time; that is, managers are not in danger of losing their jobs purely because they fail to meet control objectives or strategic plans. A longer-term, more rounded view of management competence is taken, and managers tend to be long-serving members of the company.

Toshiba

The planning and control processes in Japanese companies take place within a very different social and corporate context from that of Western companies.[12] However, we felt that it would be useful to undertake some limited research in Japan, to try to understand how leading Japanese companies handle strategic control. We met with about half-a-dozen Japanese companies, and Toshiba is a good example of the sort of approach we found.

Toshiba is of comparable size and diversity to ICI. It had sales of ¥3,572 billion ($28.6 billion) in 1988, spread across 10 business groups, ranging across sectors such as Materials and Components to Energy Systems, Consumer Products and Telecommunications (see Figure 4.8).

Toshiba's strategy is guided by a long term vision for the company that looks forward into the twenty-first century but is primarily concerned with the next decade. The vision statement is concerned with future social, economic and technical changes, and with the shape and business mix that Toshiba should aim for. It can lead to the setting up of project teams to convert broad ideas (for example, increased role in computers and telecommunications) into more specific plans. Toshiba's vision was first drawn up in 1984, but is currently being revised and updated.[13]

Figure 4.8 Toshiba Organization Chart

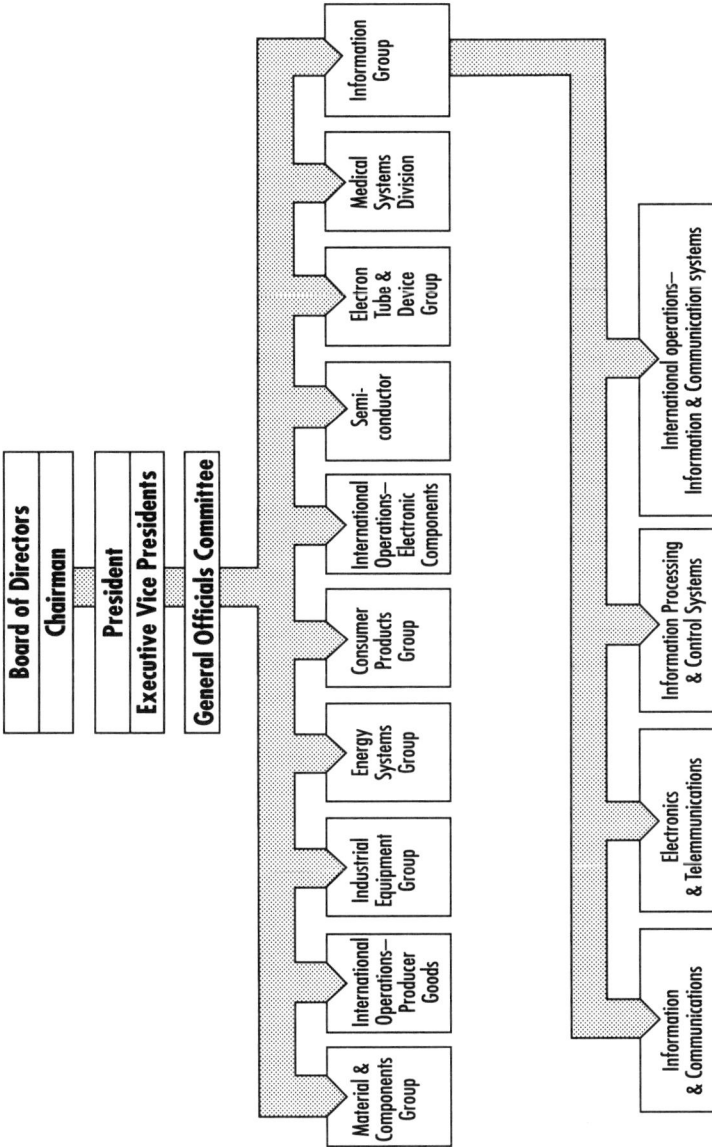

The corporate vision provides a background against which each of the 10 business groups submits a three-year medium-term plan and a one-year, more detailed operating plan and budget to the corporate centre. The medium-term plan is subject to a fundamental review every three years. In the intervening years the plan is reviewed and updated, but not fundamentally revised unless circumstances have changed. Once the plan has been approved it provides a framework for decisions for the business head. "In principle," we were told, "the business head is free to implement the plan once it has been agreed with the board. In practice, they check back frequently." The business plan includes targets for the main financial aggregates, and may also cover such variables as market share, investment, product launch dates and other aspects of the business.

The business plan for the three-year period is translated into a more detailed operating plan and budget on an annual basis. The budget is broken down into two six-month periods. It is regarded as firm only for the first six months, with the second six months subject to rebudgeting at the half year stage. It is intended that the first year of the medium term plan should be consistent with, rather than the same as, the budget. In addition, three or four non-financial objectives or commitments may be agreed between each business group and the corporate centre for each six-month period. These emerge from an informal negotiation between the business group and the centre.

Control in Toshiba involves quite detailed monitoring. There are monthly performance reviews for each business with the Keiei Kaigi (the General Officials Committee), which consists of the top 12–14 corporate managers in the company. The monthly meetings, which last about one or two hours for each group, focus on performance against budget, and take up any variances that are emerging. Non-financial objectives are less formally and frequently monitored than financial objectives, but where variances from financial figures occur, the meetings can delve into considerable detail. One manager explained, "In the event that a business is showing significant variances from the plan, the top management will put pressure on the team in question to improve the results. If they are not satisfied with measures which are being taken, then they may call in the corporate staff to provide additional advice. This is not so welcome." A similar monitoring process occurs within each group and business unit.

There is no direct link between either financial or non-financial targets and personal career promotions or bonuses. However, performance in both these areas is an important part of longer term personnel appraisals.

In addition to the formal planning process, Toshiba encourages extensive discussion and wide consultation between the levels of the company. The size and diversity of the company means that much of the initiative for strategy must be delegated to business group heads, but they maintain a close relationship with those to whom they report at the corporate level. As is typical of most Japanese companies,[14] decisions are reached through collaboration between levels and represent a consensus between them. Building the consensus involves frequent informal meetings, subtle hints, and thorough staff work.[15]

The basic belief in the desirability of decentralizing responsibility to business heads, and then leaving them as free as possible, so characteristic of Western Strategic Control companies, is at odds with this more cooperative, collaborative approach to management. In this context, less reliance is placed on defining, monitoring and rewarding a few explicit strategic control objectives, and more depends on informal agreements and pressures. Individual personal responsibility and accountability for strategy is replaced by a more collective, shared responsibility. Thus, despite the existence of formal strategic planning and control, we see the most important control processes in Toshiba as informal.

Notes and References

1 General background on the strategic management style and other aspects of BOC and Courtaulds will be found in Michael Goold and Andrew Campbell, *Strategies and Styles,* Blackwell, Oxford, 1987.

2 The Chief Executive's Office is the three-person top team, chaired by Jack Welch, which runs GE.

3 From "Jack Welch: How good a manager", *Business Week,* December 14, 1987.

4 Shortly after this point had been made, we had to break off this interview because a call had just come in from the Chief Executive's Office!

5 The bulk of the research with B.A.T was carried out before the portfolio restructuring of 1990, which took the company out of the Paper and Pulp and Retail businesses. The strategic planning and control procedures described, however, remain in operation within the new, more focused group.

6 This was a primary reason for classifying BOC as a Strategic Planning company in *Strategies and Styles*.

7 During 1989 the level of diversity was reduced by a number of disposals.

8 Digital UK, for example, has experienced a decade of growth averaging 30% a year.

9 Although the strategic account is the basis for current strategy, thinking in Digital UK is now moving towards "strategic business communities" where the focus is not on the individual company but on the community of inter-trading companies – suppliers, producers and users – whose information systems will increasingly be linked.

10 Within Digital the region is the operational unit. Within Digital Europe there are 35 regions. The larger countries may have more than one region, but some regions encompass two or three smaller countries.

11 The committee consists of nine members, who each hold specific responsibilities for particular regions, functions and product groups. The main line of reporting in Nestlé is geographic. Thus the heads of major countries report directly to regional heads, who are, in almost all cases, members of the executive committee.

12 The Ashridge Strategic Management Centre is cooperating in a broad study of Japanese corporate management styles, which is being carried out by Kimio Kase and Nigel Campbell at Manchester Business School.

13 The concept of "vision" is commonly used in debates about long-term strategy in many Japanese companies. See Gary Hamel and C.K. Prahalad, "Strategic Intent", *Harvard Business Review,* May-Jun 1989.

14 See T. Kono, *Strategy and Structure of Japanese Enterprises,* Macmillan, London 1984; R. Shimizu, *Top Management in Japanese Firms,* Chikura Shobo, Tokyo, 1986; Tadao Kagono (ed), *How Japanese Companies Work,* Nihon Keizai, Shinbunsha, 1984; Richard Pasale and Anthony Athos, *The Art of Japanese Management,* Simon and Schuster, New York, 1981.

15 Toshiba has 2,000 people working at its corporate headquarters in Tokyo.

CHAPTER 5

HOW THE STRATEGIC CONTROL PROCESS ADDS VALUE

Corporate strategic control processes need to be designed with a clear understanding of how they can help – or hinder – the performance of business units. As we examined the strategic control processes of the 18 companies described in Chapters 3 and 4, we became convinced that formal systems, although relatively rare in practice, have many special strengths. They also have certain drawbacks, which in some circumstances may tip the balance in favour of an informal strategic control process. In this chapter we describe the most significant ways in which control systems can add, and subtract, value.

HOW FORMAL STRATEGIC CONTROL PROCESSES ADD VALUE

Our analysis of formal strategic control processes identified six main sources of added value:

1. They force greater clarity and realism in planning.
2. They can encourage higher ("stretching") standards of performance.
3. They provide more motivation for business unit managers.
4. They permit more timely intervention by corporate management.
5. They help ensure that financial objectives do not overwhelm strategic objectives (thereby avoiding "back door" financial control).
6. By defining responsibilities more clearly, they make decentralization work better.

Clarity and realism in planning

As far as possible, strategies, and the objectives they imply, should be clear and realistic. Otherwise there is a danger that plans will lack substance and specificity. As Charles Roush and Ben Ball maintain: "A strategy that cannot be evaluated in terms of whether or not it is being achieved is simply not a viable or even a useful strategy."[1] It is for this reason that Peter Lorange, in his book *Corporate Planning: An Executive Viewpoint*,[2] argues that the establishment of clear control objectives is an essential final step in the planning process.

Yet, in practice, by no means all strategies are sufficiently clear and realistic. For example, one manager at BP described the situation before the introduction of strategic milestones: "People in the company were awfully good at putting together mellifluous strategic plans that didn't in fact say what they were really going to do at the end of them."

Similar concerns were expressed in a number of other companies. In these circumstances, it becomes much harder for the centre to check whether plans are being implemented, and much easier for business heads to propose broadly optimistic longer-term improvements, without thinking through realistically what will have to be done to bring them about. This approach leads to the sort of "hockey stick" forecasts[3] – downward trends magically turning up – that have done so much to discredit long-term strategic planning.

There are three ways in which a formal control process can add value by making strategies clearer and more realistic. First, the need to agree explicit control objectives ensures that business managers think through the implications of their plans. A chief executive who is interested in specific plans and targets, and who monitors achievements against them, forces business managers to push their own thinking through to clearer implementation plans. What are the key sources of competitive advantage in the business? What do we really have to achieve to make the strategy work? What critical assumptions are we making? What resources do we need? With a formal strategic control process, it is no longer sufficient to have a directional strategy ("Improve our quality image"). The businesses must also specify variables by which to measure progress with their strategies, and levels of achievement that they believe will represent good performance (defect rates, customer survey ratings). This implies a greater depth of thinking and understanding behind strategic plans. Of course, clear and specific plans may be drawn up without corporate encouragement; but formal corporate control provides an antidote to any tendency to leave the details vague.

Secondly, the control process introduces a more objective and dispassionate element into strategic decisions. It is easy for managers to become personally committed to their own pet strategies, and to escalate that commitment as time passes.[4] Often they can persuade themselves that the favoured strategy will work, even though most evidence suggests otherwise. The knowledge that there is a tough-minded corporate control process can inject realism. As a senior manager in RTZ put it: "We can stop managers falling in love with their businesses."

Thirdly, a requirement to identify some explicit strategic objectives, with personal rewards and sanctions linked to the achievement of these objectives, makes for more realistic targets and prevents over-optimism in strategic plans. In companies such as Ciba-Geigy and Pilkington, year-by-year changes in longer-term targets are also tracked to prevent managers from moving the goalposts without reference to earlier plans. This practice reduces the temptation to be unduly optimistic about the more distant targets in the plan. In addition, a control process that picks up deviations from targets creates pressure for managers to act early to correct problems. At ICI, a division head claimed: "The merit of milestones is that, having gone through the process of defining them and having them accepted, people are more attuned to seeing deviations from them as important."

Therefore a formal control process that requires businesses to define their strategic objectives more clearly and explicitly can prevent sloppy, vague or unrealistic plans. This can add value, especially for weaker management groups who may be prone to these shortcomings. As one company put it, "We have found that a more explicit strategic control process has been a tremendous focuser of debate, rather than the exchange of prejudice which we used to get into."

Stretching standards of performance

A considerable body of evidence suggests that difficult goals lead to better performance than do easy goals.[5] This is not just a matter of squeezing more performance out of the lazy or the incompetent. It also seems possible for good managers to respond to the challenge in stretching goals, and to produce results that surprise even themselves. In his classic work *The Game of Budget Control*, Gerd Hofstede[6] maintains, for example, that budgets are best seen as a game. Managers play to win (that is, to make budget), and get satisfaction from knowing that the target is a tough one. An easy target makes the game not worth playing, while a difficult one draws out extra effort and superior performance.

On the other hand, a goal that is seen as too difficult will turn people off and lead to reduced performance.[7] Managers must accept the goal, rather than rejecting it as an unachievable imposition. Reflecting on his own experiences as chairman of ICI, John Harvey-Jones claims: "Set targets which are impossible to achieve and you switch your people off. Set targets which are too easy and you also switch them off. Set targets which are difficult but just achievable, and then ensure that you achieve them, and you will switch people on."[8]

Many Financial Control companies (see Appendix 4) believe that the "stretching" of standards of performance is one of the most important ways in which corporate and divisional management add value. By insisting on "high wire" financial performance, the centre at Tarmac believes that it draws out from managers down the line levels of achievement that they would not have attained on their own. And at BTR one director claimed: "Many managers do not know what they can achieve until you ask them." In these companies the budget process is designed to arrive at financial targets that are achievable, but "only with a following wind and exceptional efforts". Managers respond to the challenge by pushing themselves to meet these higher standards, and the control process adds value by stretching managers to deliver more performance. Equally, those who consistently do make their budgets have the satisfaction of knowing that they have performed at the highest levels. They "feel like winners", and the resulting glow of satisfaction and self-confidence then leads them on to tackle further, yet more challenging targets in the years ahead. The psychology of this process is closely reminiscent of Hofstede's notion of budgets as games.

In principle, strategic controls should offer the potential for a similar sort of added value. But in practice there is much less evidence of the strategic control process being used in this way. Clearly, "stretch" is easier to introduce where strategic objectives have been made precise; otherwise it will be hard to calibrate the extra performance that is being called for. Companies without explicit strategic objectives therefore have difficulty in stretching strategic goals to make them more ambitious. But even companies that do establish explicit objectives tend not to place much emphasis on stretching them. Why should this be so? Our work suggests that there are two main reasons.

First, companies that reject the Financial Control style believe that trade-offs must be made between different sorts of goals, between different time frames, and between financial and strategic goals. These trade-offs make it impossible to focus all attention on a single goal (for Financial Control, the profit bottom line) and push for maximum stretch against it. Stretch in any one dimension carries with it the danger that other goals, of equal importance, will not be met as a consequence. The complex balance between goals makes it dangerous to apply stretch to any one of them. As we were told at Kingfisher, "Any business is a system. So a focus on any one variable may lead to pushing the system out of equilibrium."

Second, to stretch the goals proposed by the business, the centre must know what represents high wire, but achievable performance. This is a subject on which corporate managers will always have difficulty second-guessing business managers, who know much more in detail about their businesses. For the profit bottom line, however, some absolute and competitive standards of comparison are available, and the head office team may be able to reach a view on how stretching a given target is without delving into great detail. In the absence of any such comparative standards, this is more difficult for strategic objectives. Unless the chief executive has a fairly close knowledge of the business in question, he will have little choice but to accept the strategic objectives proposed by the business – or to reject the strategy in its entirety. This is where the value of good background information on the businesses comes into play.[9]

Nevertheless, some companies claim to have benefited by stretching strategic objectives. In Shell, for example, we heard about a post-acquisition programme of facilities rationalization. "We proposed a two-year timetable for completing the programme. They told us we would have to get it done within one year. And, to our surprise, we found that we were able to accomplish pretty much everything we had set out to do within the one-year time frame." ·

The added value here stems from finding ways to get things done, which, with a more relaxed time scale or no deadlines, would not have been necessary. Most of us would recognize the importance of deadlines in concentrating our attention on results, and would accept that tighter timetables can produce higher output rates.

The discussion of objectives between the business and the centre therefore provides an opportunity for the standards of performance that the business proposes to be made more ambitious. By pressing for higher standards, the centre can raise the sights of the businesses, modify their strategies and draw out more performance than was previously promised.

Personal motivation

In theoretical economics, there is an extensive literature, "Agency Theory",[10] that deals with the separation of ownership and management in public companies, and the means by which the potentially divergent interests of "principals" (owners) and "agents" (managers) can be harmonized. Within the company, there is a similar problem in motivating lower levels of management to work with wholehearted commitment towards the objectives agreed with senior management. The control system can add value by providing the personal incentives[11] that align individual and corporate goals, and by motivating managers to devote their best efforts towards them.

In *Strategies and Styles*, the term "tight" controls was used to describe the situation in which performance against planned objectives leads directly to substantial personal rewards or sanctions. Thus the "tight financial controls" of a Hanson or a BTR mean that managers who hit their budgets will automatically be rewarded with positive feedback, enhanced status and cash bonuses; and that those who miss their budgets will be directly penalized through compensation bonus schemes, and will be in immediate danger of losing their credibility as managers and even their jobs.

In our current research we have found that, even if companies have a formal strategic control process, they do not tie strategic objectives as tightly and directly to personal rewards as Financial Control companies tie profit objectives. It is more acceptable for a manager to put forward valid reasons for failing to achieve a strategic target. Incentive compensation formulae are less mechanistically tied to the achievement of strategic targets.[12] Trade-offs between different strategic goals and between strategic and financial goals are more readily recognized. And, most importantly, individuals' careers are less immediately at risk (see Appendix 3). Companies want to avoid the sort of antics that can turn the control process into an elaborate game, in which managers make enormous efforts to hit the required targets at whatever expense to the underlying strategy.[13] For these reasons, strategic controls are less tight than financial controls, and therefore tend to provide less direct personal motivation and incentives.

Nevertheless, formal identification of the criteria of good strategic performance does create extra motivation. Even if there is no direct link to compensation and a relatively forgiving attitude is taken towards missed objectives, the mere fact that results in these areas are specifically monitored is enough to give them extra importance. Add to this the expectation that, in a longer term and more indirect manner, evidence of performance against strategic objectives will matter in personal evaluation and promotion decisions, and setting explicit criteria of good strategic performance does give extra focus and priority to the selected goals. In British Petroleum Oil International, the chief executive commented: "The key value of milestones is in creating a focus on certain issues. Particularly if milestones are supported with personal career and compensation incentives, they are extremely powerful in getting movement in the organization."

In addition, it is possible to link the formal strategic control process with the Management by Objectives process. Several companies with formal strategic control processes consciously set MBO objectives for business managers in the context of the agreed strategic milestones or objectives. Shell Chemicals UK goes further by "cascading" the business managers' objectives down through the organization so that "90% of people in the organization are personally involved in the direction of the business. This leads to greater interest, improved motivation and a sensible consideration of priorities." If strategic objectives are more clearly set and communicated, managers are more likely to be personally committed to them.

Some companies also suggested to us that the sorts of goals employed in the strategic control process were more motivating than conventional financial goals, because they relate to "real" achievements (for example, to complete a product development programme) rather than to financial outcomes, which are subject to the vagaries of exchange rate shifts and other uncontrollable environmental factors. One senior manager in ICI, for example, said: "They do provide a lot of commitment – more than budgets, because they cover more meaningful things. People can associate with real objectives more closely and clearly than with purely financial ones."

For companies such as BP, ICI, NatWest, Pilkington, RTZ and Xerox, an important reason for setting explicit strategic objectives is therefore to enhance personal motivation to deliver selected goals. This adds value, provided the objectives identified do merit extra attention. If it is possible to pick a few strategic objectives that are the key to success in the business, it makes a great deal of sense to give special emphasis to them in rewarding and motivating individual managers.

A third source of added value therefore relates to the personal motivation to which the formal strategic control process gives rise. By creating personal incentives and sanctions associated with the delivery of agreed objectives, the control process can bring individual managers' motivation into line with corporate needs, and can sharpen the efforts made to implement the agreed strategy and achieve the promised results.

Timely intervention

A vital source of added value by central management comes from interventions in businesses that are following the wrong strategy or being poorly managed. The centre can exert pressure to revise the strategy or tighten up the operations, and can ultimately withhold resources from the business or change the management team. Business-level managers seldom put intervention of this sort high on the list of benefits they receive from being part of a group, but it is clear from our research that selective intervention to improve the performance of less successful businesses is a key source of corporate added value.

But knowing where and when to intervene is not easy. Financial results provide a clear enough indicator of problems, and Financial Control companies use them as by far the most important trigger for intervention. They believe that a rapid reaction to shortfalls in financial results is the best approach. Others feel that financial results very often provide too late a trigger for intervention. It is worth recalling from Chapter 4 the telling comment made by a GE manager: "If you see it in the financial numbers, then it's too late. The time to intervene is when a business begins to lose the strategic initiative." Under this view it is necessary to get behind the financial results to perceive the early warning signals of trouble ahead.

One way to do this is through close and frequent contact with the business. By following the detailed results being achieved in different areas, by spending time with the management of a business and with its customers and suppliers, by tracking a selection of pet personal indicators,[14] senior central managers develop a feel for how the strategy is being implemented and whether it is proving successful. Almost inevitably, this approach places more weight on informal controls than on explicit milestones. But, although hands-on, close control of this sort can help to pick up problems at an early stage, decentralized companies tend to regard it as excessively interfering.

Several companies therefore see formal strategic controls as a more effecive way to trigger early intervention. Without explicit targets, they argue, it is harder to know when a business is going off track. As one company put it: "Since we do not have a formal agreement on strategic objectives, there is a danger that longer-term alarm bells are missed. There is a danger of reacting only to financial information, and of overlooking strategic progress in the businesses."

A few formal strategic objectives provide a basis for deciding when a business is going off-track strategically, without requiring managers to monitor a whole range of more detailed performance indicators. Setting such objectives also broadens the scope of performance reviews to include non-financial measures of progress. Ideally, they focus on early warnings, leading indicators of future problems, which allow a more timely response from central management.

Even if there is some doubt about whether the chosen strategic objectives are indeed the most important targets or provide the earliest indication of trouble, their special status can help central managers decide when a business management team is losing its grip. For, if business managers accept four or five key strategic targets, and then consistently miss those targets, it is fair to question whether they are on top of their business. Anyone can fail once, even twice, but repeated failure calls into question a manager's judgement in accepting the targets in the first place and their ability to manage the business to any predetermined path.

Strategic milestones can therefore help corporate management to intervene in a timely fashion in a number of ways. They create explicit expectations about standards of performance; they direct attention to strategic issues in the dialogue between the businesses and the centre; and they provide a sense of how well the business can manage towards targets that it has agreed.

For many companies, the ability to see more quickly and more clearly when a strategy is either not being implemented as agreed (action controls) or not being successful (result controls) is the most important facet of strategic control. Shell, for example, de-emphasizes issues such as assessment of personal management competence, but stresses that the key value of strategic milestones is to know when to review the strategy. ("We use milestones more as signposts that tell us when the strategy is off track than as measures of management achievements.")

In similar vein, companies such as Ciba-Geigy also track the assumptions behind a strategy. Changes to the underlying premises can trigger a reconsideration of the strategy. In Chapter 3 we cited an example where the Ciba-Geigy strategic control report had picked up that the assumed rate of market growth in a business had failed to materialize, thus leading to a reconsideration of its strategy. Most companies, however, feel that it is not cost-effective, and probably not even possible, to identify clearly all the key assumptions on which a strategy rests. Making assumptions explicit is much rarer than making objectives explicit, and the vast majority of companies rely instead on a general, informal sense of changes in the business environment that need to be taken into account in reviewing the strategy.

A formal strategic control process can therefore provide a basis for head office decisions on whether and when to intervene in each business. Added value is created when these interventions lead to more successful strategies and better results than would otherwise have been achieved.

Avoiding "back door" financial control

If financial targets are clear and explicit but strategic objectives are not, it is hard for business managers to be as motivated by strategic control as by financial control. We discussed this problem with a senior manager in a consumer goods company, where the maintenance of brand strength was supposed to be a key strategic objective. "But when the going gets tough," he told us, "there's always pressure from the top to cut the advertising budget to stay on target with budgeted profit objectives." He drew his own conclusions about the relative importance of financial and strategic goals. In some companies, the importance of profit targets can make it difficult for the centre to intervene in a business that is on track financially, even if there are well-founded concerns about its strategic progress. A case in point is the business cited in Chapter 1 which avoided making cost-saving rationalizations as long as high prices allowed it to make good profits.

In these circumstances, informal strategic controls mean that strategic objectives are much less powerful motivators than financial objectives, and the control process becomes dominated by financial targets. This is Financial Control by the back door. Many companies that profess to be "strategically managed" in fact place such a heavy emphasis on financial targets in the control process that strategic plans and objectives lose credibility.

One way to overcome this problem is to introduce a more formal strategic control process, which forces explicit discussion of trade-offs between financial and strategic objectives in the planning phase, introduces personal rewards for strategic achievements as well as financial achievements, and legitimates central intervention if strategic targets are missed. A number of companies have moved towards more formal strategic controls for these reasons. For example, at ICI, a senior corporate manager maintained: "Previously the budget and the strategy process were not sufficiently linked. Now the message is that budgets are very important, but so are strategic milestones. If trade-offs arise between them, the business head is expected to come in and discuss them with us."

Ciba-Geigy, National Westminster Bank, RTZ and Xerox are among the companies that believe a formal strategic control process provides a better balance to budgetary control.

Clearer responsibilities

In companies that choose a decentralized management style, it is important that clear criteria of good performance be defined. Otherwise senior central managers cannot know whether delegated responsibilities are being effectively discharged, and business managers will be uncertain about what they should be trying to achieve. Financial Control companies encounter little difficulty in this area, since they make it quite clear that the profit bottom line is of paramount importance. But companies following the Strategic Control and Strategic Planning styles find it harder to establish appropriate criteria. A common complaint of business unit managers, especially in Strategic Control companies, is that the criteria of good performance are unclear.

> "You get the feeling that he [the CEO] does have views about what you should be achieving strategically. But you have to interpret them from his line of questioning. You may get the sense that he doesn't like what you're doing with the business, but there can be a lack of clarity in communicating about it.
>
> It's a matter of what he [the CEO] happens to be interested in at a point in time – 'flavour of the month'."

In consequence, central intervention is seen as arbitrary and unpredictable; business unit managers are less psychologically committed and confident; and motivation is sapped, since managers are unclear about their goals. All this undermines the functioning of a decentralized organization. It is liable to create an adversarial and mutually suspicious relationship between the businesses and the centre, and to break down the spirit of trust and cooperation that is essential to make decentralization work well.[15]

Our research suggests that clearly set and explicit objectives can mitigate this problem. A business manager in BP maintained: "Milestones provide a clear reference point for assessments. Without them, we would have a much more random process. They also help to foster understanding at the next level up. It forces them to focus on important strategic items."

The added clarity and focus on strategic issues may make for more strenuous discussion, but ensures its relevance. "Milestones have added to the tension, but improved the dialogue," was a comment in ICI. And in Shell it was pointed out that explicit milestones avoided the problem of managers trying to second-guess their bosses: "Milestones provide a framework that forces open discussion of the issues."

Interestingly, some commentators claim that the whole idea of control systems and management information systems (MIS) implies a lack of mutual trust between the different levels in an organization, and so damages working relationships. Chris Argyris, a noted exponent of this view, has claimed that: "An MIS that aspires to be foolproof ... indicates lack of trust on the part of the user ... Subordinates' reactions will tend to be to continuously make management's assertion that they must be monitoring and controlling a self-fulfilling prophecy."[16]

The theory is that the stress built in to the control process destroys cooperation and mutual trust between individual managers and across management levels; that control goals distort performance, since managers lose sight of the overall strategy by focusing only on the measurable output criteria; and that goals emerge as political compromises between warring factions rather than as considered milestones that measure progress.

Argyris believes that the implicit but "undiscussable" assumptions behind the control process (in particular, the assumption that the boss does not trust his subordinates) invite defensive behaviour and prevent openness. However "well designed" the control system, it will encounter resistance and cause problems as long as these assumptions remain unchallenged.

Trust and confidence are, indeed, at the heart of any well-functioning control system. No system can work well unless there is a basic belief by senior management that business managers are competent, and vice versa; a mutual agreement that control targets are suitable; and accepted limits within which decentralized responsibilities can be exercised. As one Shell manager put it: "You have got to trust people. You can't spend all your time monitoring them." Once senior management loses confidence in a business manager, these conditions will quickly cease to hold and the control process will degenerate. The verdict on performance is likely to be negative, almost irrespective of the specific results achieved. Conversely, if confidence in the manager remains high, explanations for deviations from objectives will be readily accepted. The level of trust, and the atmosphere it brings, fundamentally affect the functioning of the control system.

But our research suggests that, used well, a formal strategic control system can itself play an important part in building mutual confidence, for three reasons. First, business managers who deliver on their "contracts" earn the confidence of senior management. The concept of a manager's "track record" is important, and performance against an explicit set of control objectives provides a firm basis on which to build the track record. Secondly, discussions about strategic control targets improve senior management's understanding of the business. Finally, the existence of clear performance criteria prevents arbitrary interference by the centre. In ICI we were told: "The review of milestones is less about the detail of achievement against them, and more about reassuring the executive that the business does have a credible management and control process for achieving its strategy. Milestones raise the confidence level."

Although business heads have much to gain from more explicit criteria of good performance, the initiative for suggesting that they should be set almost always needs to come from the centre rather than from the businesses. As an experienced manager explained, "I really feel we need clearer, more explicit objectives. But, if you're running a business, you're not likely to spontaneously propose specific milestones or objectives, because that clearly puts you on the line to deliver in a more precise fashion." The onus seems likely to remain with the centre on this issue!

To sum up, explicit agreement on strategic milestones lets business managers know clearly what is seen as most important, what they need to deliver to count as good performance. It makes it harder for financial pressures to push strategic issues off the agenda for discussion with central management, and it helps to ensure a minimum level of understanding of the strategy at the centre. All this improves the working relationships between levels in the organization and makes for a more open and constructive dialogue between them. The sixth, and perhaps most important, source of added value from the control process therefore comes from its ability to clarify responsibilities and make decentralization work better.

HOW FORMAL STRATEGIC CONTROL PROCESSES SUBTRACT VALUE

Balancing these sources of added value are several drawbacks or sources of subtracted value associated with a formal strategic control process. The three most important problems are:

- inflexibility
- misdirected motivation towards the wrong goals
- added cost and bureaucracy of control process.

These are also the main reasons why some companies prefer a more informal approach to strategic control.

Inflexibility

The idea that companies should make detailed and precise plans, and move forward systematically in implementing them, has recently come under attack. James Brian Quinn, whose book *Strategies for Change*[17] challenged many of the conventional views of strategic planning, argues that most change proceeds step-by-step or incrementally. Grand designs with carefully specified plans seldom work. The best that can be achieved is to introduce some sense of direction, some logic into the incremental steps. This view stresses the messy, political nature of decisions, and brings out the need for flexibility and opportunism in strategy.

In a similar vein, Henry Mintzberg[18] draws a parallel between the potter at his wheel and the strategist. As a potter begins to work, he has some general notion of the artefact he wishes to create. But the detailed design, and even the whole conception, evolves as the potter works with the clay, seeing new possibilities emerge as the work progresses. Uncertainty about how a given design will work out in practice, and a need to allow for the creative element, lead to the conclusion that the corporate strategist as rational planner should be replaced by the craftsman analogy. Again, flexibility in strategy is more important than control.

By fixing managers on certain pre-specified objectives, a formal control process can introduce inflexibility into business strategies. A dogged pursuit of selected objectives, the criteria of good performance, may prevent managers from seeing new and better opportunities that arise, or from reacting to changed circumstances. At the extreme, a formal and inflexible commitment to pre-set objectives will obstruct the very adaptability that Quinn and Mintzberg see as the essence of good strategy. The strategic control process then subtracts value.

Similarly, some senior managers feel that a formal strategic control process is too simplistic, and fear that it prevents the use of more intuitive, judgemental skills – skills that are the essence of good management. Herb Simon is representative of this "intuitive" view of management. Drawing on his work concerning the functioning of the human brain, Simon[19] suggests that management has more in common with chess than science. Chess grandmasters proceed by pattern recognition rather than by straight logic. They scan the position on the board and draw on their experience to select a few feasible alternative moves to assess. This is not a matter of systematically checking all the alternatives and choosing the best: chess is too complex for that. Rather, it is efficient use of past experience to suggest, semi-intuitively, some good options. Too logical an approach would get bogged down, and would fail to respond in the available time.

By analogy, Simon views the senior manager as scanning a business's situation and, from a *gestalt* of all the relevant factors, arriving at a judgement of an appropriate response. "Every manager needs to be able to respond to situations rapidly ... a skill that requires cultivation of intuition and judgement over many years of experience and training."[20]

It follows that the attempt to identify a "few key strategic control variables" will inevitably screen out much information of relevance to skilful managers, and a formal strategic control process may conflict with their powers of judgement. Simon's views seem to imply that the very characteristics of formal strategic controls trivialize the art of management; they attempt to reduce an inherently complex process to simple terms and, in so doing, inhibit experienced managers more than they help them. Explicit strategic control measures are less likely to be effective than a less well-defined, more informal sense of direction that will guide the senior manager's response to events as they unfold.

These problems have been recognized by several companies in our research. "The strategy is a statement of how objectives are to be achieved at a particular moment in time. But most of our success stories are not based on a disciplined strategy but on reaction to opportunity," was the comment at Mars. And, in one retailing company, we were told:

> "We have avoided placing too much weight on any particular strategic objectives because we know that things change and opportunities come up during the year. We could, I suppose, make the store development programme an objective with big rewards attached to it. But you always need to remain open to new sites that come up' unexpectedly, and you always face some unanticipated disappointments with planning applications."

Other companies that have stressed the need for judgement and flexibility in strategy include BOC ("the really early warnings come from your feel for the business"), GE ("management judgement should spot the problem before any formal early warning system") and Kingfisher ("a focus on any one variable may lead to pushing the system out of equilibrium").

To prevent the strategic control process from causing inflexibility, these companies avoid formalizing control objectives or milestones. They do not establish a few pre-set criteria of good performance, which are then a key basis for personal rewards. Instead, objectives evolve in a more informal manner, reflecting the shifting priorities in the business. There may be some sacrifice in clarity because the control process is less systematic, but the advocates of flexibility regard this as a price worth paying.

Misdirected motivation

The benefits of stretching standards and strong motivation can become drawbacks if the goals chosen are either incomplete or incorrect. A misdirected focus on the wrong objectives, or on too few objectives, will be more damaging than helpful. We have already discussed the possibility that inflexibility in implementing strategy may prevent companies from responding to opportunities that arise; misdirected motivation is even more dangerous since it causes managers to lock on to inappropriate goals.

The danger of misdirected motivation is, of course, a major reason why Financial Control is an unsuitable style for many companies. The failure of financial controls to encompass important strategic factors is a prime motivation for introducing strategic controls. But several companies feel that an emphasis on a few explicit strategic milestones runs similar dangers. If the formal objectives chosen do not represent the right strategic goals and priorities, misdirected motivation can be damaging. The personal motivation generated by the formal control process then detracts from performance rather than enhancing it, and a more informal approach to control, which places less emphasis on a few selected targets, can be preferable.

Misdirected motivation is a particular problem in businesses where it is hard to identify good measures of strategic progress. In these businesses, strategic control is problematic. The strongest statement of this position is given by Bill Ouchi.[21] He argues that in some organizations it is

difficult to measure the outputs of individual units precisely and objectively. The desired result (for example, "increasing marketing orientation") may not be amenable to measurement, or else (for example, in
organizations with extensive shared responsibilities) the credit due to
different units may be hard to apportion. In these cases, Ouchi maintains
that controls that emphasize the measurable results achieved by the unit
are inappropriate. Ouchi claims, further, that it is sometimes hard even
to specify the sorts of actions that will be required to bring about a given
outcome. In a research laboratory, for example, considerable discretion
must be left to the scientists on the bench to decide how to spend their
time in seeking the desired breakthrough. Controls that prescribe the
actions they should take or the programmes they should implement are
liable to be counterproductive. Ouchi refers to this as a situation in
which the knowledge of means–ends relationships is low.

In situations where both the ability to measure outputs precisely and
objectively and the knowledge of means-ends relationships are low,
Ouchi believes that conventional control processes break down.
Control objectives are liable to be arbitrarily and wrongly set, and the
danger of misdirected motivation is high. In such cases, Ouchi suggests
that "clan" controls may be preferable to conventional controls.

What are clan controls? The features that Ouchi stresses are:

- a strong sense of shared values and clan traditions
- careful selection of new recruits, followed by socialization or
  indoctrination into the shared values of the clan
- ability to trust individual clan members to pursue clan goals without formal "senior management" control.

As examples of clans, he cites hospital doctors and R&D staff.[22]

The strength of the clan is that individual clan members can be relied
upon to pursue the common clan goals spontaneously. No formal control system, beyond the socialization process, is needed to bring their
personal goals into line with the organization's goals. Therefore it is not
necessary to specify and monitor particular objectives or milestones.
Individuals can be relied upon to pursue their best endeavours on behalf
of the clan, and they can be given discretion over exactly how they do
this. In an environment in which suitable control measures are hard to
define, an informal control process with these characteristics is desirable.

The "clan control" concept is interesting, and it is undeniable that
there are companies where managers derive high motivation from identifying closely with the underlying purposes, values and mission of the

organization.[23] But the circumstances that Ouchi claims are most appropriate for clan controls are very seldom, if ever, found (at least in strong form) in the companies we have researched. A number of businesses found difficulty in specifying desired outputs in a precisely measurable form, but none were wholly unable to do this. Equally, many businesses could not state exactly what means should be adopted to reach a given objective, but very few could not indicate the main directions they favoured. Indeed, if a business unit within a major company said it had no idea how to measure its outputs or how to reach its objectives, this admission would lead, in all probability, to a rapid change of management! Identifying and measuring suitable strategic control objectives is often difficult, but seldom impossible.

We do not reject the notion of clan motivation, however, since we believe that clan motivation and control motivation are not mutually exclusive alternatives. Rather, clan motivation, or a sense of mission as we prefer to call it,[24] can operate alongside and reinforce strategic controls. Control-based motivation ties strategic objectives to personal rewards, while clan-based motivation depends on values and purposes that individual managers believe are intrinsically worthwhile and sound. Ideally, as in some of the most successful Japanese companies such as Matsushita and Toshiba, these two sources of motivation can reinforce each other.

The clan approach to control tends to fit more naturally with less formal strategic control processes. But this is not inevitable. For many years, Shell has relied heavily on its shared culture and values as a source of motivation. Now some sectors in the company are introducing formal milestones, not to supersede but to complement the more "clannish" approach to control and motivation. A formal control process that recognizes no goals or value other than those embodied in the explicit objectives will conflict with clan motivation, but one that sees the formal objectives as part of a wider vision can be compatible with it.

Cost and bureaucracy

Unfortunately, all control processes incur costs and overheads. And the more extensive the efforts necessary to establish, measure and monitor suitable control parameters, the higher the costs are. To the extent that strategic control measures cannot be based on existing reports or information flows and require extensive one-off analysis, the cost of establishing formal strategic control measures may be substantial. Companies such as Courtaulds and GE, which in principle recognize the value of explicit strategic control objectives, may balk at the practical cost of defining them.

In Courtaulds, we were told that relative competitive cost levels were the key measure of strategic strength in one business. The centre had sponsored a major consulting study in the early 1980s to arrive at an estimate of where Courtaulds stood in terms of this measure. But relative cost position had not been made into an ongoing strategic control measure. "The work needed to estimate competitive cost positions is neither cheap nor easy to carry out. I wish we could find a cost-effective and simple way of getting at it, but we haven't yet. The main problem of using a measure of competitive cost position as a strategic control is that it would be too time consuming and expensive." A similar point was made to us in GE:

"Any system you put in place costs money. Therefore it must have an incremental benefit. Financial numbers are, on the margin, cheap to produce because financial data has to be produced for legal and shareholder purposes. But calculating competitive position is very expensive if you do it well. It's like checking the health of the average person. You could take his temperature every hour and give him a check-up once a week. But it would be too costly. It makes more sense to rely on individuals to report their feelings of ill health rather than to have continuous monitoring."

The issue here is simply a matter of cost/benefit analysis. How much will it actually cost to set up a suitable formal control measure? How much benefit will we derive from having it? If the cost outweighs the benefit, informal controls will be preferable.

In addition, the more bureaucratized the control process, the slower and the less responsive are decisions that result from it. Where a series of structured meetings and a stack of reports are necessary before decisions can be taken, the bureaucracy of the control process gets in the way of good strategy. GE's lament ("We had financial measures and strategic measures and financial analysis and strategic analysis, and we lost focus on the issue of insight") must strike a chord with many companies. As a result, the company has moved towards a more informal approach to control. "If you're looking for more speed and more responsiveness, that requires more trust. This means that formal, written-down objectives are less essential."

The danger that formal control processes can become weighted down with bureaucracy is generally recognized. Some companies believe that the danger can be avoided, however. ICI, for example, has designed its strategic milestone system to be as flexible as possible and to avoid unnecessary bureaucracy. And National Westminster Bank tries to set objectives for which the measurement data are already routinely collected, so that new reporting systems involving added cost and bureaucracy are not needed. But for companies such as GE, the prevention of bureaucracy has been the prime motive in adopting a more informal type of control process, in which explicit strategic objectives are not formally defined, documented and monitored.

FORMAL OR INFORMAL CONTROLS?

Formal strategic control processes bring several benefits in terms of clarity and realism in planning, stretch, motivation, timely intervention, avoidance of backdoor financial control, and clearer responsibilities. But they can also cause problems of inflexibility, misdirected motivation, cost and bureaucracy. It is the balance between these advantages and disadvantages that should guide the choice of a strategic control process.

The importance of these different sources of added and subtracted value differs according to the circumstances in which each company is operating. For some companies, and some management teams, the advantages of a formal process will appear overwhelming; for others, an informal approach will be preferable. This is because the appropriate degree of formality depends both on the sorts of businesses in the company, and on the way in which the control process will be used. The choice between formal and informal controls must fit, therefore, with a company's business mix, and with its management skills and priorities. We shall explore the factors underlying this choice further in Chapters 6 and 7.

NUMBER OF PERFORMANCE CRITERIA

How the strategic control process adds value also depends on the number of performance criteria that it encompasses. Increasing the number of objectives makes for more timely intervention (more trigger points) and reduces the danger of misdirected motivation (less chance of objectives being an incomplete reflection of what matters most). The observation in BP was: "As one moves down through the levels, the milestones tend to become more detailed and specific. The further down you go, the clearer are the milestones. You know what you need to do each year to keep on track."

On the other hand, a control process that specifies many detailed milestones can reduce the degree of focus on those that matter most, and can lead to interference from the centre on detailed issues that should be left to the business. If, at the extreme, legitimate control is replaced by nit-picking interference, the results are usually counterproductive, since independent-minded business managers are liable to react badly. A typical comment from a business head was: "My attitude is basically: tell me what is wanted and I'll do it. But then don't interfere in the details of the business." For this reason many senior corporate executives prefer to focus control on only a few key objectives. This attitude was summed up by one chief executive who maintained: "The last thing to do to a good manager is tell him what to do. You can tell him what you want." Furthermore, close and detailed control can bring with it additional cost and bureaucracy, especially with more formal control processes. There are therefore drawbacks to more detailed control processes that use multiple objectives which can, in some circumstances, outweigh their benefits.

The balance of advantage and disadvantage between more and fewer performance criteria largely mirrors the strengths and weaknesses of the Strategic Planning and Strategic Control management styles.[25] These important trade-offs need to be taken into account, in addition to the degree of formality, in designing a strategic control process that will match the needs and circumstances of a company.

Notes and References

1 See C. H. Roush and B. C. Ball, "Controlling the implementation of strategy", *Managerial Planning,* vol. 29, no. 4, Nov/Dec 1980, 3-12, p 6.

2 P. Lorange, *Corporate Planning: An Executive Viewpoint,* Prentice-Hall, Englewood Cliffs, NJ, 1980.

3 See Michael Goold and Andrew Campbell, *Strategies and Styles*, Blackwell, Oxford, 1987, p. 189.

4 "... a high level of commitment can be dangerous. Examples ... show that individuals, businesses, and countries sometimes continue to commit large resources to failing projects despite continued negative feedback." C. R. Schwenk, "Information, cognitive biases, and commitment to a course of action", *Academy*

of Management Review, vol. 11, no. 2, 1986, pp. 298-310. See also B. M. Staw. "The escalation of commitment to a course of action", *Academy of Management Review,* vol. 6, 1981, pp. 577-87.

5 See E. A. Locke *et al.,* "Goal setting and task performance, 1969-1980", *Psychological Bulletin,* vol. 90, no. 1, 1980, pp. 125-52.

6 G. H. Hofstede, *The Game of Budget Control,* Van Gorcum, Assen, 1967.

7 A. C. Stedry and E. Kay, "The effects of goal difficulty on performance", *Behavioral Science,* vol. 11, 1966, 459-70.

8 J. Harvey-Jones, *Making it Happen; Reflections on Leadership,* Collins, 1988, p. 102.

9 See Chapter 2, pp. 31-2.

10 M. C. Jensen and W. H. Meckling, "Theory of the firm: Managerial behaviour, agency costs and ownership structure", *Journal of Financial Economics,* vol. 3, 1976, pp. 305-60. S. Baiman, "Agency research in managerial accountancy: a survey", *Journal of Accounting Literature,* vol. 1, 1982, pp. 154-213.

11 See V. Govindarajaran and A. K. Gupta, "Linking control systems to business unit strategy: impact on performance", *Accounting, Organisations and Society,* vol. 10, no. 1, 1985, pp. 51-66, and M. S. Salter, "Tailor incentive compensation to strategy", *Harvard Business Review,* Mar-Apr 1973, pp. 94-102. There has been extensive research into the type of goals and objectives that motivate people. Widely accepted results are that goals and objectives should be: specific, clearly defined and preferably measurable, rather than "do your best" (E. A. Locke, L. A. Saari, K. N. Shaw and G. P. Latham, "Goal setting and task performance, 1969-80", *Psychological Bulletin,* vol. 90, no. 1, 1980, pp. 125-52); stretching – difficult but attainable, (A. C. Stedry and E. Kay, "The effects of goal difficulty on performance", *Behavioral Science,* vol. 11, 1966, pp. 459-70); set participatively rather than imposed, if the task to be achieved is complex (D. J. Campbell and K. F. Ginrich, "The interactive effect of task complexity and task performance: A field experiment", *Organisational Behaviour and Human Decision Processes,* vol. 38, no. 2, 1986, pp. 162-80.)

12 In Courtaulds the idea of tying bonuses to strategic objective achievement was described as an "absolute minefield – just another area for conflict between the centre and the businesses".

13 See *Strategies and Styles,* op. cit., p. 190, on "control games".

14 In one company, we were told that the first question the CEO always asks of business heads concerns their success with graduate recruitment. In another company, the CEO maintains a personal filofax (a "black book") of performance statistics on each business, to which he always refers during performance reviews.

15 This point is stressed by Lawrence Hrebiniak and William Joyce in *Implementing Strategy,* Macmillan, London, 1984. They argue: "When measurable performance

criteria are lacking, performance appraisal and review are subjective, at best, and, at worst, political, arbitrary and capricious," (p. 118).

16 C. Argyris, "Organisational learning and management information systems", *Accounting, Organizations and Society*, vol. **2**, no. 2, 1977, pp. 113-23, See also C. Argyris and D. A. Schon, *Organisational Learninig: A Theory of Action Perspective*, Addison Wesley, Reading, Mass., 1978, and C. Argyris, *Strategy, Change and Defensive Routines*, Pitman, Mass, 1985.

17 J. B. Quinn, *Strategies for Change*, Richard D. Irwin, Homewood. Ill, 1980.

18 H. Mintzberg, "Crafting Strategy", *Harvard Business Review*, Jul-Aug 1987.

19 H. A. Simon, "Making management decisions: the role of intuition and emotion", *Academy of Management Executive*, Feb 1967, pp. 57-64.

20 ibid, p.63.

21 W. G. Ouchi, "A conceptual framework for the design of organisational control mechanisms", *Management Science*, vol. 25, no. 9, Sept 1979, pp. 833-48; "Markets, bureacracies and clans", *Administative Science Quarterly*, vol. 25, Mar 1980, pp. 129-41.

22 This type of control is part of what is referred to by Kenneth Merchant (*Control in Business Organisations*, Pitman, 1985) as "personnel" control.

23 Many authors in fields ranging from leadership to motivation have identified that purpose, values and culture can help to establish standards and behaviour patterns in organizations. Some of the more interesting sources are: T. J. Peters and R. H. Waterman, *In Search of Excellence: Lessons from America's Best Run Companies*, Harper & Row, New York, 1982, Chapter 3; R. T. Pascale and A. G. Athos, *The Art of Japanese Management*, Simon & Schuster, New York, 1981, Chapter 7; W. Bennis and B. Nanus, *Leaders: The Strategies for Taking Charge*, Harper & Row, New York, 1985, pp. 87-109; P. Selznick, *Leadership in Administration: A Sociological Interpretation*, University of California Press, 1957, pp. 1-28; E. H. Schein, *Organizational Psycholgy*, Prentice-Hall, Englewood Cliffs, NJ. 1980, pp. 33-39.

24 See A. Campbell and K. Tawadey, *Mission Statements and Business Philosophy: Winning Employee Commitment*, Heinemann, London, 1990, and A. Campbell, M. Devine and D. Young, *A Sense of Mission*, The Economist Books/Hutchinson, London, 1990.

25 See *Strategies and Styles*, op cit., Chapters 11 and 12. The appropriate degree of detail also depends on the level in the corporate hierarchy. See Appendix 2.

CHAPTER 6

CONTROLS THAT MATCH A BUSINESS'S CIRCUMSTANCES

As we have seen, different approaches to strategic control have distinctive strengths and weaknesses. For this reason, companies should think carefully about how well their control processes fit the businesses in their portfolios. The control process will work well only if its strengths and weaknesses match the circumstances of the businesses that are being controlled.

In our research we have identified several factors that should influence the choice of control approach for a business.[1]

- The length of time-lags between actions and financial results.
- The nature of the portfolio of which the business is a part; in particular the potential for linkages with other businesses in the portfolio and the diversity of the portfolio.
- The level of risk; in particular the prevalence of "bet your company" investment decisions, the extent of uncertainty, and the speed of change in the business's environment.
- The sources of competitive advantage in the business.

The length of time-lags determines whether profit controls or strategic controls are needed. The other factors determine whether strategic controls, if chosen, should be formal or informal, and whether they should encompass many criteria of good performance or few.

TIME-LAGS

The length of time it takes for decisions to pay off is a fundamental consideration in the choice of a control approach. If profits do not respond quickly to actions and initiatives, an exclusive focus on profits as the key criteria of good performance is obviously dangerous. Good strategies can then, at least in the short term, be compatible with a poor or declining profit trend and vice versa, as discussed in Chapter 1.

Long delays between actions and results occur in many businesses. The sort of capital equipment needed in the paper industry, the steel industry or the industrial gases business often takes several years to build, commission and utilize at anything close to full capacity. In such businesses, capital investment is likely to depress short-term earnings, even if it pays off handsomely in the long run. In Wiggins Teape the view was: "In the paper business, you have to put up £200 million for a new machine, with the prospect of not getting a payback for up to ten years. You have to look at investment more in terms of whether you can afford the short-term cash flow to do what's right for the long-term strategy."

Expense investments can also take time to have an impact. Companies like Mars and Nestlé accept that the current year's earnings can always be boosted by cutting back on brand support spending, since the downturn in profits caused by eroding brand strength usually shows through only in later years. Equally, BP and Shell can improve short-term profits by reducing their current spending on oil exploration, ICI by squeezing research spending. ("If we terminate a drug development programme, that helps our profits this year. But in ten years time, we may have nothing worth selling.") All these companies recognize that decisions to cut expense investments will increase current profits, but will in due course – maybe several years later – come home to roost. Because expense investments cannot be capitalized for purposes of financial reporting, the trade-offs between current spending and future profits are particularly hard to handle.

A further influence on the speed with which current actions show through in financial results is the nature of competitive conditions in the industry. If competition is indirect, with many competitors able to prosper,[2] decisions that weaken competitive position may have little impact on profitability until the industry matures and competition becomes more intense. For a period, in the early 1980s, almost all participants in the personal computer industry were able to make money, irrespective of their underlying strategic position, provided they had a product that worked. Now, with growth slowing and product designs converging, a shakeout has taken place, and only those companies that had built some competitive edge are surviving.[3]

Conversely, if competitive conditions are unusually fierce, so that profits are depressed for everyone, the benefits of decisions that strengthen competitive position may not show through until and unless a more stable competitive equilibrium is re-established. British Steel began ten years ago to take the measures that have now made it one of the most profitable steel producers in the world. But it was not until a degree of stability returned to its markets in the late 1980s that profitability became more satisfactory.

In any business where there are long time-lags between actions and their eventual impact on profitability, short-term profit controls run a serious risk of causing misdirected motivation. If Hanson, with its tight financial controls, were to take over the ICI Pharmaceutical business, there would be a grave danger that the control process would focus too much attention on current year's results, thereby preventing investment in the sort of 10–15 year research programmes on which the long-term future of the business depends. In this sort of business, strategic criteria of good performance must supplement profit controls. A strategic control process is of fundamental importance.

Conversely, in businesses where there are short time-lags between actions and financial results, getting day-to-day operations right is more important than focusing on long-term competitive position.[4] Courtaulds distinguishes between the bulk of its businesses, where a strategic approach is needed, and the converting operations where it is more questionable. ("In converting businesses, success depends more on detailed operational issues and good management than on overall competitive position.") In these businesses, it may be best to focus on pure profit controls. Then corporate management need not try to understand the detail of the business; the complex operating decisions and trade-offs are left to business management (where they belong), and motivation towards the bottom-line result is appropriately clear and strong.

In RTZ's Pillar Merchanting business, which distributes engineering and building supplies, the emphasis is firmly on decentralized responsibility and profit controls. "It's not worth thinking ten years out in this sort of business, since things can change totally in a couple of years," we were told. "There is little fixed capital and low customer loyalty. You can play tunes with the business on very short time scales." RTZ believes that "The main thing we can offer a business like this is freedom from bureaucratic reporting and control. The key strategic decision is not to burden them with too much strategy".[5]

The first essential step in devising a control approach is therefore to determine whether there are long time-lags between actions and their profit consequences. If there are, a strategic control process is needed. If not, a profit control process is probably preferable.

In the remainder of this chapter, we will assume that long time-lags are characteristic of the business in question, and that the issue is therefore what type of strategic control process to adopt.

NATURE OF THE PORTFOLIO

Strategic control is easier in companies whose portfolios are made up of stand-alone businesses in a relatively small number of different sectors. High levels of linkages between the businesses and a high degree of diversity both complicate the task.

Linkages

Companies like IBM and Digital must coordinate product development and marketing strategy between different organizational units that have responsibility for specific components, systems, geographical areas and market segments. Each of these units can be regarded in some sense as a business, and controls can be established for the performance of that business as a stand-alone entity. But to do so makes it more difficult to achieve the sort of cooperation and coordination that is required by the nature of these businesses. Thus, although Digital is keen to promote a sense of personal responsibility, it now avoids allocating too much decentralized responsibility for individual businesses' performance, and concentrates more on collective efforts.

"We had a structure based on product-market businesses and accountabilities up to 1982. But there were lots of difficulties and problems. Because of separate accountability it was difficult to provide an integrated approach to large accounts. There were lots of boundary disputes. Instead of being strategists, the product people were being policemen, accountants and lawyers. Now we are trying to encourage people to work together in a more flexible fashion."

If there are important linkages between businesses in a corporate portfolio, a fully decentralized approach to strategy is questionable. To achieve the benefits and synergies that can come from collaboration, the company needs a more cooperative approach to strategy in which businesses share decisions and responsibilities. In Mars, the situation was described as follows: "Many of the brands are global and need to be managed from a corporate perspective that may be different from a business unit's perspective. In this sense the autonomy of a business unit is constrained."

Strong accountability and incentives for business-specific performance are then less possible and less desirable.

Control processes for such companies need to avoid performance criteria that undermine cooperation and misdirect motivation. An exclusive focus on the profit bottom line for individual businesses is clearly unsuitable, and explicit strategic objectives that focus on business-specific performance (as they nearly always do) will also cause problems, particularly if they are linked strongly to personal rewards. A more informal approach to strategic control, which allows value to be placed on softer objectives, such as cooperative attitudes and team spirit, often seems to work better. In addition, a larger number of objectives and less emphasis on business unit profitability can make it easier to incorporate goals concerned with linkage management in the control process.

Figure 6.1 summarizes the appropriateness of different strategic control processes for companies with important linkages between businesses in the portfolio.

Figure 6.1 **Choosing a Control Approach: Important Linkages Among Businesses**

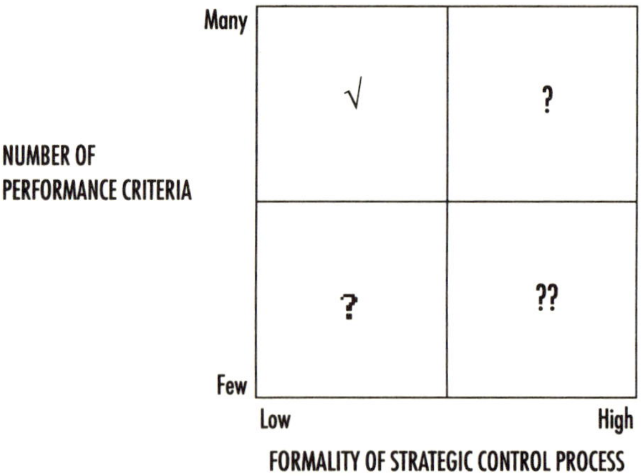

Misdirected motivation (lack of cooperation) is the key source of subtracted value to avoid
    Explicit milestones and a focus on a few criteria of good performance will be satisfactory only if they include cooperative objectives

Key: √ = appropriate
        ? = questionable
        ?? = highly questionable

Diversity

In highly diverse portfolios, it is hard for top management to have the depth of knowledge of individual businesses and their managers, and the frequency of contact, that are needed to make informal controls work well. In one large and highly diverse company that follows an informal strategic control process, we were told by the director of planning: "We must question whether, given the industrial and geographical diversity of our interests, we have too many units reporting to the centre to control in this way. This is a particular issue at a time when simpler problems, such as eliminating areas of low profitability, are now less important."

If top managers are not closely familiar with the businesses, the quality of the informal debate may not be high enough to identify the right objectives clearly and to see that progress is genuinely being made.

Strategic control is particularly tricky in diverse companies where the businesses have very different key success factors. "There is a real problem in controlling a complex, technology intensive business in an area which is largely unfamiliar to most of us," said the CEO of one company.

Figure 6.2 **Choosing a Control Approach: High Diversity Among Businesses**

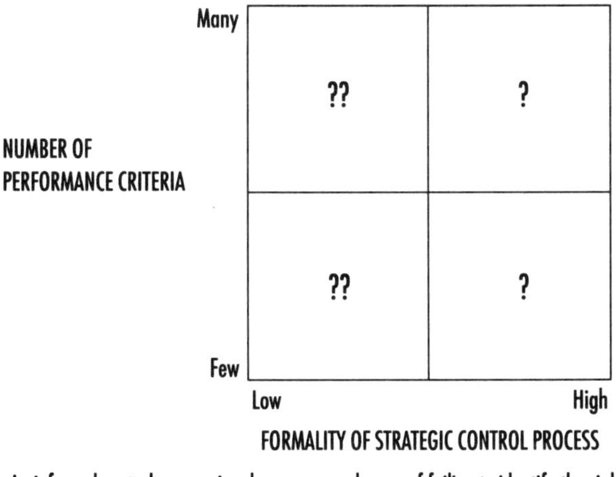

An informal control process involves a severe danger of failing to identify the right strategic objectives
    Formal process helps to structure the debate, but high diversity causes problems under any strategic control process

Key: ? = questionable
        ?? = highly questionable

The business in question was relatively new and no members of the top team had personal experience of managing it. "It is hard for us to know what matters most. All our knee-jerk reactions are liable to be wrong." Since informal controls rely heavily on the right knee-jerk reactions, they had proved unsatisfactory in this company.

A formal strategic control process forces a more open and structured debate about what strategic objectives are right for each business, and how much progress is being made. With a highly diverse portfolio, this tends to be an improvement on more informal processes. However, our research suggests that there is a limit to senior managers' ability to identify and comprehend strategic objectives across a large number of different businesses. In our view, high diversity is likely to lead to misidentification of strategic objectives at the centre, and hence a focus on the wrong criteria of good performance. This is a problem, whether the approach to control uses explicit objectives or is more informal.

Figure 6.2 (on page 153) shows how diversity affects the suitability of different strategic control processes.

LEVEL OF RISK

High levels of risk make it more difficult to identify specific future targets for the achievement of which business management can be given unequivocal responsibility. Three related but distinct factors influence risk levels: "bet your company" investment decisions, uncertainty and speed of change.

"Bet your company" investment decisions

In some businesses, large, infrequent, risky decisions are unavoidable. Developing and launching a new model range in automobiles, a new public switch in telecommunications, a new generation of computer equipment in IT – these are all "bet your company" investments that can make or break a whole company. In such cases, top corporate managers need a control process that allows them to monitor the success of decisions closely, so they can intervene quickly at the first sign of trouble. The centre cannot afford to stand back and judge business management by the overall results they achieve, since the cost of mistakes is unacceptably high. Timely intervention is the key added value from the control process.

In businesses that must make "bet your company" investment decisions, decentralized responsibility for strategy is less viable.[6] A more hands-on style of corporate management is needed in which the centre helps to set the strategy and monitors all relevant performance indicators, so that emerging problems will be quickly detected. In these sorts of businesses, control against a few clear criteria of good performance is inappropriate, and business managers are unlikely to see close corporate monitoring of results as interference. Figure 6.3 summarizes the implications for strategic control of "bet your company" investment decisions.

Figure 6.3 **Choosing a Control Approach: Many "Bet Your Company" Decisions**

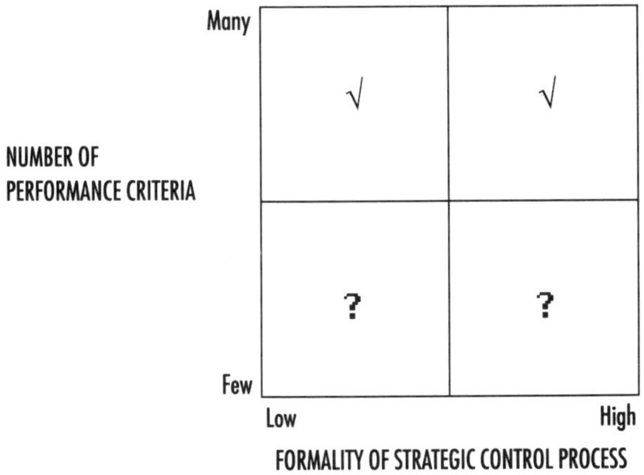

Timely intervention is the key source of added value from strategic control
   It is less appropriate to concentrate on only a few criteria of good performance in the control process

Key: √ = appropriate
       ? = questionable

Uncertainty

Several companies talked about the impact on the control process of high levels of uncertainty in their businesses.[7] The oil companies, for example, face large and unpredictable shifts in oil prices: "With the volatility of the oil price, we need to focus more on 'real' things such as reserve levels and success rates in exploration than on financial returns." A similar situation exists in research-based businesses. In ICI, one manager argued that in businesses like Pharmaceuticals and Seeds technical milestones were possible, but commercial returns were much less easy to forecast. "In Pharmaceuticals, much depends on the development and registration process, where events are largely out of our hands, and on the market reception for a new drug, which again is hard for us to control. Therefore, milestones are less personal performance measures, than key events along the path for the business, which help the centre to decide on an appropriate level of resourcing."

Uncertainty has two main consequences for the control process. First, it means that tight accountability for targets is less feasible. If everyone knows that events for which business managers have no responsibility may cause targets to be missed, the control process cannot hold them personally accountable for hitting or missing the targets. As one company put it: "We find it difficult to distinguish between the effects of management action and changes in the operating environment. It is difficult to decide whether failure to meet strategic milestones should be met by altering the milestones or blaming the manager. We tend to take the former course."

If specific objectives are set, absolute objectives (such as achieve a 10 per cent cost reduction) are less appropriate than objectives set relative to the competition (such as achieve 5 per cent lower cost than any other competitor). The fundamental goal is to do better than others in the industry, even if unpredictable events influence absolute performance levels.

Uncertainty and changes in the environment also increase the danger in a tenacious pursuit of pre-set objectives. Pressing on quickly with the costly development of a drug that has begun to show signs of toxicity is not desirable. Instead, the programme needs to be re-evaluated, and new directions set. Explicit milestones and formal controls may be undesirable if they cause managers to lock onto certain targets too firmly and inflexibly.

It is for this reason that Ciba-Geigy's strategic control process monitors the background assumptions as well as the strategic objectives that have been agreed. The company can then take account of changes in these assumptions in the formal control process. National Westminster Bank also recalculates objectives in the light of changes in the bank's operating environment, such as shifts in interest rates or exchange rates. But, in both cases, there is an assumption that the effects of changes in the environment are relatively predictable. In businesses where such effects are not predictable, tight, formal control processes are much less feasible.

Figure 6.4 shows the implications of high levels of uncertainty for strategic control processes.

Figure 6.4 **Choosing a Control Approach: High Uncertainty**

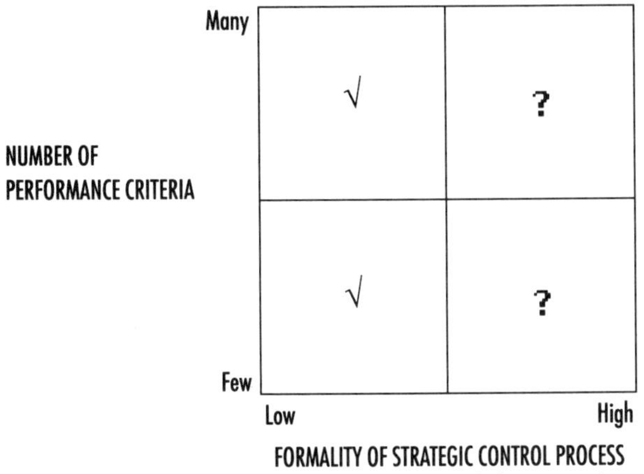

Inflexibility (failure to adjust to changing circumstances) is the key source of potential subtracted value to avoid
    Formal controls may be dangerous unless they are flexibly administered, set in terms relative to the competition, and can be adjusted to take account of change in the environment

Key: √ = appropriate
        ? = questionable

Speed of change

In some businesses, rapid response to changes in the environment is especially important. Manufacturers of fashion goods, for example, always face uncertainties about the level of demand for their products; their success depends on detecting and responding quickly to trends as they emerge. More and more companies see their markets developing in this direction. In these circumstances strategic planning and control processes must be faster moving, more flexible and less bureaucratic. The centre needs to delegate more, interfere less and reach decisions more quickly. These have been GE themes, but we have heard them echoed in a number of other companies. In Nestlé, for example, one senior manager stated: "We generally discuss decisions and results pretty thoroughly. In most of our markets, things don't change fast and this is suitable. But in faster changing areas such as chocolate count lines and ice cream bars you have to delegate more, so that country managers can respond more quickly to their markets."

Even IBM[8] has recently tried to decentralize more responsibility and reduce the amount of central monitoring. One manager explained, "The purpose of the change is to create a faster response to the changing market place. We want to make IBM move from being a product-driven to a market-driven company."

In addition, rather than providing incentives to implement a pre-agreed strategy or to reach pre-set objectives, the control process needs to encourage managers to be flexible enough to come up with new strategies as appropriate. Close control against objectives set in the last strategy review is not desirable or possible in fast-changing businesses. Instead, the control process must allow quick decisions on changing strategy.

In businesses that face rapid change, more decentralized management styles and less formal control processes are indicated. If explicit strategic objectives are set, they should concentrate on a few key results rather than numerous more detailed actions, thereby allowing business managers more flexibility in how they achieve the objectives. Figure 6.5 summarizes these implications.

Figure 6.5 **Choosing a Control Approach: Rapid Change**

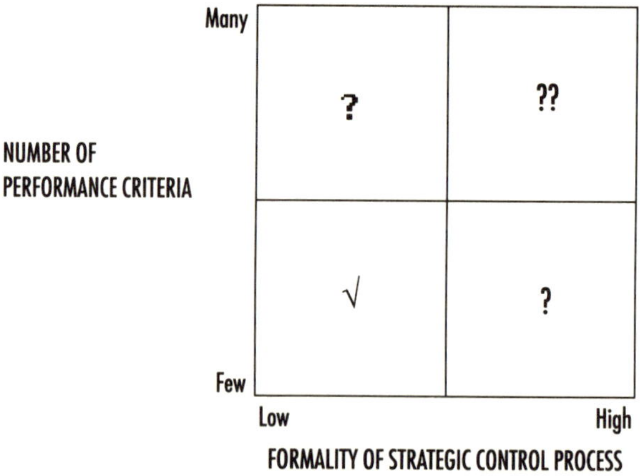

Inflexibility, interference and bureaucracy are the key sources of subtracted value to avoid
  Explicit objectives and formal monitoring of a wide range of performance criteria run the risk of tying the business down too much, unless they are administered in a flexible and unbureaucratic fashion

Key: √ = appropriate
        ? = questionable
        ?? = highly questionable

SOURCES OF COMPETITIVE ADVANTAGE

An understanding of the sources of competitive advantage in each business must lie behind whatever strategic control objectives are established. If strategic objectives are to capture the criteria of good long-term performance, they must focus on the underlying key success factors that drive competitive advantage. As one company put it: "Milestones are simply timetabled key success factors, together with statements about the level of achievement to be attained."

But identifying the sources of competitive advantage for a business can be a difficult and time-consuming process. It requires both analysis of the strategies and results of different competitors, and insight into the causes of success and failure in the business. Since the nature of competitive advantage differs between businesses, there is no general answer to the question of what variables the strategic control process should focus on. Consequently, different companies define very different sorts of strategic objectives.

Our purpose here is not to propose how to analyse competitive advantage or to identify which particular sources of advantage matter most in specific businesses.[9] There are, however, some differences in the nature of competitive advantage between businesses that are important for the control process. The distinctions we shall stress are between:

- Businesses in which a few simple sources of advantage drive profitability versus those in which a larger number of more complex factors matter.
- Businesses in which the sources of advantage can be readily measured versus those in which they cannot.

Businesses driven by a few simple sources of advantage

In some businesses, one or two key variables drive profitability. The Boston Consulting Group made its reputation by arguing that, in businesses where the experience curve operates (for example, semi-conductors), cumulative volume or market share is the dominant factor in determining relative competitive profitability. More recently, the Total Quality movement has placed similar emphasis on quality as the underlying source of success.[10] And, in our research, we have encountered several managers who believe that one or two factors have overwhelming importance for their businesses. In consumer goods businesses, for example, market share is typically seen as a key source of advantage and is closely monitored. "Market share has great value as a key proxy for our ability to reach the market and therefore to earn high levels of profitability. A simple objective of maintaining or increasing market share is possible, and we can exercise strategic control just by watching trends in market share in addition to trends in profitability."

This statement, from a manufacturer of household durables, is typical of the spirit behind the control processes of several consumer goods companies.

If a few factors, such as market share or quality, are the key to competitive advantage, strategic control can focus on them as the criteria of good performance. A comparatively simple strategic control process is possible and, provided the sources of advantage have been correctly identified, the risk of misdirected motivation is limited. In such businesses, a formal control process using a few explicit strategic objectives is feasible, and can offer valuable benefits, in terms of clearer and more realistic plans, stronger and more stretching motivation, timely intervention and clearer responsibilities.

If, moreover, the sources of advantage can be measured with reasonable ease, the cost of establishing explicit objectives will not be prohibitive. For example, if good public data are available on competitors' market shares – as is true in many consumer products – it is not especially costly or difficult to make relative market share an explicit strategic objective.

Figure 6.6 shows the suitability of different control processes for a business in which a few easily measurable sources of advantage drive profitability.

Businesses driven by multiple, complex sources of advantage

The PIMS (Profit Impact of Market Strategy) programme has been collecting data on business unit performance since the early 1970s. In all, some 450 companies, covering the USA, Canada and Europe, have provided data, and around 3,000 SBUs are currently being tracked. For each SBU, the data cover financial performance, about a dozen variables concerned with competitive position or strategy (for example, market share, relative product/service quality, new products as a proportion of sales), and about ten factors concerned with market or industry structure (for example, market growth rate, stage of market evolution). The purpose of the programme is to identify, through regression analysis, the variables that are the most important drivers of profitability.[11] The analysis can be carried out for eight major industry sectors (consumer

Figure 6.6 **Choosing a Control Approach: Few, Easily Measured Sources of Advantages**

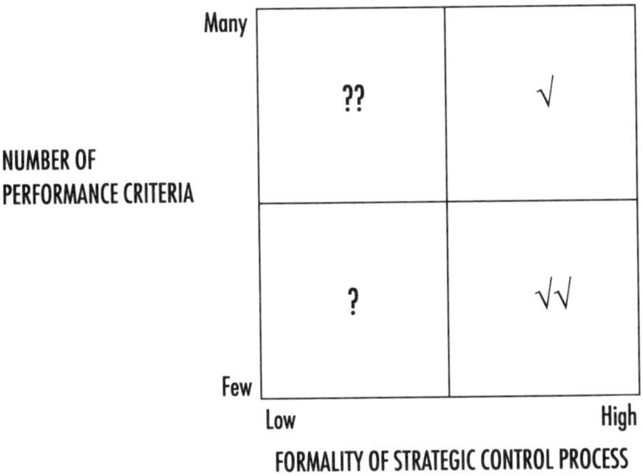

Benefits of a formal control process are possible to achieve without misdirected motivation or high cost
More informal approaches to control are liable to lose some of these benefits

Key: √√ = very appropriate
 √ = appropriate
 ? = questionable
 ?? = highly questionable

durables, consumer non-durables, capital goods, raw and semi-finished goods, components, supplies, services and distribution).

The results of the PIMS analysis are interesting.[12] The amount of the variation among SBUs in return on investment (ROI) that is explained by all the competitive strategy and industry structure variables together varies from 53 per cent in capital goods and consumer non-durables to 65 per cent in consumer durables.[13] Put more negatively, 35–45 per cent of the variation in ROI remains unexplained, even after a 20-variable multiple regression. In some industries, certain variables are specially important. For example, market share accounts for 30 per cent of the variation in ROI in consumer durables and 28 per cent in consumer non-durables. But in other industries (raw and semi-finished goods, services, distribution), the single most important variable accounts for less than 10 per cent of the variation in ROI.

The regression equations do not, of course, provide a tailored analysis of the specific sources of advantage for individual businesses, which might yield more powerful relationships.[14] But the PIMS work does suggest that the search for a few dominant sources of advantage is often likely to be fruitless. Unfortunately, in many businesses it is just not possible to find one or two factors that are the key to success. Instead, the competitive battle is won by doing well across a variety of areas, and no simple success formula can be found.

This view is borne out by our research. Managers in businesses as different as speciality chemicals, international logistics and industrial services have argued that no simple system of strategic controls is possible, because their businesses are intrinsically complex. Strategic controls need to reflect this complexity by avoiding a focus on one or two variables. "Trying to be too cut and dried about specific, measurable performance variables is counterproductive. It is important to have controls, but difficult to express them in terms of a few key variables," was a typical comment from a chief executive who believed in more informal controls.

A good example is provided by the lubricants business in BP.

"Lubes is a very different business from retail gasoline. It depends less on major programmes, such as site developments. It is about higher added value, more marketing-intensive, more complex products going into many different segments. You can look at overall market share, but it's only a very crude shorthand. What you need is a focus on mechanisms by which market share can be improved in specific products and markets."

Problems arise not only from the number of factors that must be considered, but also from the difficulty of identifying and understanding the relationships. In retailing, it is necessary to take account of market share, purchasing scale, segment focus, sales mix, pricing policy, store costs, and other factors. But some retail companies with whom we talked believe that a relatively simple model can be built to show how each of these factors contributes to profitability. Controls can then be geared to specific objectives in terms of these factors. In RTZ Pillar's aviation support business, on the other hand, no simple model is seen as adequate.

"We provide product support over lifetimes of up to 25 years on things such as undercarriage equipment and aircraft engines. It takes a long time to break into the business, but, once having done so, you can enjoy sustained profits provided your service is right. You have to keep track of a whole range of customer and supplier contacts to know how the relationship is developing, and the only way to do this is by working closely with the business unit management. You have to be fully familiar with all the issues; there is no substitute for this."

Businesses that are technically difficult to comprehend and have multiple sources of advantage present the greatest control problems for corporate management. In these businesses, it is difficult to identify and understand what the sources of advantage are, let alone to reduce them to a small number of readily measured variables. A relatively informal control process that embraces a range of objectives and can shift attention on to priority issues as they emerge is in some ways preferable, although such an approach can lead to excessive interference, especially if corporate managers do not fully understand the business. If, furthermore, the sources of advantage can be measured only by extensive, one-off analysis, the cost of establishing explicit objectives may become prohibitive.[15] These are the sorts of situations in which Ouchi favours clan controls, as described in Chapter 5.

In businesses where the sources of advantage are numerous, complex and hard to measure, formal controls with explicit objectives are difficult to define and run a significant risk of focusing attention on the wrong goals. Also, control approaches that use only a few criteria of good performance are problematic. Informal approaches that can comprehend a

Figure 6.7 **Choosing a Control Approach: Multiple, Complex Hard to Measure Sources of Advantage**

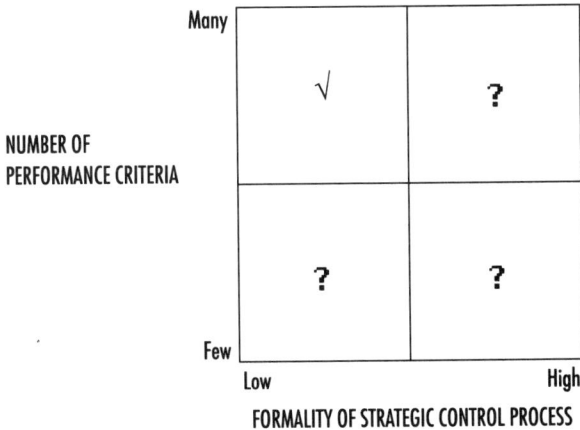

The greatest dangers are misdirected motivation (focus on inappropriate objectives) and high cost (problems in measurement of performance)
  Explicit objectives may be wrongly chosen or too costly to measure
  A focus on too few criteria of good performance is also dangerous

Key: √ = appropriate
     ? = questionable

wider range of objectives have some advantages in these circumstances. Figure 6.7 (on page 163) diagrams these observations.

Nevertheless, the attempt to define clearly the criteria of good strategic performance remains valuable. Many managers overestimate the complexity of their businesses, and so avoid making a serious attempt to isolate suitable strategic objectives. And even if the business is genuinely complex, there are benefits to defining some explicit objectives. The formal control process may not capture everything that matters, and may need to be buttressed by informal or clan controls. But the very difficulty of control in complex businesses means that wholly informal controls can easily become no controls.

SUMMARY

Relatively formal strategic control processes are indicated in diverse companies with few important linkages between businesses in their portfolios; in businesses that do not face high levels of uncertainty and rapid change; and in businesses where competitive advantage depends on a relatively small number of identifiable and measurable variables. More informal strategic control processes are suitable in less diverse companies, especially if there are important linkages between businesses in the portfolio; in businesses that operate in unpredictable and fast-changing environments; and in businesses where the sources of competitive advantage are hard to identify and measure.

Control processes with few criteria of good performance are suitable for companies with largely stand-alone businesses, in which the businesses do not face "bet your company" decisions and can build competitive advantage around a small number of key success factors. A larger number of performance criteria is appropriate if there are strong linkages between businesses in the portfolio, the businesses face large risky investment decisions, the rate of change in the businesses is not too rapid, and the sources of competitive advantage are complex and numerous.

INDUSTRY EXAMPLES

Figures 6.1–6.7 are consolidated in Figure 6.8, which summarizes the choices and trade-offs that must be made in matching a strategic control approach to a business's circumstances. As a means of pulling these

Figure 6.8 **Matching a Strategic Control Approach to a Business's Circumstances**

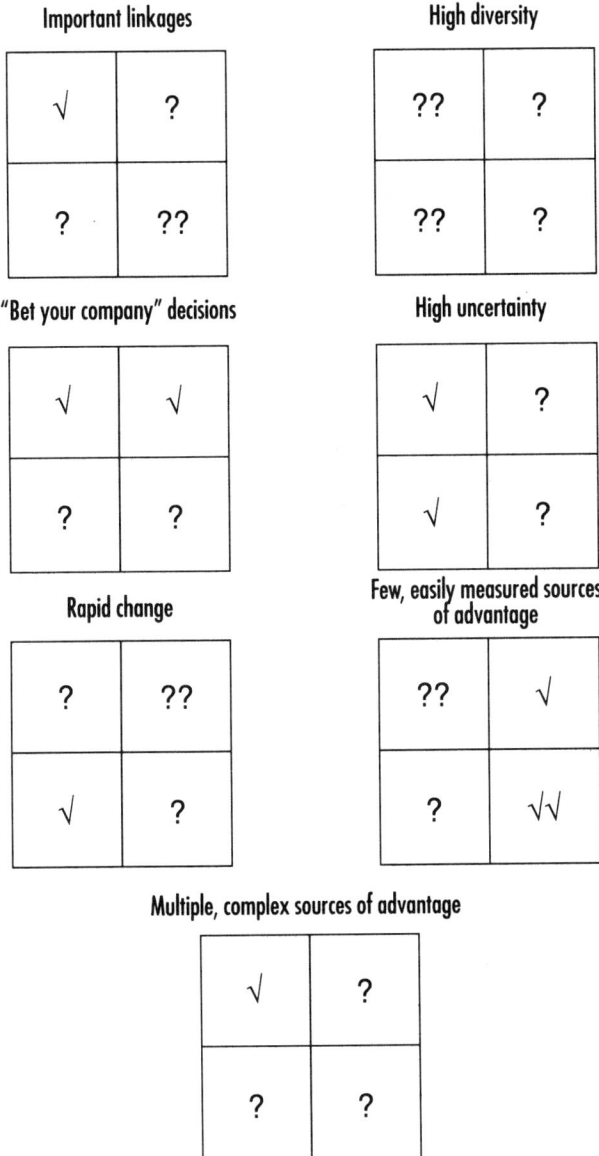

Important linkages

√	?
?	??

High diversity

??	?
??	?

"Bet your company" decisions

√	√
?	?

High uncertainty

√	?
√	?

Rapid change

?	??
√	?

Few, easily measured sources of advantage

??	√
?	√√

Multiple, complex sources of advantage

√	?
?	?

Key: √√ = very appropriate
      √ = appropriate
      ? = questionable
      ?? = highly questionable

observations together, some industry illustrations may be useful. These illustrations are intended as schematic examples only. We shall give a simplified description of the characteristic features of each industry, and then draw out the implications for the control process. In reality, of course, a company designing a strategic control process would wish to undertake a much more in-depth analysis of its situation, covering these and other factors more carefully and more fully, and relating them to their own particular priorities.

Consumer products

Consumer product businesses are characterized by:

- Fairly long time-lags between actions and results, especially in building a brand position.
- Some potential for linkages between similar businesses that can transfer skills to each other; but no strong need for coordination of strategies or sharing of resources.
- Few, if any, "bet your company" decisions; instead incremental investments are typically possible, in both marketing and manufacturing.
- Limited uncertainty, since demand is relatively predictable in most mature segments.
- Slow rate of change in most segments, though there are some more fast-moving product areas.
- Relatively few, simple, clear, measurable sources of competitive advantage: market share and brand recognition matter most, with good market research data available on competitors' shares, media spending, product launches, and so on.

These features imply that a strategic control rather than a profit control process is needed. The availability of a few, simple, measurable sources of advantage suggests that a more formal and explicit approach would be useful and feasible, particularly given the absence of strong linkages and high uncertainty. The need for fast response, which might argue against formal controls, is limited to certain segments.

Research-intensive/extractive industries

Research-intensive and extractive industries are characterized by:

- Very long time-lags in research/exploration.
- In general, few important linkages, since both research and exploration are typically product specific.
- Some large, "bet your company" decisions, especially in exploration.

- A high level of uncertainty, since the outcome of investments is hard to predict.
- Little need for rapid response to changes, since time cycles are generally long.
- Moderately complex sources of advantage, but with some ability to identify and measure progress against key milestones.

Here a pure financial control approach is clearly impossible. The size, importance and complexity of decisions argues for a hands-on approach to planning and control, while the uncertainties of the business suggest a flexible and/or less explicit approach to defining objectives. An informal approach to control that covers a number of criteria of good performance and does not overemphasise short-term profitability would be sensible; an alternative possibility is a more explicit approach that focuses on research/exploration milestones but is not tightly administered.

Commodity manufacturing

Commodity manufacturing businesses fall into two groups. Capital-intensive process industries, such as paper, base chemicals and steel, involve:

- Long time-lags, especially associated with new capacity investments.
- Some linkages, especially if there are multiple manufacturing sites with related products in different geographical areas.
- Large, risky decisions on major investments.
- Some uncertainties associated with the cyclical pattern of demand and fluctuations in raw material prices and exchange rates.
- Fairly slow response rates, since rates of change are not great;
- Simple sources of advantage, related to relative competitive cost position, which, however, is often hard and costly to measure.

Converting businesses, such as carton or bag manufacturing, are quite different. They typically involve:

- Short time-lags, since capital investments are small and operating factors matter more.
- Very few, if any, big decisions.
- Little need, or potential, for linkages with other businesses, with each unit working best as a stand-alone entity.
- Some uncertainties associated with demand patterns, the level of competition and input cost levels.
- Need to move quickly and opportunistically to respond to market opportunities before competitors and to contain operating costs.

- Success dependent less on sustainable sources of competitive advantage and more on good operations.

Businesses in the first category (capital intensive, process industries) need strategic controls. They will probably do best under a Strategic Planning style, with multiple criteria of good performance, because of the magnitude of decisions and the linkage potential. Explicit strategic objectives are possible, but may be costly to define and will need to be flexibly administered.

Businesses in the second category (converting) do not need long-term strategic controls. Indeed, they will probably do best under a Financial Control style. Pure profit controls will give maximum bottom-line motivation, while allowing plenty of freedom to business unit management to respond to opportunities as they arise.

New/emerging/fast growth businesses

In new businesses, where patterns of competition have not yet been firmly established, the typical characteristics are:

- As yet, unclear time-lags.
- Linkages dependent on nature of business and portfolio of which it is part; probably low initially.
- Initially small decisions, but a possibility of "bet your company" decisions later.
- Extensive uncertainty and, quite possibly, a need to respond rapidly to changes as they arise.
- Nature of key success factors and sources of competitive advantage not yet fully clear.

A pure profit control approach is liable to stifle an emerging business and prevent it from making strategic decisions that may be necessary for its long-term success. But the uncertainties about the future of the business and about the best ways to build competitive advantage, together with the need to be able to respond quickly, make it hard to set clear, precise and explicit objectives.

A relatively informal, less precise approach to control may therefore be best. Whether this should focus on only a few control parameters, to allow business managers the scope to fine tune the business as they see fit, or on a greater number, to give the centre more influence over the development of the business, depends on the specifics of the business and the management team in question. In BP, we were told: "New businesses come more under the spotlight than established or mature businesses.

This is because the new business is less familiar, so we don't want to be so delegative in running it. We look at the results being achieved carefully, but usually without having set specific targets." Alternatively, more explicit milestones can be set, but with the understanding that they may need to be changed as the business develops.

These examples show the relationship between business characteristics and appropriate control approaches. However, the final choice of a control approach will also depend on the issues top management wishes to emphasize in the management process, and on the skills and attitudes of the management team. These factors influence the development of control processes over time, as we discuss in Chapter 7.

Notes and References

1 Several of these factors overlap with those discussed in Michael Goold and Andrew Campbell, *Strategies and Styles,* Blackwell, Oxford, 1987, Chapter 12, where the broader question of how to match a company's overall management style to its businesses is explored.

2 In *Competitive Strategy,* Free Press, 1980, Michael Porter identifies the level of rivalry between competitors as a key determinant of industry profitability. See, also, the discussion of "open competitive battles" in *Strategies and Styles,* Chapter 12.

3 See, for example, "PCs: The big three get bigger and clones feel the squeeze", *Business Week,* December 12, 1988, pp. 54-5.

4 See "Strategy for the 1980s", *Perspective 241,* The Boston Consulting Group, 1981.

5 Companies that believe that their skill lies in strategic management are typically uncomfortable with businesses in which day-to-day operations are the key to success. GE is an example. "We are not good at low-tech, low value-added businesses where scale is not important, where it is difficult to get a sustained advantage. The levels of profitability that General Electric expects can only be sustained if we win in businesses where there is a chance for significant competitive advantage. That is why we allocate resources to those businesses where we can be number one or two, and where the industry characteristics result in leadership having value" (M. Carpenter, Speech to the Conference Board, February 13, 1986). These views have led to a significant programme of investments and divestments under Jack Welch.

6 See *Strategies and Styles,* op.cit., Chapter 12.

7 Several writers have argued that risk and uncertainty play a vital role in determin-

ing the right management process. See, for example, P. Lawrence and Jay W. Lorsch, *Organisation and Environment,* Harvard School of Business Administration, Boston, 1967; R. E. Miles and C. C. Snow, *Organisational Strategy, Structure and Process,* McGraw-Hill, New York, 1978; H. I. Ansoff, *Corporate Strategy,* McGraw-Hill, New York, 1965.

8 See, for example, "Reinventing IBM", *Fortune,* August 14, 1989, and "Big changes at Big Blue", *Business Week,* February 15, 1988.

9 See Michael Porter, *Competitive Advantage,* Free Press, 1985, for a detailed discussion. See also George Day and Robin Wensley, "Assessing advantage: a framework for diagnosing competitive superiority", *Journal of Marketing,* April 1988, for a good summary of different techniques, which integrates both a customer and a competitor perspective of the necessary analysis.

10 See, for example, *Quality Improvement through Defect Prevention,* Philip Crosby Associates Inc., 1985; Philip Crosby, *Let's Talk Quality,* McGraw-Hill, New York, 1989; David Gaverin, *Managing Quality,* Free Press, 1987; J. M. Juran, *Juran on Planning for Quality,* Free Press, 1987.

11 For a full description of the PIMS approach, see, Robert D. Buzzell and Bradley T. Gale, *The PIMS Principles; Linking Strategy to Performance,* Free Press, 1987.

12 We are grateful to Keith Roberts, PIMS' development director in London, who provided us with the detailed results for the eight industry sectors.

13 In services the R^2 is 81 per cent, but in this sector there are relatively few SBUs, so that a high R^2 is easier to attain.

14 PIMS do provide a "par" ROI for individual businesses, based on the profit performance of "lookalike" businesses, and using the results of the regression equations.

15 There are particular problems if the quality of publicly available data on competitors is poor, as it often is in industrial goods and services.

CHAPTER 7

DEVELOPING A STRATEGIC CONTROL PROCESS

In talking with managers about their companies' approaches to strategic planning and control, we were struck by how often people found it necessary to tell us about how their company had arrived at its current approach, where it had come from, in order to explain what it was doing now. It seems difficult to understand how things are today without an account of the history. The reason lies in two vital influences on management process: the shifting priorities of the top team and the gradual development of skills and attitudes throughout the company.

To understand both the historical changes in a company's planning and control process, and its current approach, we need to trace the way in which the senior management agenda has evolved over time. Different issues call for different emphases in the planning and control process, and the right approach for a company has to take account of the concerns that are currently most pressing. Developments in management skills and attitudes, on the other hand, are often a precondition for the successful introduction of new approaches to planning and control. As such they are an essential infrastructure for strategic management and control. But skills and attitudes change slowly, and constrain the options that are realistically open to a company. An evolutionary view of management processes is therefore necessary, which takes account of both top-level priorities and management capabilities.

General Electric represents one of the most interesting examples of how strategic control processes develop over time. Although its story has been well publicized,[1] it is worthwhile to review the stages through which the company has passed, for its experience is relevant to a wide range of other companies.

DEVELOPMENT OF STRATEGIC PLANNING AND CONTROL AT GE

GE was one of the first truly diversified companies. During and after the Second World War, it moved into a number of new business areas.

Between 1940 and 1968 its revenues grew from $457 million to $8,382 million, and by 1968 it was competing in 23 of the 26 two-digit Standard Industrial Classification (SIC) industry categories. As a result, the company's centralized management style came under strain, and in the 1950s a new, more decentralized structure was put in place. By the late 1960s GE had established nearly 200 departmental profit centres.[2] These decentralized units were held together by sophisticated systems of budgeting, capital expenditure authorization and financial reporting.

At first the decentralized structure seemed to work well, enabling the company to cope with its rapid growth in size and diversity. But, by the mid-1960s, the chief executive, Fred Borch, was concerned that GE had fallen into a pattern of "profitless growth". Too much investment was going into businesses that were insufficiently profitable. The source of the problem, he decided, was that the decentralized units were not really self-sufficient businesses; in addition they were focusing too much on short-term growth, and not thinking enough about the development of longer-term strategies to attain strong competitive positions. This was the beginning of a move towards a strategic planning culture at GE. The move had three components: a new strategic structure designed around strategic business units (SBUs), the introduction of strategic planning at the business level, and an attempt to allocate resources in accordance with some corporate strategic priorities.

GE's SBU structure, which paralleled but did not replace the regular operating structure, is discussed in Chapter 3. Essentially, the idea was to define business units that could have viable stand-alone strategies, and make them the basic units for strategic planning. Without an SBU structure of this sort, the management responsibilities created by the operating structure would always impede the creation of valid strategies. The SBU structure was introduced in the late 1960s, with 43 SBUs emerging from the 190 operating departments.

At around the same time, GE began a major effort to improve the quality of strategic thinking in the businesses. Training was provided for all senior general managers and planners through special strategy seminars at GE's Crotonville management development centre. Strategy staff, many of whom were recruited externally, burgeoned, with approximately 200 senior-level planning posts in GE by 1980. And consulting companies such as Arthur D. Little, the Boston Consulting Group and McKinsey were brought in to help introduce new strategic thinking and techniques, both corporately and in the SBUs. Developing skills in strategic planning, then a very new field, took time and perseverance. But by the mid-1970s most of the SBUs were in a position to provide sophisticated and well-analysed strategic plans.

The third prong of the new strategic planning culture was an approach to portfolio resource allocation that has since become well known.[3] SBUs were positioned on a grid, whose axes measured the strength of the business unit's position and the attractiveness of the industry in which it was competing. The grid provided a background for greater selectivity between SBUs in corporate investment and divestment decisions, and led to the establishment of different portfolio roles (build, hold, harvest) for SBUs in different positions on the grid (see Figure 7.1).

As the 1970s progressed, the strategic planning process began to work increasingly well, and led to major improvements in strategy thinking. Jack Welch, GE's current chief executive, commented: "Our planning system was dynamite when we first put it in. We had the best financial controls in the world at General Electric. We did not have an outstanding planning process. We put one in. So you put thinking across good numbers; there's nothing like thinking to go with good numbers. The first years of the planning process were sensational."

During the 1970s, strategic controls and milestones were introduced to ensure that SBUs were implementing their agreed strategies (see

Figure 7.1 **Investment Priority Screen**

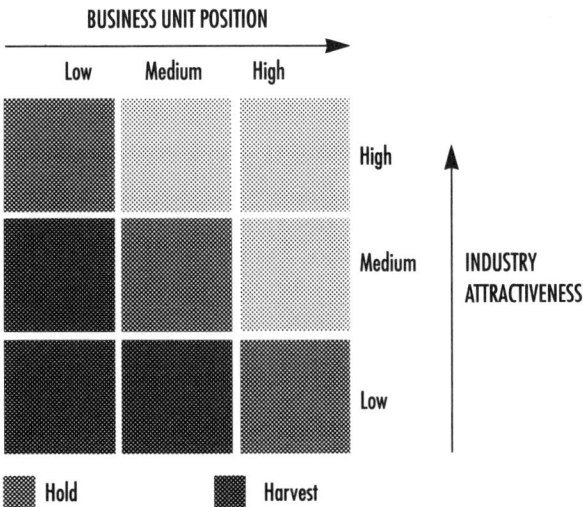

Chapter 3), and that managers were not sacrificing their strategic programmes in order to achieve their short-term profit targets. Over time,
considerable progress was made with integrating the strategic planning
process, the budget and the personnel appraisal processes. Budgets were
set in the light of strategic plans, and included specifically earmarked
funds for strategic programmes and development; and management performance reviews and incentive compensation included a systematic
assessment of how far strategic goals had been met. This integration of
strategic control with operating control was intended to align personal
incentives and corporate objectives.

But, as time passed, the sophistication of the planning process began
to get in the way. Jack Welch again:

"The books got thicker, and the printing got more sophisticated and
the covers got harder and the drawings got better. So the thinking
kept going down. The meetings kept getting larger. One of the problems was the size of meetings: nobody can say anything with 16 or 18
people there. You might as well come in with robes and incense. You
can't talk, and as a result, it was unhealthy.

There were some people who spent the week between Christmas
and New Year planning for a meeting with me in July. Now think of
the data I'm receiving in July. We could have had an Arab oil em-
bargo, we could have 15 different things between times."

The structure of the company had also become more complicated.
Because the Chief Executive's Office had felt it was unable to do justice
to all the plans it was asked to review, another layer, the sector, had been
introduced into the organization in 1977. The result was a further prolif-
eration of meetings and reviews. Indeed, we were told of one business
that had 27 formal reviews during a single calendar year in the late
1970s, in many cases covering the same topics at different levels. And,
because there were so many SBUs, even a business facing major strategic
issues might have no more than 15 minutes to present its case to the
Chief Executive's Office. As we were told by a senior member of the
corporate staff, the formal structure of the management process became
a barrier to good strategy:

"During the 1970s we built a planning process which was very complete and became very complex. We had formalized ways of measuring strategy, focusing on variables such as market share, customer
satisfaction measures, market attractiveness and so on. But, on balance, the process did not work very well. There were too many SBUs

to understand in any detail, and the intricate planning processes were regarded as time consuming and not particularly important parts of the decision-making process by the SBU heads. Line managers tended to delegate planning to 'mandarin' planners."

During the 1980s under Jack Welch, GE has therefore moved away from a formal, structured approach to strategic planning and control, towards the more informal approach described in Chapter 4.

Welch's goal has been to combine "the strength, resources and reach of a big company [with] the sensitivity, the leanness, the simplicity and the agility of a small company. We want the best of both." He believes that GE has now achieved this: "The new arrangement has proved breathtakingly clean, simple and effective. Ideas, initiatives and decisions move, often at the speed of sound – voices – where once they were muffled and garbled by a gauntlet of approvals and the oppressive ministrations of staff reviews."[4]

The current emphasis is on dismantling the unnecessary bureaucracy of planning and control through a programme called "work-out": "an intense and continuing programme to liberate employees from the cramping artefacts that pile up in the dusty attics of century-old companies: the reports, meetings, rituals, approvals, controls and forests of paper that often seem necessary until they are removed." The essence of "work-out" is to dispense with any aspect of the formal process that cannot be shown to have clear and specific value.

There is obvious appeal in this latest phase of GE's development. But it would not work for every company. Particularly, it would not work for companies that had not been through many of GE's prior steps, which have gradually built up the skills and attitudes needed under the current process. This is what Mike Carpenter, GE's head of planning from 1982 to 1986, had to say: "If the new process seems ad hoc – it is. If it seems dependent on openness and honesty – it is. If it seems dependent on both corporate and SBU management being competent strategists and well informed – it is."

Carpenter cited four factors essential to GE's ability to move in this direction:

1. A historical commitment to a strategic planning process, which has given GE "a very high proportion of businesses with well-defined, successful strategies and a group of general managers with good strategy skills".

2. The Chief Executive's Office's extensive knowledge of each business.

3. The presence of "powerful strategic thinkers" in the Chief Executive's Office.

4. An environment in which "open and honest dialogue on strategic issues, however difficult and unresolved, is at a premium and where covering up problems is the kiss of death."

Summarizing his views, and those of most others in GE with whom we talked, Carpenter said: "We couldn't have got to where we've got without having gone through the more formal phase in the 1970s. This has given us a history of rigour and analysis in the company which is carried on now despite the fact that the process is much more informal."

There are of course dangers in the more informal process. One business manager claimed:

"Because there is no longer formal identification of strategic measures or milestones, we may be missing some emerging issues. The problem is compounded by the fact that the finance department are the major providers of data in the company. They are seen as being the primary, or only, source of timely and reliable information. This may lead to a tendency to over-rely on financial information as opposed to strategic information about the businesses."

Despite these reservations, most GE managers feel that the more informal approach to strategic planning and control of the 1980s has worked well, and GE's results speak for themselves.[5]

Figure 7.2 summarizes the development of GE's approach to strategic planning and control, showing the approximate sequence and timing of the stages the company has passed through. Each stage can be seen either as a reaction to problems or opportunities that emerged or as a refinement of the process as it developed. And the elapsed time reflects the difficulty of building management skills and systems quickly.

DEVELOPMENT OF STRATEGIC PLANNING AND CONTROL IN OTHER COMPANIES

Other companies appear to have moved through some of the same steps as GE, in a not dissimilar way, for not dissimilar reasons. For example, the current era of strategic planning and control at Ciba-Geigy dates back to the merger, in 1970, between Ciba and Geigy. In the years immediately after the merger, the prime strategic task was to integrate the two companies into a single organization. Once this objective had been accomplished, the emphasis shifted to forward planning for the

Figure 7.2 **GE's Development Of Strategic Planning And Control**

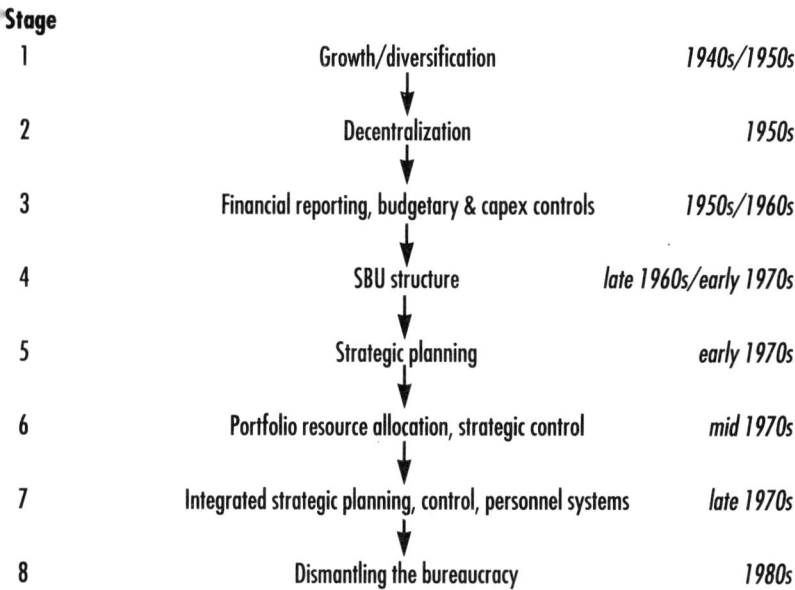

Stage		
1	Growth/diversification	*1940s/1950s*
	↓	
2	Decentralization	*1950s*
	↓	
3	Financial reporting, budgetary & capex controls	*1950s/1960s*
	↓	
4	SBU structure	*late 1960s/early 1970s*
	↓	
5	Strategic planning	*early 1970s*
	↓	
6	Portfolio resource allocation, strategic control	*mid 1970s*
	↓	
7	Integrated strategic planning, control, personnel systems	*late 1970s*
	↓	
8	Dismantling the bureaucracy	*1980s*

businesses in the group. So, in 1973, each division was asked to establish its own "Leitbild" (vision and long-range plan). In 1975, these division "Leitbilds" were used as the basis of a corporate "Leitbild". Since 1975, the divisions have been asked to focus their medium-range plans (MRPs) on how their "Leitbilds" would be implemented. The intention is that these MRPs should emphasize specific timetabled strategic projects rather than long-term numerical projections. Each division can decide how to put together its MRP; for example, how extensively to consult with local companies. This allows each division to plan in the way that it considers most appropriate.

In 1980, the company faced a down-turn in profitability which led the executive committee to implement a number of turn-around projects. The aim was to improve profit by 1 billion Swiss francs over three years. Each of these turn-around projects was headed by an executive committee member, and in aggregate they produced almost exactly the profit improvement that had been called for.

As a second response to the profit down-turn, fresh emphasis was placed on the corporate portfolio strategy. The executive committee wanted to be able to distinguish more clearly between the more and less mature segments of the business, and between those that had high and low development potential. Accordingly, the company was divided into 32 so-called corporate segments (similar to GE's SBUs). This segmentation was not easy, since there were many shared costs between divisions. But, in principle, the attempt was made to define business areas that were reasonably separate from each other strategically. Over time the operating line management structure has been moving closer and closer to the corporate strategic segmentation. Recently the corporate segment structure has been reduced to 18 business sectors, each of them with its own SBU portfolio.

Having defined the corporate segments, the executive committee called for a strategic plan for each segment. To formulate and agree good-quality plans for each segment proved to be a major task, and took a number of years. Eventually, in 1984, a corporate strategic plan was made, and a portfolio role or category was assigned to each segment.

Only after this did the process of monitoring strategic achievements begin.

"In introducing strategic planning and control, you need to take account of the gradual evolution of the company. There must be flexibility and a willingness to wait for the right moment to introduce new processes and systems. These cannot be pushed on an unwilling management. Don't tell everyone that at the end of all this there will be strategic controls. Move forward step by step instead. Otherwise you create reluctance and people say, 'This is just more and more planning and control, simply for and by the centre.'"

Figure 7.3 shows the stages that Ciba-Geigy has passed through. The nature, sequence and timing of the steps is not the same as at GE, but there is clearly some parallelism in the issues that have been faced and in the way planning and control skills have developed gradually over time.

Other companies that stress the historical developments behind their current approach to strategic planning and control include ICI, BP, Shell, Courtaulds, Kingfisher, Vickers, Inchcape and Thorn-EMI. At ICI, many people feel that genuine business strategies could not be developed effectively until the 1980s, when most businesses were reorganized to have international rather than UK responsibilities. At the same time, businesses with significant overlaps, such as Petrochemicals and Plastics, were amalgamated into single units. In 1982 the chairman, John Harvey-Jones, introduced a requirement for all businesses to prepare and present strategy alternatives, as a background for corporate

Figure 7.3 **Ciba-Geigy Planning Instruments**

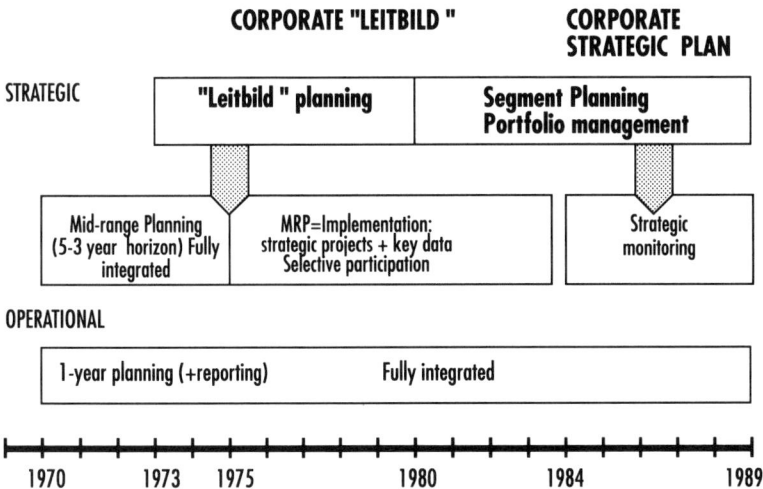

	CORPORATE "LEITBILD "		CORPORATE STRATEGIC PLAN
STRATEGIC	**"Leitbild " planning**	**Segment Planning Portfolio management**	
	Mid-range Planning (5-3 year horizon) Fully integrated	MRP=Implementation; strategic projects + key data Selective participation	Strategic monitoring
OPERATIONAL	1-year planning (+reporting)	Fully integrated	

| 1970 | 1973 | 1975 | 1980 | 1984 | 1989 |

resource allocation decisions. Then, in the mid–1980s, explicit strategic controls and milestones were introduced to provide greater clarity on strategic objectives, and to counterbalance the forces of financial, budgetary control. BP has followed a rather similar path, with much of the new strategic thinking dating back to the reorganization into business streams around 1980.[6] Shell Chemicals' introduction of explicit strategic milestones, on the other hand, was prompted primarily by the need to ensure that agreed strategies were implemented, and to provide clearer signals on when an unsuccessful strategy should be reviewed.

At Courtaulds and Kingfisher, the emphasis is upon the length of time it takes to raise the level of strategic planning skills within the business units. Both companies' CEOs, Chris Hogg and Geoff Mulcahy, feel that progress has been made – but the rate of progress has been slow, despite major investments in training in both cases. A timescale of at least five, and probably ten, years seems necessary to achieve the required depth and sophistication of thinking. Admittedly, these companies may have begun from a low base. Mulcahy maintains that, when he took over at Woolworths in 1982, "to have started out sweeping the shop floor was not just compatible with promotion to the top levels in Woolworths, it was a requirement." And Hogg was highly critical of the quality of strategic thinking at the time of his accession.[7] But both men stress the importance of expecting only a gradual improvement in strategic planning skills.

This point is borne out at Vickers, where consistent progress was made during the 1980s in rationalizing the portfolio and improving the quality of business strategies. The company lays particular stress on competitive analysis and competitive position in developing strategy:

"The first base is to do good competitive analysis. The second stage is to set competitive objectives in terms of strategy. And the third – and perhaps optimal – stage is to build competitive targets into financial bonus schemes for individual managers. We do not yet have a regular formal monitoring of competitive objectives, but it will come in due course. We have made a lot of progress with analysing the basic competitive position of the main Vickers businesses, but we have not yet got so far as control."

In other words, strategic planning skills are now quite well developed in Vickers, but the strategic control phase remains to be tackled in a formal sense.

Managers in many other companies told us that their priorities lay in developing their strategic planning skills more fully, and that, until this had been done, it would be premature to embark on any sort of formal or explicit strategic control process. At Inchcape, for example, we were told: "In a company that is in the early stages of applying strategic planning, the planning is unlikely to be sophisticated and the controls have to be more basic. For example, the need to make a substantial change in the organization structure may come before the specification of particular control variables." These companies perceive a need to move sequentially; to start by concentrating on organization structure and strategic planning skills, moving on to strategic control only when strategic planning is well accepted, and well done, within the company.

Thorn-EMI stresses its evolution from a financial crisis in the mid-1980s, towards a more strategic view in the last year or two: "When we were focusing on turn-around, there were no strategies, no planning, just delivery. All that mattered was profit. The CEO made it very clear that this was what performance meant."

Having successfully negotiated the turn-around phase, the company is now grappling with the problems of introducing a more strategic approach to encourage development and growth, without losing the benefits of tight financial control:

"There is a lot of pressure to meet short-term financial results, and a business manager not up to budget would get a tough time if he suggested any strategic development. But as the company moves from turn-around to build, the organization's behaviour and processes must also change. We need to relate organization structure and process to strategy as the basis for future development."

Accordingly, Thorn-EMI is just in the process of introducing strategic benchmarking to complement financial objectives. This shift in emphasis from pure financial control to a more balanced form of strategic control is characteristic of several companies that have survived a financial crisis and are now looking for a more expansive future.

We believe that there are two main forces behind the developments in GE and the other companies we have discussed: responses to particular management issues or priorities, and gradual skill-building over time.

MANAGEMENT PRIORITIES

In many companies, the historical development of strategic planning and control shows the influence of shifting management priorities at different points in time. Among the most important issues that have shaped the management process are corporate overload, financial crises, the need to encourage strategic thinking and to discriminate in resource allocation, the search for linkages among businesses, implementation problems, a need to offset budget pressures, and undue bureaucracy.

Corporate overload

In GE, the initial push to decentralize was a response to a period of rapid growth and diversification, which threatened to overload the previously more centralized management structure. Much the same thing has happened in many other companies, including BP, Courtaulds and ICI.

In such situations, top management's priorities are to reduce interference by the centre in business unit affairs, and to create extra performance motivation. This leads to a need for clear performance goals, often with a strong focus on profit and cash flow measures. Even if control does not emphasize short-term profitability and tight accountability as much as in Financial Control style companies, it typically stresses financial results as key criteria of good performance. Budgetary systems and capital expenditure processes then become the primary means through which the decentralized businesses are managed and controlled.

Financial crisis

In the aftermath of a financial crisis, companies often introduce stricter financial controls. Sometimes, as in the case of Thorn-EMI, this is a temporary reaction. In other companies, it leads to the continuing adoption of a Financial Control style, with tight financial controls applied across all businesses in order to discourage unnecessary risk taking and to emphasize that the profit bottom line should receive top priority.

Need for strategic, long-term thinking

Although high levels of decentralization create extra motivation, and strict profit controls lead to strong short-term performance, corporate managers, as at GE or Thorn-EMI, may begin to question whether sufficient attention is being paid to the long-term development of the businesses. Is enough thought being given to trends in the market or the competition? Are products being developed that will allow for continued growth over the coming years? Is there too much concern with operating or tactical issues? In addition, the central team may feel too remote from the main issues faced by the businesses. Particularly after a period of decentralization and financial control, there is often a desire for more dialogue on strategic issues between the centre and the businesses.

If top management has such concerns, it may introduce some form of structured strategic planning process to balance financial, short-term goals and to shift attention onto longer-term trends in competitive position. A preliminary step is often to identify those business units for which separate strategic plans can sensibly be drawn up (such as GE's SBUs, Ciba-Geigy's corporate segments, BP's business streams), and to restructure the organization accordingly. Until this step has been taken, strategic planning is unlikely to make much useful progress. Thereafter there will probably be a lengthy process of skill-building in thinking through and presenting strategic plans before the companies are capable of preparing valid, insightful and well-documented strategies.

During the early, relatively unsophisticated phase of strategic planning, plans are seldom pushed through to clear, well-specified strategic objectives or milestones. An explicit strategic control process is unlikely to exist, and such strategic controls as there are will be largely informal. With the emphasis on producing and discussing believable strategic plans for each business, the control loop is often somewhat neglected.

More selective resource allocation

In GE, the spur to more selective resource allocation was the "profitless growth" problem of the 1960s. In other companies, resource allocation has reached the top of the management agenda for different reasons. Cash constraints, with demands for capital from the businesses well in excess of available funds for investment, have been the problem in some companies; in others the centre has simply perceived that a more differentiated approach to resource allocation would enhance the overall performance of the company. Whatever the reason, many companies have gone through a period when the need for more selective resource allocation was their top priority issue.

The resource allocation issue often leads to the adoption of some form of portfolio planning, in which different objectives are established for each SBU in the corporate portfolio, as a function of the attractiveness of the industries in which they are active and the strength of the business's competitive position. Thus growth may be pushed in some businesses, while profits or cash flow arc at the top of the agenda in others. B.A.T, for example, has been pushing for growth in the financial services sector, which is seen as an industry with more long-term attractions and growth potential than the base tobacco business, where profits and cash flow are the key targets.

Since portfolio planning is about selective resource allocation and differentiated objectives, it requires clear agreement on the key objectives for each business. This imperative can lead to increased emphasis on the strategic control process, and to pressure for the establishment of a more explicit objective-setting process.

Lack of linkages

When heads of decentralized business units are under pressure to improve the performance of their own units, they may pay very little attention to the performance of other businesses or even to the company as a whole. In some cases, incentives to focus narrowly on one's own business can be so strong that it becomes very difficult to share skills and experiences and to benefit from potential linkages between businesses. As we discussed in Chapter 6, some companies, such as Digital, have responded to this problem by de-emphasizing the separate, individual accountability of each SBU. This move leads to less decentralization, and less tight controls against business specific performance.

Failure to implement agreed strategies

In recent years, several companies have become disillusioned with strategic management, because strategies that were agreed in the planning process were never successfully implemented. Amongst the causes of this problem are plans that are too vague or too unrealistic, or else management teams that are insufficiently committed to them. Several companies have reacted, as described in Chapter 5, by introducing more formal strategic controls, in order to create more rigour in establishing objectives, more follow-through in terms of personal rewards for successful implementation, and a better basis for decisions on when to intervene in businesses that are failing to implement their strategies successfully. Almost all the companies that have introduced more formal strategic controls have shared these goals.

Budget pressures crowd out good strategies

A particularly common problem with strategy implementation arises where business heads feel under so much pressure from their budget contracts that they allow their longer-term strategies to be blown off course. Budget pressures may stem from short-term business difficulties, from top management's perceived attitudes, or from the company's reward system (see Appendix 3). Some companies try to offset such pressures (as did ICI in the mid-1980s) by establishing a more formal strategic control process, with associated rewards and penalties. Ultimately, it is possible, as in the GE of the late 1970s, to attempt to integrate the various elements of the budget, the strategy and the personnel processes into a consistent and mutually supportive whole.

Too much bureaucracy

The GE experience of the 1980s is clearly a reaction to a process that had built up too much bureaucracy in the 1970s. The danger of a highly sophisticated formal strategic planning and control system is that it will stifle creativity and insight, and lead to slow decisions and high overheads. To address these problems, GE has moved away from elaborate, regular, written strategic plans, explicitly recorded and formally monitored strategic objectives, and formula-based links between strategic objectives and personal rewards. It has replaced them with a rolling dialogue between the centre and the businesses, focused around specific issues rather than calendar deadlines, with face-to-face communications, and with more broadly-based, subjective personal incentive systems. Strategic control is exercised more informally, through the periodic meetings and contacts between business heads and the Chief Executive's Office. GE's dismantling of the bureaucracy of planning and control is intended to lead to more effective communication about the criteria of good strategic performance and about progress against them; and to a more flexible way of reaching decisions and seeing that they are implemented.

SKILLS AND ATTITUDES

The development of the planning and control process also depends on the skills and attitudes of managers. This is the infrastructure on which strategic management is built.

Building skills

For many companies, the greatest challenge in making strategic planning and control work is to raise the level of skills in strategic thinking throughout the company. Simply going through the motions of strategic planning and control is no guarantee of success. Without good thinking, the strategic plans will be of little value and the objectives agreed will not be a suitable basis for control.

Unless managers agree on how to approach and analyse strategic issues, a formal planning process is likely to do more harm than good. As one business manager said:

"Strategic planning is a good thing, as long as both sides speak the same language. But it's rather like trying to get to the Gare du Nord. If you both speak French, then you'll get there quickly. If neither of you speaks French, then you'll get there by means of sign language. If you think you speak French but in fact don't do so very well, then that will probably complicate the process of getting there."

If there is to be a common language of strategic planning, everyone must agree, for example, on the importance and meaning of concepts such as competitive advantage, and on the analysis and information needed to make use of them. It is also necessary for business managers who have had less experience in devising and presenting strategies to improve their skills in these areas.

But the time needed to build the skills of strategic planning throughout a company is long. Major investments in training, an extended period of learning by doing, and continuous feedback and reinforcement from top management are required. Companies in our research talked in terms of several years, even a decade, before real progress was made. It is probably easier to establish these skills now than it was 20 years ago when GE embarked on the task, but it is wrong to imagine that skills can be built overnight.

Strategic control is unlikely to be effective until progress in strategic planning has reached a certain level. Strategic control depends on having objectives that are accepted as valid, by both the business and the centre. If the strategic plan from which the objectives have been derived is of dubious quality, the strategic control process will be a waste of time and effort. As one chief executive bluntly put it: "Until we have improved the quality of our businesses' strategic plans, we will not be tackling strategic control. There is no point in controlling rubbish."

Excellence in strategic planning is especially necessary to support informal strategic controls. Most people in GE welcome the move towards the current informal approach, but they acknowledge that it would not work unless the company had already gone through the "structured" stage of the 1970s, which established a common language and a commitment to strategic thinking and skills. GE managers also agree that the current approach depends heavily on the personal skills and energy of Jack Welch and his management team. Without these pre-conditions, informal strategic controls can very easily degenerate into confusion, inconsistency and laxity.

Creating the right attitudes

There is a natural, and justified, suspicion of formal planning and control processes in most companies. Proposals to introduce new and improved systems in these areas are often greeted with scepticism ("just more overhead") or even hostility ("What are they trying to prove now?"). Furthermore, many business heads find that the pressure of day-to-day events makes it hard for them to spend time on defining and spelling out strategic objectives. Any new formal process therefore needs to prove its worth in practice before it will receive widespread support; as a Courtaulds senior manager stated: "You have to educate and persuade managers of the benefits of strategic control before you will get them to accept the process."

This argues for moving forward step by step (as suggested by Ciba-Geigy), rather than setting up some new grand design. Managers must see that the planning process is actually helpful to them before they are asked to accept a control process. And they must appreciate the value of clearer and more explicit objectives, before these are linked into reward systems. There is a constant danger that formal processes will add more cost than value, and a corresponding need to move slowly in adding to them.

Conflicts over the proper approach to strategic control sometimes stem from the attitudes of, and the relationships between, the strategic planning and financial control staffs. In one company that had tried to establish a formal strategic control process, but without much success, we were told: "You have to convert the finance people to incorporating strategic measures into the control system. Convincing sceptical finance people that strategic milestones are practical and worthwhile hasn't been easy." It is partly for this reason that BP Oil International has now combined its planning and financial control functions into one department entitled "strategic control".

The centre must therefore plan to overcome attitudinal resistance when changing the strategic control process. New roles and relationships will take time to be accepted, and the rate of progress will depend on active and continuing support from the chief executive and the top management team.

THE EVOLUTION OF STRATEGIC CONTROL PROCESSES

In Chapter 6, we argued that the nature of the businesses in a company's portfolio should influence its choice of a strategic control process. In this chapter we have seen that other influences are equally, if not more, powerful; the issues that rise to the top of the senior management agenda and the developing skills and attitudes in a company are also vital. These are the factors that lie behind many of the changes in planning and control processes introduced into the companies we have studied.

Progress or pendulum?

Over time, new issues, skills and attitudes cause the nature of the planning and control process to change in nearly all companies. Is this progress or just the swing of the pendulum? Are the changes real, evolutionary improvements or just ways of addressing specific problems, which will themselves be superseded as priorities change – indeed, which may even contain the seeds of other problems which will bring about their own demise?

In many cases, we believe, changes are introduced as ad hoc reactions to problems, as responses to currently fashionable management theories, or even as means of freshening up a process that has become stale with use. It is hard to argue that such changes represent real progress. But, to some extent, the nature of the issues that a company faces does reflect the level of sophistication of its management processes. Before decentralization, few of the issues we have discussed in this book are likely to be relevant. Corporate resource allocation issues are hard to address, and seldom even emerge, until an SBU structure has been set up. Problems with implementing strategies presuppose some mechanism for drawing up and agreeing the strategies in the first place. And the bureaucracy of planning and control becomes an issue only after a fair degree of formal structure has been introduced. Progress may be too strong a word, but there is some sort of evolution in the issues that a company typically faces. Moreover, where changes in management process are driven, or facilitated, by the gradual building up of skills, this can be interpreted as genuine progress. For these reasons, we do see some sort of evolution, somewhat along the lines of GE, as natural.

To suggest that all companies must move through precisely the same sequence of steps as GE is, of course, too strong. Other companies may face a different development of management priorities; they may be able to avoid mistakes made by GE; and they may be able to build skills more quickly. GE, after all, was in many respects the pioneer of strategic planning, so that others should be able to benefit from its prior experience and learning. Companies such as ICI and National Westminster Bank, for example, have been concerned from the outset to avoid bureaucracy in their strategic control processes. As a result they may not need to go through the dismantling stage that we have described at GE. It may also be possible to omit or combine certain steps, or at least to compress the time needed to move from step to step. But we do feel that some evolution of priorities and skills over time is inevitable, and that it is unrealistic to expect to move rapidly through different management process stages.

Current status and future outlook

It is our impression that the large majority of companies that aspire to strategic management are currently either still at stage 4 or 5 or are just entering stage 6 in Figure 7.2. That is, they are working out a suitable SBU structure, setting up a strategic planning process or embarking on portfolio resource allocation. Few have yet reached the point of emphasizing strategic control. As one senior and experienced director of strategic planning put it to us: "It has taken us 15 years to get a firm grip on the budget process and to set budget targets. We are just starting on the road to getting a more effective strategic control process."

During the next decade, as companies become more sophisticated and effective in their management of strategy, we believe that interest in strategic control processes will become more and more widespread.

Notes and References

1 See, for example, "General Electric Company: Background note on management systems: 1981" in R. F. Vancil, *Implementing Strategy: The Role of Top Management*, Harvard Business School Press, Boston, 1982; "General Electric: Strategic position: 1981", Francis J. Aguilar and Richard Hamermesh, Harvard Business School Case No 381-174; "Planning vs strategy – which will win?", Michael A. Carpenter, *Long Range Planning*, 1986 (50–53); "Life under Jack Welch: opportunistic and tough," Christopher Lorenz, *Financial Times*, May 16, 1988; "Why strategy has been put in the hands of line managers", Christopher Lorenz, *Financial Times*, May 18, 1988; "Speed, simplicity and self confidence; An interview with Jack Welch", *Harvard Business Review*, Sept-Oct 1989.

2 Alfred Chandler's pioneering work, *Strategy and Structure*, (MIT Press, 1962) describes a similar, but earlier process in Du Pont, General Motors, Standard Oil and Sears Roebuck.

3 See, for example, Richard Hamermesh, *Making Strategy Work*, John Wiley, 1986.

4 GE's Annual Report, 1988, p.3.

5 After 40 consecutive quarters of growth in earnings during the 1980s, GE's return on shareholders' equity reached 20% in 1989. The stock market value of the company increased from $12 bn in 1980 to $58 bn at the end of 1989.

6 See Michael Goold and Andrew Campbell, *Strategies and Styles*, Basil Blackwell, Oxford, 1987, Chapters 4 and 5.

7 "In the strategic reviews of 1979-80, most group businesses had a hard time: first, in getting and laying out relevant information; and then in believing it. Acting on it was of course more difficult still. Most plans described (imperfectly) the competitors of two years back, contrasted with themselves in a year or two's time, assuming a following wind. The habits of thinking widely, fearlessly and straight about the environment, the industry and the competition were largely absent." (Chris Hogg, quoted in *Strategies and Styles, loc. cit.*, p. 27).

CHAPTER 8

MAKING STRATEGIC CONTROL WORK

CHOICE OF A STRATEGIC CONTROL PROCESS

More companies need to devote serious attention to the strategic control process. Too often, strategic control is neglected and, as a result, strategies that look attractive on paper are not successfully implemented. As companies become increasingly concerned about the implementation of strategy, we believe that strategic control will assume greater importance in the management process. Strategic control is particularly vital in companies where there are long time-lags between decisions and their eventual profit consequences, and where the prime responsibility for proposing and implementing strategy is decentralized to the business level.

Some companies opt for a strategic control process in which objectives are explicitly agreed and formally monitored; others prefer a more informal approach. Companies also differ in the number and detail of their strategic objectives. Some companies, typically those with a more decentralized management style, emphasize a small number of objectives, and profitability is of particular importance. In other companies, a wider range of objectives receives attention, and profitability, though important, is set within a broader context.

Few companies today define and monitor strategic objectives as systematically as they track budget objectives. Most use an informal strategic control process. In explaining why they prefer an informal approach, managers typically stress flexibility, balanced motivation, low cost and lack of bureaucracy. Informal strategic controls are particularly suitable if:

- There is a need for cooperation among businesses in the portfolio, making it hard to define clear criteria of good performance for which an individual business can be held accountable.
- The environment is highly uncertain, so that pre-set targets are liable to lose validity as events unfold.
- There is a need for fast changes in strategy, so that the criteria of good performance alter rapidly.

- There are multiple sources of competitive advantage in the business, which are difficult and complex to identify and measure.

Formal and explicit strategic controls will also be inappropriate in companies that have not yet developed strong strategic planning skills, so that valid strategic objectives cannot be reliably defined.

But the drawbacks of a formal strategic control process should not be exaggerated. It is possible for objectives to stress cooperative goals, for corporate management to accept that unpredictable events influence the performance of a business, and for the control process to allow for some flexibility in strategies and in the results they achieve. A rigid, bureaucratic control process with oversimplified objectives may be damaging, but formal strategic control does not need to have these undesirable characteristics. Many companies that use informal strategic controls seem either to have overestimated the problems associated with a more explicit process, or, more commonly, to have not yet given the matter serious consideration. Informal strategic controls are frequently chosen by default, rather than as a deliberate matter of corporate policy. In such cases, informal controls usually lead to unclear criteria of good strategic performance, and hence to frustration, conflict and lack of mutual trust.

While a case can be made for informal strategic controls in certain circumstances, we believe there are real benefits to a more formal process. Most of these benefits flow from having clearer criteria of good strategic performance. Clear targets reduce confusion and enhance motivation amongst business heads, sharpen up plans, and make it easier for central management to intervene in a timely manner if things are going wrong. We therefore expect that, in future, more companies will decide to adopt a formal and explicit strategic control process.

The success of a strategic control process depends critically on the quality of thinking behind strategies that are agreed, the quality of communication on the criteria of good performance, and the quality of the centre's response to results that are achieved. We advocate a more formal strategic control process because we believe that it can often help to raise standards in these vital areas.

MAKING FORMAL STRATEGIC CONTROL WORK

The basic characteristics of a formal strategic control process have been described in Chapters 2 and 3. Our research has brought out several issues that need careful handling if such a process is to work well. In particular, a company that wants to establish formal strategic controls must:

- Select explicit objectives that are good indicators of strategic performance.
- Set targets that are suitably stretching.
- Create the right level of pressure for strategic performance.
- Build a strategic planning process that will support the strategic control process.
- Introduce formality and explicitness, but minimize bureaucracy.

Selecting the right objectives

The centre must take the lead in insisting that clear and explicit objectives are agreed for each business. These objectives should include both financial and non-financial performance measures. But there are dozens of possible non-financial performance indicators in any business. How should suitable strategic objectives be selected?

- Strategic objectives should be based on an analysis of the sources of long-term competitive advantage in the business. They should be indicators of progress in establishing or defending positions of long-term advantage. There are no universal indicators of competitive advantage, and each business needs to identify the variables that are most important to it. Time and attention devoted to identifying the best measures of competitive advantage is an essential starting point for strategic control.[1] Without good analysis of the sources of advantage in each business, the strategic control process will be built upon flawed foundations.
- Strategic control should concentrate on a small number of key objectives. If objectives are too numerous, they cease to have any real motivational force. In companies that wish to decentralize responsibility for strategy as far as possible (followers of the Strategic Control management style), no more than 4–6 key objectives[2] per business per year should be agreed. Even where the centre is more influential and involved in strategy formulation (as with the Strategic Planning management style), 10–15 key objectives per business per year seem to be the maximum that can be set without causing confusion about priorities and interference with operating decisions.
- Objectives may cover long-term goals, but should concentrate on progress measures, or milestones, for the coming year. More distant

objectives do not have the same force as objectives on which rela-tively near-term feedback will be received. Changing business con-ditions may require modifications in more distant objectives before they can be reached, and changing management responsibilities make it hard to hold individuals accountable for long-term goals.

- Milestones should focus on leading indicators of future results. The strategic control process will then provide early warning of poten-tial problems before financial results turn down.[3] Too little atten-tion is usually given to searching for milestones that will serve as early warning signals.

- Objectives can focus either on the completion of major projects that are vital for strategic success ("launch new product line by January 1, 1991") or on measures of results achieved in key areas (product quality ratings, market share levels). The balance between project measures and result measures should reflect the manage-ment style and priorities of the company. Particularly with more decentralized management styles (Strategic Control), objectives should concentrate on results rather than projects or action pro-grammes, allowing the centre to exercise control without interfer-ing with business management's operating responsibilities. Project-based objectives, by contrast, tend to stress the implemen-tation of agreed action programmes more than the overall perform-ance and success of the business. For example, an objective such as "Bring on stream new plant by January 1, 1991" can beg the ques-tion of whether or not achieving the objective will enhance the competitive position and performance of the business. Project-based objectives can be useful in strategic control, but only if they are clearly linked to the achievement of long-term competitive advantage, and do represent major steps towards it. Strategic con-trol should be distinguished from the detailed follow-up on action items in an operating plan.

Setting suitable targets

Once objectives have been identified, target achievement levels must be set. Ideally, these targets will elicit additional effort and achievement from business managers. But it is hard to know how much "stretch" is appropriate, particularly for a corporate management team that has decentralized operating responsibility to the business level. How can tar-gets be set at the right levels?

- Targets should be as precise and objectively measurable as possible. Vague, non-quantifiable objectives should be avoided,[4] in order to reduce confusion and increase motivation. But, in contrast to financial targets, there are often no readily available, precise measures for the strategic objectives in question. It then becomes necessary to identify a proxy measure of achievement, and to gather data on it. If, for example, "customer satisfaction" is a vital objective, it may be necessary to undertake market research specifically to create a measure of achievement in this area. Whenever possible, however, strategic control should use currently available data. Costly, one-off information gathering should be avoided unless the measure is vital for strategic success.[5]

- The objectives and targets should be proposed, in the first instance, by the business heads. They should be in the best position to identify the sources of advantage in their businesses, and to know what level of achievement to aim for. Otherwise the targets may be seen as imposed by the centre, and those running the businesses may lack ownership of them.

- But the centre should aim to sharpen and stretch the targets proposed by the businesses. Currently, although strenuous negotiation of targets is common in the budget process, it rarely occurs with strategic control.[6] We believe that, as companies gain experience with strategic control, this should change. The centre should know enough about each business to tell whether a given target represents stretch performance and should negotiate targets with the businesses that represent ambitious, but achievable performance.

- Targets should be set in the light of the performance of other leading competitors. Competitive benchmarking of this sort allows a suitable degree of stretch to be introduced into the targets.[7] In addition, targets should be defined, where possible, as measures relative to the competition (relative market share rather than absolute market share). Such targets link directly to the ultimate goal of outperforming the competition. However, very few companies at present build competitively set targets into their control process. Reasons given include a lack of competitor data and of simple, objectively measurable indicators of competitive position. But although competitive targets may be hard to define, much more could and should be done to develop and use competitive measures.

- Strategic targets should be re-examined and made consistent with financial targets at the time of the operating plan or budget. Many companies that prepare strategic plans provide either no link, or only a weak link, to their operating plans; strategic plans concentrate on competitive position and long-term goals, while operating plans are driven by the need to deliver acceptable profits in the coming year. Consequently businesses often feel encouraged to propose creative, expansive strategies in their strategic plans, but are brought down to earth sharply by tough negotiation of financial targets in the budget. In some companies, the strategy discussions and the budget discussions seem to take place under quite different ground rules. If strategic targets are not formally incorporated in the operating plan, we believe they should at least provide the background in relation to which budgets and operating plans are set. Strategic targets should be consistent with financial, profit-based targets, and any trade-offs between budget targets and strategic targets should be made explicit. Indeed, an important benefit of a more formal strategic control process is to bring these trade-offs into the open, and to ensure that they are argued through to a conclusion. It is essential to avoid setting budget targets that are incompatible with strategic targets without a consequent renegotiation of the strategic targets.

Creating pressure for strategic performance

By monitoring results, providing personal incentives and sanctions, and intervening in poorly performing businesses, the centre creates pressure for strategic performance. But strategic objectives are less amenable to monthly progress reports than financial objectives, and are less suitable as the basis for compensation bonus formulas. Moreover, the right response to missed strategic objectives is often unclear, because of trade-offs between financial and strategic objectives and changed circumstances. Strategic control is inevitably looser than strict financial control. But how tightly should strategic control processes be operated?

- Progress against the agreed strategic targets should be systematically reviewed. Formal reports on strategic progress will be less frequent than financial reports, but should be made at least annually.
- Managers' personal rewards[8] should reflect strategic performance as well as financial performance. In particular, bonus plans that depend exclusively on performance against budget profit targets should be avoided, since they conflict with the more balanced

motivation that the strategic control process aims for. Although there is value in a simple, objectively measurable formula with bonuses geared to profits, the logic of strategic control demands that personal rewards should also be affected by strategic factors, even if this makes for greater complexity. Tight, mechanical links between progress against strategic objectives and personal bonuses are, however, inappropriate, especially in businesses that face high levels of risk and uncertainty. More indirect links, which accept that some element of subjective judgement on the strategic performance of a business and its managers is both necessary and desirable, can achieve prominence for strategic objectives with less sacrifice of flexibility[9] (see Appendix 3). While such links may lack the immediacy and motivating power found in the tight financial control processes of companies such as Hanson and BTR, they can nevertheless bring long-term personal interests into line with the strategic goals of the business.[10]

- The explicitly agreed strategic objectives must be seen to matter to top management. Senior managers must show personal interest in following up on progress that is being made, and must take missed targets seriously. A not uncommon problem seems to be the CEO who likes to be closely involved in setting strategy for the businesses, but lacks the tenacity, patience or interest to follow through in the implementation phase on the strategic objectives that have been agreed. It is equally damaging to shift the emphasis away from the agreed objectives onto a new set of priorities without warning and without discussion of the rationale and implications of the change in emphasis. Simply defining strategic objectives without making them matter sets up a control process without delivering any corresponding benefits.

- Although missed financial goals will probably remain the most important triggers for corporate intervention, missed strategic targets should also prompt action. Options include: calling for more information on other aspects of performance, reviewing the validity of the strategy, withholding further investment until targets are met, or, at the extreme, changing the management. The choice is always difficult, and it cannot be made by any control "system".[11] Senior corporate managers must decide whether the problem is temporary and will resolve itself; or whether a tougher response is in order. This is a matter of judgement, and there needs to be some flexibility in interpreting the simple fact of a missed target. But, while missed milestones should not lead to an automatic response, they should direct corporate attention towards strategic issues. The formal strategic control system cannot tell the centre how to intervene, but it can pinpoint important questions.

Strategic planning and strategic control

The formal strategic control process follows on from the strategic planning process. In particular, objective setting is both the final stage of planning and the departure point for control. How can strategic planning most effectively reinforce and complement strategic control?

- The value of the strategic control process depends on the quality of the strategic plans from which the strategic objectives are derived. A company that has not yet built up the skills of strategic planning, or whose organization structure is not based on strategically defined business units, is unlikely to select valid strategic objectives. Until a company has reached a relatively high level of sophistication and insight in its strategic planning, a formal strategic control process will not be worthwhile.

- An annual strategic planning process can supplement formal strategic controls by providing the centre with a broader, more in-depth assessment of a business's strategic progress. The strategic plan can discuss progress in areas not covered by the formally agreed objectives or milestones, go into more detail concerning the business's markets and competition, and test the assumptions behind the strategic objectives. But, for these purposes, the annual strategic "planning" process should focus on monitoring past progress rather than on planning for the future. A regular in-depth check of progress makes sense, but an annual attempt to produce wholly new plans for the future will usually become a repetitive waste of effort instead of an opportunity for fresh thinking and ideas. A fundamental re-thinking of future strategy should be undertaken only if the monitoring of strategic objectives, or of general progress, indicates that the strategy is no longer on track.

Formality without bureaucracy

A formal and explicit strategic control process helps to clarify the criteria of good strategic performance. But formal processes can easily become rigid and bureaucratic. How can the strategic control process be formal and explicit, but not bureaucratic?

- Large staff departments and lengthy reports should be avoided. Line managers themselves should be in the best position to identify the sources of advantage in their businesses, and should not have to hire planners simply to fill in corporate reports.[12] Reports should focus on the few key targets that have been identified, and should not become glossy and extensive documents.

- Most of the information needed should already be available. If it is not, it should be specially gathered only if it is likely to help in running the business. Information on progress against key strategic objectives should, of course, be an important part of the data base of any business, whether or not it is called for as part of a corporate control process.

- Face-to-face meetings and discussions help to prevent formal control reports from becoming simply a bureaucratic routine. Written reports that are greeted only with a resounding silence do not add value for the businesses, and should be avoided.

- The existence of formal strategic control reviews should not preclude wider, less formal background reviews of progress that are not limited to the explicitly defined strategic objectives. These reviews, which should occur as part of the ongoing line management contacts between the businesses and the centre, are needed to allow the centre to gain an understanding of the sources of competitive advantage in the business and to determine what issues are most important for the business to address. They should also assist the centre in determining whether the agreed milestones are suitably stretching and in deciding on how to react to deviations from planned achievements.

- A structured and systematic control process should not stop important decisions from being taken as and when issues arise. A formal strategic control process provides a safety net to prevent issues being missed, but it is not intended as a substitute for an effective and speedy line management decision process, and it should not interfere with the functioning of such a process.

Summary

Establishing a formal strategic control process that adds value is not easy. It is much harder to agree targets that measure strategic progress than it is to specify financial objectives. It is often more difficult to know how to react to missed strategic targets than to missed budgets, and there is a danger that a formal strategic control process will bring with it unacceptable overhead and bureaucracy.

But these difficulties are not insurmountable. Table 8.1 summarizes our main recommendations for dealing with them. A good strategic planning process will identify explicit milestones that monitor competitive position and progress; stretching targets can be formally agreed and monitored in a way that does not lead to bureaucracy; and a formal control process can provide pressure for strategic performance without becoming rigid and inflexible. Under these conditions a formal strategic control process will be valuable in the vast majority of businesses.

Table 8.1 **Making Formal Strategic Control Work**

Issues	Recommendations
Selecting the right objectives	– Based on analysis of competitive advantage – Few in number – Milestones that measure short-term progress – Leading indicators of future performance – Projects or action programmes only if important for competitive advantage
Setting suitable targets	– Precise and objectively measurable, if possible – Proposed by business managers, but stretched by the centre – Competitively benchmarked – Consistent with budget targets: trade-offs openly confronted and resolved
Creating pressure for strategic performance	– Systematic progress monitoring and reviews – Personal rewards indirectly tied to achievement of strategic targets – Performance against strategic targets matters to top management and is the basis for corporate interventions
Strategic planning and strategic control	– High-quality strategic planning needed as basis for strategic controls – Strategic planning process used to review strategic progress
Formality without bureaucracy	– Avoid large staff departments and lengthy reports – Avoid specially gathered data – Conduct reviews face-to-face – Supplement formal reviews with informal contacts – Be prepared to short-circuit formal process if necessary

MAKING INFORMAL STRATEGIC CONTROL WORK

Despite the advantages of a formal strategic control process, some companies will feel that a more informal process suits their circumstances better. To make an informal process work well, several of the recommendations made in connection with formal strategic control remain relevant. In particular, performance reviews should still be based on an assessment of progress relative to competitors; strategies should be consistent with budget targets; and personal rewards and corporate intervention should take account of strategic performance and progress.

But the greatest problems for informal strategic control processes come from lack of clarity on the criteria of good performance. How can these difficulties be avoided?

- To an even greater extent than with formal control processes, the value of informal strategic control depends on the quality of strategic planning that lies behind it. Without a formal requirement to spell out explicit objectives, strategies can easily remain woolly and directional. This can be avoided only if managers in the businesses and at the centre nevertheless discipline themselves to push their strategic plans through to action implications. Without the crutch of a formal strategic control process, a high level of strategic planning skills and self-discipline is particularly vital.

- For business managers, the lack of explicit strategic targets can make it difficult to establish priorities. Close contact and frequent meetings with the corporate centre are then the only way to convey what is regarded as most important. If either the centre or the businesses wish to shift objectives or priorities, the changes should be openly debated and agreed at the earliest opportunity.

- For the centre, too, the absence of a formal control process places more weight on the frequency of informal, line management contacts with the business. Central managers must possess a considerable depth of knowledge and feel for their businesses, in order to identify important issues without the formal triggers of missed objectives or milestones. For this reason, informal controls tend to work better in smaller, less diverse companies, where the chief executive has personal experience in the main business areas.

- If specific strategic targets are not agreed, more emphasis should be placed on the overall mission of a business. Given a clear and widely accepted mission, business managers can be allowed more latitude and flexibility in deciding how to proceed towards the ultimate goal.

- Since the nature of the business head's "contract" under an informal control process is looser, there needs to be a higher level of mutual trust, confidence and goodwill to make the process work. Unless, and until, a working relationship of this sort has been built between the levels, the opportunities for miscommunication and cross-purposes created by an informal strategic control process will be dangerous.

Advocates of informal control maintain that objectives can be clear, even if they have not been explicitly written down and agreed. Table 8.2 summarizes ways to achieve such clarity. To work well, informal strategic control requires excellent line management communication on directions and priorities, consistency in reactions to results that are achieved, and a depth and sophistication of strategic understanding at all levels of a company.

Table 8.2 **Making Informal Strategic Controls Work**

Issue	Recommendations
Unclear criteria of good strategic performance	– High level of strategic planning skills and self-discipline needed – Close contact between businesses and centre – Depth of knowledge and feel for businesses at centre – Clear and widely accepted missions for businesses helpful – Mutual trust between levels essential

TOP MANAGEMENT ROLE AND PORTFOLIO DIVERSITY

The role of the chief executive and top management team is vital in making any strategic control process a success. To add real value, top corporate management must:

- Understand the strategic situation in each business well enough to have a view on what objectives are most important for competitive advantage.
- Know what represents a "stretching" level of achievement in terms of these objectives.
- Determine the right sort of pressure to apply to businesses that are missing their objectives.
- Avoid interfering in operating details that should be left to the business managers.

- Create a constructive atmosphere in performance reviews, using them mainly to motivate managers and to put forward suggestions for improving results, rather than to find fault.

In large diversified companies, it is particularly difficult to know each of the businesses well enough to fulfil these requirements. It helps if the top management group has, collectively, recent personal experience in running the major businesses in the portfolio.[13] But ultimately it is a question of whether the top managers have the skills and energy to become sufficiently knowledgeable about the strategies and the progress of each of their businesses. Chief executives who do add value in the control process invariably receive high marks from their subordinates for their ability to get themselves well briefed on each business, and to follow through on the genuinely important aspects of strategy.[14]

A reasonably homogeneous portfolio also facilitates strategic control. It is easier to exercise strategic control in companies that specialize in particular sorts of businesses, such as Unilever and Nestlé which concentrate their portfolios on fast-moving consumer goods, than in more diverse companies. If the businesses in the corporate portfolio share a common strategic logic[15] – facing similar issues, building competitive advantage in similar ways, defining their objectives in similar terms – the centre can much more readily add value in the strategic control process.

The greatest problems in strategic control arise in highly diverse companies, especially if top management favours a distant, hands-off relationship between the businesses and the centre. In these circumstances, there is a grave danger that the chief executive will not know enough about the businesses to exercise effective strategic control, and that the control reviews will fail to help and motivate business managers. It is our conviction that too much diversity is incompatible with good strategic control.

Notes and References

1 Common parameters, such as market share and product quality, are by no means always the most insightful measures of competitive position. Objectives that track success rates in attracting highly qualified new recruits can, for example, be more vital than anything else in professional or research-based organizations; and the Boston Consulting Group now argues that cycle times (whether in design, delivery, processing, service or any other important activities) are the real key to advantage in many businesses.

2 This covers both key financial and non-financial objectives.

3 Early warnings are most valuable in businesses where there are unusually long time-lags between decisions and their impact on financial results. In the pharmaceutical business, milestones that measure the progress and prospects on new drugs being taken into development are an essential part of strategic control.

4 Even apparently measurable targets ("Achieve 15% market share") may be amenable to a variety of different interpretations (nature of served market, source of data used, and so on). To establish unambiguous targets and to avoid game playing by managers who wish to present their results in the best possible light, it is important that definitions of measures and sources of data be clearly agreed when the targets are set.

5 Reliance on existing data should not be taken as too binding a constraint. We met with a hospital administrator who told us that one reason why strategic control was difficult for him was because the statistics that he received on discharges from the hospital lumped together those who left because they had recovered and those who died.

6 Part of the problem is the difficulty of stretching performance in more than one dimension. Strategic control introduces trade-offs that make stretch less easy to define; the more targets, the harder it is to stretch any one of them.

7 See the section on Xerox's approach to benchmarking in Chapter 3.

8 This includes career progression as well as monetary compensation.

9 One interesting scheme that we encountered involved setting "minimum acceptable" and "outstanding" targets for 6-8 key objectives. Managers were severely penalized if they failed to achieve the minimum targets for any objective, and were strongly rewarded if they hit outstanding levels for any objective. Rewards and incentives for those managers whose performance fell between the two extremes on all objectives involved a subjective judgement about their overall performance.

10 A longer-term, more indirect link to personal rewards also reduces the danger of control "games", in which managers dress up results to meet formally specified targets, to the detriment of the overall strategy and results of the business.

11 Probably the best system response is to require, as ICI does, that business heads who see problems emerging in meeting both their financial and strategic objectives come in for a further discussion of trade-offs with the centre.

12 Complaints about the need to add staff to administer the strategic control process should be seen in the context of the size of staff already in place to administer the financial control process. Given the armies of controllers and accountants typically involved with the budget process, the resources needed to cope with strategic controls may seem relatively modest.

13 The fact that the three members of the Chief Executive's Office in GE have, between them, run nearly all GE's main businesses at one time or another makes it more possible to exercise strategic control in a vast and highly diverse company.

14 It is also necessary for central managers to avoid giving conflicting signals about the criteria of good performance. In one company that we researched, the CEO tended to focus on the main financial results and one or two key strategic objectives only. Another main board liaison director preferred to get into much more detail in monitoring achievements. There was then constant confusion and ill feeling between the businesses, the board member and the CEO, with no one quite sure what would count as good performance and where the limits of decentralized responsibility lay.

15 For a discussion of the idea of a shared strategic logic, see C. K. Pralahad and R. A. Bettis, "The dominant logic: a new linkage between diversity and performance", *Strategic Management Journal,* Nov-Dec 1986.

METHODOLOGY AND COMPANY BACKGROUND DATA

This book is based on case studies of companies exemplifying alternative approaches to strategic control. The methodological problem faced at the beginning of the research programme was how to identify and obtain the cooperation of such companies.

Initially, 33 companies were identified as having potentially interesting approaches to strategic control and were contacted directly. These companies included members of the Ashridge Strategic Management Centre, companies that previous research contacts suggested would be worth pursuing, and companies identified from press and other published sources. Interviews were carried out in all these companies.

A letter was sent to a further 196 UK companies asking about their experience, if any, with strategic control systems. These were the top 250 companies in *The Times 1,000* for 1988, after excluding companies that had already been contacted directly, or that were in sectors that were less suitable for our research (commodity brokers, trading houses). The letter was addressed to named individuals, usually the planning director or equivalent. Forty-seven companies replied to this letter, of which just five companies (or 11 per cent) claimed to be using explicit strategic milestones or objectives. Figure A1.1 shows the distribution of replies. These results, although we would claim no statistical rigour for them, tend to confirm previous research findings that the incidence of formal strategic controls is low.

The third phase of the study involved following up these replies with personal interviews in order to identify a smaller number of companies (from the 33 approached directly and the 47 that had replied to the letter) for more in-depth interviewing. In total we carried out interviews in over 50 companies, leading to more in-depth work in the 18 companies that form the basis for the case studies reported in this volume. Figure A1.2 lists the companies interviewed in depth, and shows their size and their range of activities (by product and by geography).

Figure A1.1 **Claimed Use of Explicit Strategic Objectives or Milestones**

Use strategic controls	No of companies	% of total	% excluding companies unwilling to discuss
Yes[2]	5	11	15
Developing/considering	7	15	21
No	14	30	41
Possibly[3]	8	17	24
Unwilling to discuss	13	28	–
Totals	47	100	100

Notes

1. In subsequent interviews it became clear that at least two of the companies claiming to use explicit strategic objectives did not do so and, conversely, that one company that claimed not to use explicit strategic objectives did.

2. It is reasonable to suppose that companies using or developing explicit strategic objectives would be more likely to respond than companies doing nothing about such controls, so the table probably overstates the incidence of explicit strategic objectives. Among the companies claiming to use explicit strategic objectives were one subsidiary of a Japanese company and one of an American company.

3. Some respondents felt unable to give definite responses, as they were unclear as to the meaning of the term "explicit strategic milestones or objectives".

The interview programme in these companies involved both planning and control staff and line management, particularly the general managers responsible for the individual businesses or strategic business units. We also collected documentary data concerning the strategic plans and objectives and the performance of these companies. We thus obtained several different perspectives on the strategic control systems employed in the 18 companies. This allowed for cross-checking, and significant inconsistencies were pursued in subsequent interviews.

Depending on the complexity of the companies and of their strategic control systems, and on the level of access we were given, the number of interviews conducted within these 18 companies varied from 4 to 25. A total of 210 people were interviewed during the course of the study, of whom 147 were in the companies described in Chapters 3 and 4.

Table A1.2 Company Background Data

Company	Country of Headquarters	Year End	Turnover	Profit before tax	Business sectors[1]	Turnover %	Profit %	Geographical regions[1]	Turnover %	Profit %
B.A.T Industries[2]	UK	31/12/88	£17,653m	£1,604 m	Tobacco	40	47	UK	14	13
					Retailing	23	12	Europe	34	15
					Paper	11	13	North America	31	52
					Financial services	22	27	Australasia	1	1
					Other	4	1	Latin America	11	11
								Asia	6	5
								Africa	3	4
BOC	UK	30/9/89	£2,309m	£331m	Gases and related products	56	62	Europe	24	44
					Health care	28	26	Africa	7	12
					Special products and services	14	11	America	35	22
					Other	2	1	Asia/Pacific	34	22
BP	UK	31/12/89	£29,641m	£2,533m	Exploration and production	20	54	UK	35	26
					Refining and marketing	60	25	Rest of Europe	25	18
					Chemicals	10	18	USA	30	45
					Nutrition	7	1	Rest of world	10	10
					Coal	2	1			
					Other	1	–			
Bunzl	UK	31/12/88	£1,746m	£93m	Services and distribution:			UK	24	40
					– Paper and packaging	63	51	Europe	11	9
					– Industrial products	17	10	North America	61	43
					Specialist manufacturing:			Rest of world	4	8
					– Paper and plastics	10	23			
					– Filters	10	16			

Company	Country of Headquarters	Year End	Turnover	Profit before tax	Business sectors[1]	Turnover %	Profit %	Geographical regions[1]	Turnover %	Profit %
Ciba-Geigy	Switzerland	31/12/88	SF17,647m	SF1325m[3]	Dyestuffs	15		Europe	45	47
					Pharmaceuticals	29		North America	29	7
					Agricultural	21		Latin America	8	18
					Additives	9		Asia	13	16
					Plastics	9		Africa/Australasian/		14
					Pigments	4		Oceania	5	
					Ilford	3				
					Electronic systems	6				
					Ciba Vision	3				
Courtaulds	UK	31/3/89	£2,610m	£197m	Fibres	17	19	UK	58	47
					Chemicals and materials	11	12	Rest of Europe	15	7
					Coatings	20	25	North America	17	18
					Films and packaging	14	16	Africa	2	16
					Textiles[4]	38	29	Rest of world	8	14
Digital	USA	1/7/89	$12,742m	$1,421m				US	50	29
								Europe	33	47
								Canada/Far East/Americas	18	24
GE	USA	31/12/89	$54,574m	$5,703m	Aerospace	9	8	US	88	86
					Aircraft engines	12	13	Other	12	14
					Financial services	24	26			
					Industrial	12	11			
					Major appliances	10	5			
					Materials	9	13			
					Broadcasting	6	8			
					Power systems	9	6			

Company	Country of Headquarters	Year End	Turnover	Profit before tax	Business sectors[1]	Turnover %	Profit %	Geographical regions[1]	Turnover %	Profit %
(GE)					Technical products/services	8	4			
					Other	<1	<1			
ICI	UK	31/12/88	£11,699m	£1,470m	Consumer/speciality products	38	39	UK	41	43
					Industrial products	44	54	Continental Europe	20	19
					Agriculture	16	7	The Americas	23	22
					Miscellaneous	2	<1	Asia/Pacific	13	13
								Other	3	2
Kingfisher	UK	28/01/89	£2,660m	£224m	Retailing:			All UK		
					– Out of Town		44			
					– High Street		31			
					Property		25			
National Westminster Bank	UK	31/12/88	£4,764m[5]	£1,407m	Domestic banking	71	39			
					Related banking services	13	54			
					International banking	20	7			
					Investment banking	(4)	<1			
Nestlé	Switzerland	31/12/88	FF40.7bn	FF3.3bn	Drinks	28		Europe	46	46
					Dairy products	15		North America	26	26
					Chocolate and confectionery	12		Asia	12	12
					Culinary products	12		Latin America/Caribbean	10	10
					Frozen foods and icecream	10				
					Refrigerated products	9		Africa	3	3
					Export foods and dietetic products	6		Oceania	3	3
					Petfoods	4				

Company	Country of Headquarters	Year End	Turnover	Profit before tax	Business sectors[1]	Turnover %	Profit %	Geographical regions[1]	Turnover %	Profit %
(Nestlé)					Pharmaceutical and cosmetic products	2				
					Hotels and restaurants	1				
					Other	1				
Philips	Netherlands		DFL56,079m	DFL2,428m	Lighting	12	32	Netherlands	22	11
					Consumer electronics	32	11	Rest of Europe	46	47
					Domestic appliances	12	23	USA/Canada	17	2
					Professional products and systems	27	15	Latin America	4	22
					Components	14	14	Asia	9	16
					Miscellaneous	2	5	Australia/New Zealand	1	1
Pilkington	UK	31/3/89	£2,573m	£325m	Flat and safety glass	77	85	UK	24	26
					Insulation and reinforcements	6	5	Europe	28	24
					Visionware	11	10	North America	30	18
					Optronics	3	(<1)	Rest of world	18	31
					Other	3	<1			
RTZ	UK	31/12/88	£3,961m	£879m	Metals	41	54	UK	28	19
					Energy	8	11	USA	24	18
					Industrial minerals	11	17	Australia/New Zealand	17	19
					Related industries	41	17	Africa	7	22
								Canada	17	13
								Papua New Guinea	2	5
								Mainland Europe	3	2
								Other	2	2

Company	Country of Headquarters	Year End	Turnover	Profit before tax	Business sectors[1]	Turnover %	Profit %	Geographical regions[1]	Turnover %	Profit %
Shell	Netherlands/ UK	31/12/88	£55,823m	£5,541m	Oil and gas: – Exploration and marketing	18	42	Europe	46	37
					Oil and gas: – Manufacturing marine and marketing	68	29	USA	25	28
					Chemicals	12	29	Other Eastern hemisphere	17	19
					Other	2	2	Other Western hemisphere	12	16
Toshiba	Japan	31/03/88	¥3,572bn	¥125bn	Information/communications systems and electrical devices	43		Japan	69	
					Heavy electrical apparatus	24		Americas	12	
					Consumer products and others	33		Europe	9	
								Asia	8	
								Other	2	
Xerox	USA	31/12/88	$16,441m	$1,005m	Business products and systems	70	38[6]	USA	63	50[7]
					Financial services	30	62	Rank Xerox area[8]	25	23
								Other	11	27

Notes:
1. The business sectors and geographical regions are those identified in the respective company accounts.
2. B.A.T Industries' geographical analysis omits the Financial Services activities.
3. Profit after tax.
4. Courtaulds have announced the de-merger, as from March 1990, of the Textile business into a separate company.
5. Income (interest plus non-interest) rather than turnover.
6. The profit before tax figure for the Business Products and Systems (BPS) business of Xerox was greatly reduced in 1988 by restructuring costs. Without these costs BPS would have represented 62% of Xerox's profits.
7. The restructuring costs referred to in Note 6 fell primarily on the USA. Without these costs the profits contribution would have been 65% USA, 19% Rank Xerox, 10% other.
8. Rank Xerox area is 97% Europe.

The typical interview lasted one to two hours and covered: the budgetary and strategic planning processes; strategic objective setting, including the use of short-term milestones; criteria of good performance, especially good strategic performance; monitoring of strategic performance; conditions for senior management intervention in the businesses; and the reward and sanctions system.

This field work among companies was enriched and put into a broader context by interviews with about 25 consultants and management academics, and by a full review of the management literature on strategic control processes.

Notes and References

1. The literature review has been written up separately in Michael Goold and John J. Quinn, "The paradox of strategic control", *Strategic Management Journal,* Jan 1990.

CONTROL AT DIFFERENT LEVELS IN AN ORGANIZATION

In most large companies, including those in our study, there are several levels of general management. For example, the organization structure may include corporate headquarters, business groups, divisions, business units and other units focused on specific market segments. Figure A2.1 is an illustrative organization chart for a company structured in just this way.

The presence of multiple general management levels raises some important questions. How can so many general managers each add value and avoid duplication? What differences in management style and control approach are appropriate at each level? RTZ (discussed in Chapter 3)

Figure A2.1 **Multi-Business Company Organization Structure**

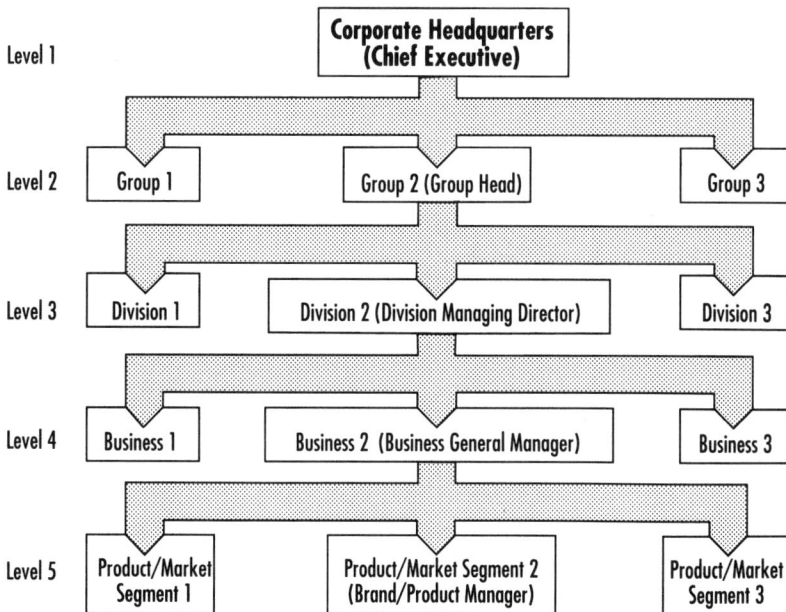

Level 1		**Corporate Headquarters (Chief Executive)**	
Level 2	Group 1	Group 2 (Group Head)	Group 3
Level 3	Division 1	Division 2 (Division Managing Director)	Division 3
Level 4	Business 1	Business 2 (Business General Manager)	Business 3
Level 5	Product/Market Segment 1	Product/Market Segment 2 (Brand/Product Manager)	Product/Market Segment 3

provides a good illustration of how different levels can each make their own contribution to strategic management and control.

Figure A2.2 shows the RTZ corporate organization structure, and, within it, a partial view of the structure of RTZ Pillar, one of the main subsidiary companies. In RTZ, the primary profit responsibility resides at the business unit level (for example, Aviation Engineering & Maintenance Ltd, H&S Aviation Ltd) – corresponding to level 4 in Figure A2.1 on page 213. The general managers of these business units are intended to have authority over the resources and decisions that are most important for strategic success in their businesses. Although a business like H&S Aviation has some links to the other businesses in the Aviation & Defence division, it could operate as a viable stand-alone competitor.

Within H&S Aviation there may be distinct market segments (specific customers or geographical areas). These are tactically important arenas in which the business unit's strategy is implemented, but they are not themselves separate SBUs. The business units exercise operating control in reviewing segment performance rather than strategic control.

Attewell-Mycroshims, Aviation Engineering & Maintenance and H&S are all part of the Aviation & Defence division. Each of the busi-

Figure A2.2 **RTZ Organization Structure**

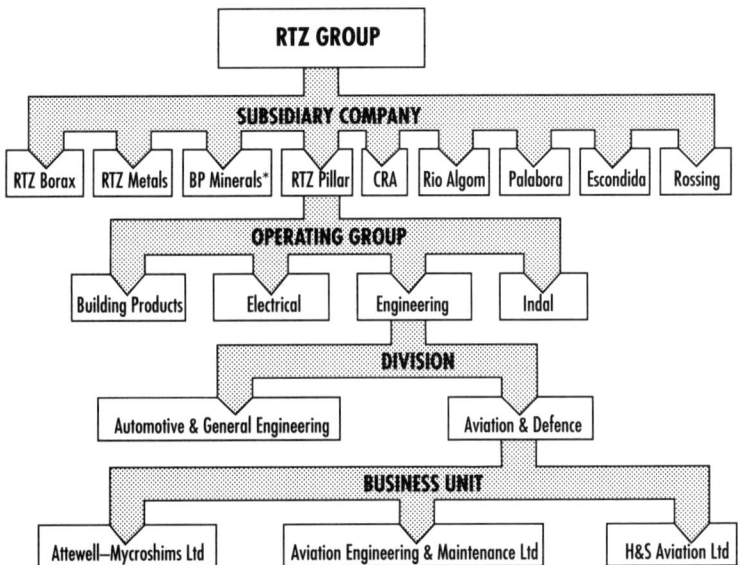

* Recently acquired

nesses in the division is concerned with similar customers (the airlines), they share a common computer system, and the division as a whole has dealings with important regulatory bodies such as the Civil Aviation Authority. In general there is little real cost synergy between businesses in the division, but market place synergies do exist which create opportunities for coordination. There is, for example, potential for sharing of information and contacts in the airline industry.

Because the division directors chair the management boards of the business units, they are closely familiar with all the issues in their businesses. Control is detailed and informal. The division follows a Strategic Planning management style,[1] reflecting the synergies between the businesses in the division and the long lead times in some of these businesses.

In Pillar's Building Products operating group, by contrast, there is a stronger emphasis on decentralization to the business units and on tight financial controls. This division's management style falls somewhere between Strategic Control and Financial Control,[2] reflecting again the nature of the businesses in this group (see Chapter 6).

"We try to tailor the management styles of each operating group to make the most effective contribution to the businesses they are managing. The style, and the nature of control, is somewhat different in each case, though I suppose you could say they are all variants of Strategic Control, but at different levels of detail."

The relationship between Pillar and the operating groups is somewhat more distant than between the operating groups and the business units. The importance of financial control is taken for granted, but beyond this the identification of strategic issues is a softer process. In the words of the chief executive of RTZ Pillar:

"How we should be controlling is a subject of extensive debate for us. We take a view of whether operating group management are too far from their businesses or too near, and we seek to influence that. We also influence where they lay the emphasis, for example, on growth or profitability. Strategic objectives are established for some of the businesses in Pillar, and achievements monitored, but, in others, it's more a matter of profitability and operating effectiveness."

Pillar, in its turn, reports to the corporate centre of RTZ. The RTZ centre's style is classic detached Strategic Control, with formally established plans and milestones. The corporate centre's role in relation to Pillar is similar to Pillar's role in relation to its operating groups, but with a greater degree of distance and formality.

Figure A2.3

LEVEL	MANAGEMENT STYLE	CONTROL APPROACH
Corporate HQ	Strategic Control (detached, formal)	Focus on a few key objectives (main financial results and explicit strategic milestones)
Subsidiary company (e.g. Pillar)	Strategic Control	Several criteria of good performance, strong emphasis on financial results
Operating group/division (e.g. Aviation and.Defence)	Strategic Control/ Strategic Planning	Depends on businesses in group. Ranges from close, informal controls using multiple criteria of good performance to something closer to Financial Control
Business unit (e.g. H&S)	Primary source of strategy (SBU)	Operating controls

The relationship between the various levels in RTZ is summarized in Figure A2.3. Each level has a distinctive role, and can make a value-added contribution, given the nature of the businesses that report to them. At higher levels in the hierarchy, there tends to be less detailed involvement in planning, and the emphasis shifts increasingly to resource allocation and control. This is an appropriate separation of roles.

In nearly all companies, control at lower levels tends to be closer and more detailed. In BP, we were told: "In the businesses, the further down you go, the clearer are the milestones. You know what you need to do each year to keep on track." At lower levels it is also relatively easier to operate a less formal control process. A Courtaulds director, who had worked at different levels during his career, stated: "A good manager running a business will know what other competitors are doing in a semi-intuitive fashion. This is much more difficult for the next level up."

A Strategic Planning style with informal controls is therefore most likely to be found at lower levels in the organization. Conversely, at least in highly diversified organizations, control typically becomes more formal and concentrates on a smaller number of key objectives at higher levels in the hierarchy. There is some danger that the control process will lose contact with real performance ("As you move up in the organization, perception becomes more important than reality; and perception always lags reality," was the comment in one company), but this is where the need for well-defined and clear strategic milestones is greatest. The corporate headquarters in highly diversified groups is more likely to adopt a Strategic Control style, and to need formal and explicit strategic milestones, than are lower levels in the organization.

Each level in an organization should make a distinctive value-added contribution in the overall management process and structure. If the upper levels simply try to make the same sort of contribution to strategy setting and control as the next levels down – which have better information and are closer to the market place – it can legitimately be asked whether the company would not be better off broken up into smaller, separate chunks. In a well-designed organization, each level of the hierarchy has its own role, and a control process appropriate to that role.

Notes

1 See Appendix 4 for a fuller description of this style.
2 See Appendix 4 for fuller descriptions of these styles.

HOW COMPANIES REWARD STRATEGIC PERFORMANCE

Performance-related pay (PRP) has become an increasingly common feature of managers' compensation packages. A survey[1] showed that 63 per cent of larger companies in the UK had a PRP scheme in 1986 compared with 24 per cent in 1981. PRP schemes can take a range of forms including bonuses, merit increases, profit sharing and stock options.[2] The most common form of PRP is the annual cash bonus, which is now used by an estimated 50–60 per cent of UK companies.[3] In addition to (or instead of) PRP, performance can also be recognized through more traditional ways. Increased salary, promotion, public acknowledgement and capital-expenditure authority are among the steps that can be taken.

The purpose of PRP and other reward schemes is to influence managers' performance,[4] both by inducing extra effort and by redirecting managers' efforts towards targets the company wishes to achieve.[5] Whatever approach is taken, it is important to reward those aspects of performance that matter most to the organization.[6] In particular, for companies that have adopted a strategic control process, it is important that some element of reward for strategic performance be included in the total performance-related rewards package.

PRP LINKED TO FINANCIAL PERFORMANCE

The most common form of PRP for corporate managers is an annual bonus based on the company's pre-tax profits for the year.[7] The bonus may also be related to some other corporate financial indicator (such as return on assets or earnings per share). For divisional or SBU managers, the bonus may include elements based on divisional/SBU financial performance as well as (or instead of) corporate performance and elements based on indicators linked to an aspect of the manager's personal responsibility (such as sales or expenses).

Such PRP schemes have several desirable features. In general, they are clearly understood, relatively easily and objectively measured through the accounting system, personally motivating and capable of allowing for stretching performance standards.

Unfortunately, such schemes can be dysfunctional from a strategic control perspective, especially if they are the sole element of PRP and are applied mechanistically. They focus management attention purely on the annual financial performance figures; strategic factors, important to the long-term competitive position of the company, then may be neglected or unwisely traded-off against short-term performance considerations.

Two main variants on the annual bonus scheme try to overcome this problem of short-term focus, but still retain the link to financial performance indicators and the positive features of such links. The first alternative is to pay a bonus based not just on annual performance but on performance over a number of years (typically three). The idea behind this is that it should dissuade managers from managing for the year-end figures to the detriment of next year's figures (for example, deferring a cost from year 1 to year 2). It should also discourage management from viewing longer-term expenditure (on assets, research and development, training, and so on) purely as a cost, rather than an investment.

Thus, one of the companies in our study employed a series of overlapping three-year bonus schemes:

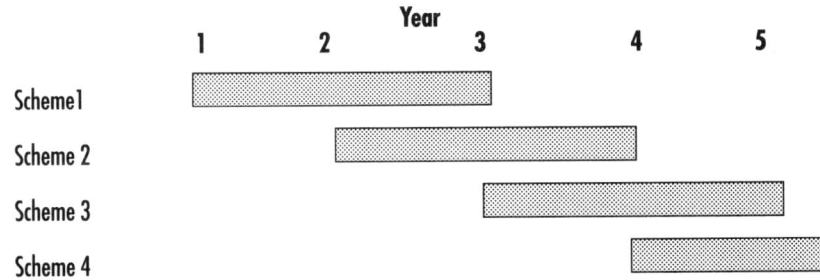

	Year				
	1	2	3	4	5
Scheme 1	▭▭▭▭▭▭				
Scheme 2		▭▭▭▭▭▭			
Scheme 3			▭▭▭▭▭▭		
Scheme 4				▭▭▭▭▭	

The second alternative awards stock options, rather than cash bonuses, based on financial performance.[8] Here the thinking is that, although the level of options is based on current financial performance, the value of the options depends on the future performance of the company as reflected in the changing value of the company's shares. Indeed, in some schemes the options may not be exercised until some future performance target is reached.

Both these alternatives are unsatisfactory in some respects. Basing the PRP on the results over a set number of years immediately raises the question "How many years?" Too few, and the problem of short termism remains, if somewhat mitigated. Too many, and two further problems are encountered. First, many managers will have changed jobs – perhaps more than once – during the time frame of the bonus scheme. This makes the scheme difficult to administer and reintroduces the problem of short termism. Second, the scheme will not be as motivating as a straightforward annual bonus scheme, which gives early feedback on short-term goals.

The motivational force of stock options based PRP schemes is also questionable, both because of the time-lag between the action rewarded (current performance) and the incidence of the reward (the exercised option) and because of the uncertainty of the level of the reward, which may depend as much on the overall performance of the stock market as on the performance of the company concerned. That is, managers' rewards come to depend on factors beyond their control – a situation that conflicts directly with the rationale for PRP.

In summary, PRP schemes based on year-to-year financial performance focus management attention on short-term financial performance to the possible detriment of long-run performance. Nevertheless, they have a number of strengths including simplicity, objectivity and motivational force. They are particularly appropriate forms of reward in industries or at management levels where long-term strategic factors are of less importance, or if used in combination with schemes that also reward strategic performance.

STRATEGIC PERFORMANCE

Given that strategic performance is important for a company, how should such performance be rewarded? Are there any alternative forms of PRP that reward aspects of performance that contribute to the company's longer-term competitive position?

Obviously, for a reward scheme to encourage good strategic performance, it must be perceived by the managers concerned to reward such performance and in a non-arbitrary way. In a number of the companies interviewed during the course of our research, senior managers indicated that strategic performance was rewarded indirectly – often through longer-term career progress. But in several of these companies, whilst this was the theoretical position, in practice the people who were promoted were those who delivered the best annual performance figures.

We found several instances in which the managers being rewarded had a different perception of the rewards process from the senior management; in such situations incentives may have unintended effects.

In deciding on their managers' financial rewards, over and above salary, almost all the companies profiled in this study make some assessment of strategic performance. This strategic performance based reward usually supplements (and complements) an element of reward based on current financial performance. Indeed, in several cases the annual profit target is a minimum constraint that must be satisfied before other elements of the PRP can be earned. Conversely, in some cases the reward based on financial performance is modulated by strategic performance. "Bonus based on profit can be up to 100%+ of salary, but this can be greatly reduced if key tasks are not fulfilled. Profit performance gets a manager into a certain bonus 'band', but where he is placed within the band depends on key tasks performance."

Whereas most companies use a predetermined formula to calculate the element of reward related to current financial performance, the element related to strategic performance tends to be based on a subjective assessment by the manager's superiors. This is not unexpected in companies that lack a formal strategic control process, although in these companies strategic performance tends to be assessed within a MBO framework. Thus, BOC has an Incentive Compensation Plan for its senior managers that includes a component based on broad indicators of financial performance and a component based on personal objectives.

"The personal goals are not explicitly linked to strategic plans but the sorts of goals agreed are clearly strategic in nature. Review of performance against these goals is a collective matter for the Executive Committee, and it is a judgemental decision concerning the degree to which these goals have been achieved that determines individuals' bonuses."

Another company with a largely informal control process had an incentive scheme for main board and subsidiary company directors based on a number of measures of performance. The performance of the subsidiary company directors was judged by the main board. "Wherever possible, the directors' objectives are quantitative, and an overall judgement of performance is possible because it is normally fairly easy to see whether a given strategic priority has been met or not. However, there must be an element of subjective judgement and balance between the objectives in arriving at the overall judgement."

But, even in those companies that employ a formal strategic control process, strategic performance and the concomitant rewards appear to be assessed rather subjectively by a manager's superiors. As noted elsewhere in this book, strategic objectives tend to be "softer" than financial targets. In assessing strategic performance at the end of the year, the question asked is not so much "Have the objectives been reached or not?" but rather "What progress has been made towards the objectives?" or "How well has the manager tackled the strategy?" Thus, in our interview programme, we heard comments such as:

"It would be difficult to use strategic controls as part of a bonus scheme because, in contrast with budget targets, they are not sufficiently precise yardsticks." (ICI)

"The strategic objectives are less precise, and in any case you seldom manage to hit them all." (RTZ)

"We want the business manager to be open about the status of his strategy and whether it needs to be changed rather than going all out for the milestones for their own sake." (BP)

These companies, then, believe that strategy is important and reward their managers according to strategic performance as well as current financial performance. But they do not believe that the assessment of strategic performance can use mechanistic, formula-based techniques; rather it needs the judgement of senior managers. Such companies, therefore, often employ a PRP scheme with two components: a formula-based component related to current financial performance, and a non-formula-based component, subjectively assessed, related to strategic performance.

In contrast, two companies in our study (the National Westminster Bank and Xerox Corporation) use systems involving tighter, formula-based links between reward and aspects of strategic performance. Each company has identified quantifiable and measurable key factors influencing strategic success and incorporated them into its calculation of management rewards.

NatWest, for example, explicitly recognizes that certain activities are important for the bank's long-term position but detract from a manager's current-year figures. To counteract any tendency to pay insufficient attention to these activities, targets are set for them and built in to the rewards formula. For example, student accounts are generally unprofitable to the bank in the short run but highly profitable in the long run, because students after graduating tend to become valuable customers for the bank. Managers are therefore set targets in terms of market share of student accounts to ensure the implementation of the bank's strategy of attracting such accounts.

Xerox Corporation uses a rewards formula based on four measures of performance: profit (against budget), return on assets, market share and customer satisfaction, which is seen within the company as being of particular importance for future competitive success. Each year and in each business area Xerox's customer satisfaction rating is measured using a standard survey instrument. The results of this survey are an important factor in determining the manager's reward.

SUMMARY

Companies use reward schemes to influence managers' behaviour. Companies for which long-term strategy is important try to reward good strategic behaviour as well as the achievement of short-term financial figures. Performance may be rewarded through a formal PRP scheme or, more broadly, through career progression and status. PRP schemes have particular importance, however, both as direct incentives and as signals of what top managements regard as most important. The nature of PRP schemes therefore often dominates managers' perceptions of what is regarded as good performance.

Ideally, PRP schemes should function as objectively as possible: using a predetermined formula limits the room for subjective judgement and hence disagreement. However, most of the companies in our research have not adopted such a formula-based approach to rewarding strategic performance. Instead they employ a more subjective assessment of performance by a manager's superiors. This approach recognizes that strategic goals cannot always be wholly precise and allows senior management flexibility in rewarding performance.

Two companies in our study (National Westminster Bank and Xerox) do use a formula-based approach to rewarding strategic performance. These companies have identified a number of measurable outputs that are of clear strategic importance and they have built performance with respect to these outputs into their rewards formulae. They believe that, given the importance of these goals, the benefits from offering people incentives to achieve them outweigh the disadvantages from focusing too strongly on a narrow set of performance indicators.

Notes and References

1 Michael Skapinker, "Now cash is clean again: UK performance related to pay", *Financial Times,* January 20, 1987 (citing figures from a Hay Management Consultants' report).

2 Michael Armstrong and Helen Murlis, *Reward Management: A Handbook of Salary Administration,* Kogan Page, 1988 (includes descriptions of the mechanics of different PRP schemes).

3 Tom Nash, "Top Salaries: the package game", *Chief Executive,* Feb 1988, pp. 14-16.

4 The link between PRP and performance is a matter of debate. On the one hand, it has been argued that PRP, like the company car in Britain, is just one more prerequisite that must be offered to attract good staff (David Hume, "Everyone wants a share option", *Management Today,* Dec 1986, pp. 66-7). On the other hand, it is claimed that there is a strong, positive correlation between PRP for top executives and corporate performance (Kevin J. Murphy, "Top executives are worth every nickel they get", *Harvard Business Review,* Mar-Apr 1986, pp. 125-32). Although this debate is obviously relevant to our study, our principal argument is that if there is a PRP scheme in operation then it should give the desired signals. That is, if strategic performance is important it should be rewarded.

5 K. A. Merchant, *Rewarding Results: Effectively Motivating Profit Center Managers,* Harvard Business School Press, Boston, 1989. On the basis of extensive research and consultancy the author examines alternative forms of "contract" for profit centre managers, including contracts designed to reward long-term as well as short-term performance.

6 T. Peters, *Thriving on Chaos,* Alfred A. Knopf, New York, 1988, Section P-6.

7 A. Vernon-Harcourt, *Monks Guide to Cash Incentives for Management,* Monks Publications, 1985.

8 In many instances the level of stock options depends less on performance and more on the basic salary of the manager. This weakens their motivational force in the PRP scheme.

CONTROL UNDER DIFFERENT STRATEGIC MANAGEMENT STYLES

In *Strategies and Styles,*[1] Michael Goold and Andrew Campbell distinguished several management styles, or ways in which the corporate centre attempts to add value to the company's business units. The main styles discussed were labelled Strategic Planning, Strategic Control and Financial Control. The styles were defined in terms of the two primary ways in which the centre influences its business units: by helping to shape the plans of the businesses (planning influence) and through the control process (control influence). Figure A4.1 was used to show the nature of planning and control influence under the three styles.

In companies that follow the Strategic Planning style, the centre is involved and influential in the formulation of plans for the businesses, and stresses long-term objectives in the control process. These companies are more flexible about the achievement of short-term targets. Financial Control companies are highly decentralized in their approach to the planning of strategies, but exercise tight short-term financial control. Strategic Control companies fall between the other two styles. In terms

Figure A4.1 **Strategic Management Styles**

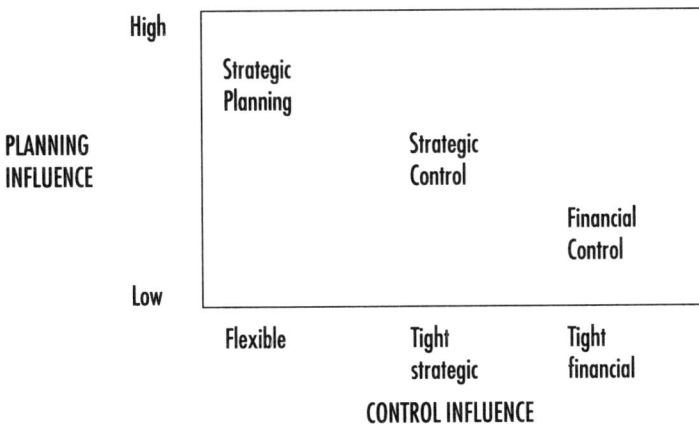

of planning influence, they are less decentralized than Financial Control companies, but less hands-on than Strategic Planning companies. In terms of control influence, they see the need for long-term, strategic objectives, but also place considerable emphasis on delivering short-term profit targets.

Strategies and Styles also identified a centralized style, in which central managers themselves make the major strategy decisions in their businesses. Only the day-to-day implementation of strategy is delegated to those at the business level. Since this style is less suitable for diversified, multi-business companies, it was not analysed in detail.

As a background to our discussion of strategic control processes in this book, it may be useful to draw out the control aspects of these styles rather more fully.

FINANCIAL CONTROL COMPANIES

Financial Control companies lie at one extreme of the control spectrum, since their control process relies almost entirely on budgeted profit targets. In the UK, the prime exponents of this management style are highly diversified companies such as BTR and Hanson. Tarmac, one of the UK's largest construction companies, also adopts the Financial Control style.

The Financial Control style is built upon two key assumptions about how to optimize the performance of a diverse portfolio of businesses.

1. Managers perform best if they have maximum freedom to run their own businesses without interference from the corporate centre, together with clear and stretching objectives for the results they must achieve.

2. Short-term profit represents the best possible measure of business performance, and should be used as the basis for a tight control process.

The first assumption follows from the belief that business heads know much more than the centre about their specific product-markets, and will be most highly motivated if they have autonomy to set and pursue their own strategies. Accordingly, they should be encouraged by the centre to make their own decisions without relying on corporate planning processes, coordination committees or central staffs for advice and support. But this freedom must be balanced by responsibility for delivering an agreed set of results. The centre's most essential role is therefore to ensure that clear objectives are established for each business; that these objectives are "owned" by the business, but are suitably ambitious or stretching; and that there are important rewards and incentives for achieving the objectives. Financial Control companies believe strongly in decentralizing both the responsibility for setting strategy and the accountability for results. They stress the importance of business-level autonomy balanced by tight control, and see the control process as by far the most important way for top management to add value to the businesses in their portfolio.

The second assumption – that short-term profit is the best measure of business performance – is more distinctive and controversial. But it is closely linked to the Financial Control companies' philosophy of decentralization, since short-term profit is seen as particularly suitable as a motivating objective for business heads. Short-term profit is an objective which:

- provides business managers with the fullest discretion on how it will be achieved; it is the ultimate "bottom-line" objective.
- can be measured with (reasonable) clarity and precision, in accordance with generally accepted accounting principles.
- will be reached (or missed) soon enough to provide powerful motivation for business heads and timely feedback for the corporate centre.

By contrast, objectives that are too detailed, or imprecise, or will be reached only in the distant future, are unsuitable as the basis for a motivating, stretching and tight control process.

Furthermore, Financial Control companies aim to operate in businesses where there are few trade-offs between short-term profits and long-term competitive position, and hence little need to invest now for a pay-off in the distant future. In such businesses it is positively desirable for the corporate centre to increase the focus on next year's profits, and on a year-on-year improvement in profits. Convinced advocates of the Financial Control style also claim that there are, in fact, very few businesses where strict short-term profit disciplines of this sort are not appropriate. As Sir Owen Green, Chairman of BTR, put it: "The view that you have to make investments with a vague view that you might get your money back in ten years is a cop out. As we have gained experience, we have not found it necessary to take these long-view investment decisions."

Financial Control companies regard short-term profit as the best objective for measuring performance and motivating management.

They reject the distinction between "financial" controls and "strategic" controls, arguing that profit should be the pre-eminent objective for business heads, since it represents the best single indicator of their stewardship in all dimensions.

CENTRALIZED COMPANIES

At the other extreme from the Financial Control style are companies in which senior central managers essentially drive and determine strategy themselves. Business units have an important role in day-to-day implementation of the decisions taken at the top, but they are not expected to play much part in shaping the strategy. This style of management is common in smaller companies and in firms with very strong chief executives (who are often the founders or majority owners of the company). The approach is also found in some large, but essentially single-business, companies; major retailers, such as Argyll or Sainsbury's, are often quite highly centralized in their management style.

In centralized companies, the issue of strategic control does not arise. Since business unit heads are not free to propose their own strategies, they cannot be held responsible for the overall results they achieve. If central managers set the strategy, they, rather than the business unit heads, must accept ultimate responsibility for results. The corporate control process therefore focuses on checking whether agreed decisions have been implemented, rather than trying to find a few key strategic performance measures by which to assess whether the business as a whole is on track. Detailed operating controls are established, but strategic controls, in the sense that we have used the term, are not appropriate.

In more centralized companies, profit remains an important goal for business heads. But it is seen primarily as a test of implementation effectiveness, reflecting the contribution that things such as cost control or good salesmanship can make, within the constraints of the strategy laid down by the centre.

STRATEGIC CONTROL COMPANIES

Strategic Control companies, such as ICI and Courtaulds, admire the clarity and simplicity of the Financial Control style and have much in common with its control philosophy. They share a basic belief in delegating strategy to the business unit, although the centre in Strategic

Control companies may provide some advice, questioning and support on major strategic issues that affect the long-term health of the business. Strategic Control companies also recognize the importance of motivating managers to deliver on an agreed set of objectives. Like Financial Control companies, therefore, they are keen to find a few clear measures of overall business performance, which will indicate how well individual businesses are performing, but will not compromise the freedom of the managers to run the businesses as they see fit.

In selecting performance measures, Strategic Control companies typically consider short-term profit the single most important indicator. But they recognize that profit is not the only or paramount goal, for in many of their businesses short-term profits may not reflect longer-term trends in competitive position. To control purely on the basis of short-term profits would provide the wrong motivation for the businesses and the wrong signals for top management. Strategic Control companies acknowledge the need to complement financial controls, based on short- term profit, with strategic controls that get at other indicators of competitive position.

In *Strategies and Styles,* the Strategic Control style was described as involving a "tight strategic control" process: that is, managers were held tightly to account, in terms of personal rewards and sanctions, for meeting both their strategic and their financial control targets. But it was recognized that several Strategic Control companies found difficulty in identifying good strategic control measures, and that, in practice, their tight strategic control processes were often confusing and ambiguous. In this book, we have confirmed that Strategic Control companies need to identify a small number of key strategic performance measures, and we have found some companies, particularly those with more formal strategic control processes, that succeed in doing so. We have also confirmed that they place considerable emphasis on meeting short-term profit targets, which may be linked quite tightly to personal rewards. But we have concluded that control against strategic targets is, in fact, very seldom tight. The distinctive features of the control processes of Strategic Control companies are, therefore:

- Identification of a small number of strategic targets or milestones to complement annual financial targets for profit and cash flow.
- Fairly tight links between short-term profit targets and personal rewards.
- Indirect links between strategic targets and personal rewards.

STRATEGIC PLANNING COMPANIES

Companies that adopt a Strategic Planning style (for example, Shell, National Westminster Bank and Digital) are less decentralized than either Financial Control or Strategic Control companies. Their basic assumption is that the business heads and the corporate centre should be jointly responsible for setting strategy. By bringing together the insights, experience and broader perspective of the centre and the detailed knowledge and ideas of the business, they expect to reach better decisions. But Strategic Planning companies accept that primary responsibility for proposing strategy and for day-to-day tactics and implementation should be delegated to the business unit. The centre will only slow down or impede decisions if it becomes too deeply involved.

In principle, Strategic Planning companies have less need for one, or a small number of "bottom-line" indicators of overall business performance. The centre is sufficiently closely involved in the businesses' strategies to be able to agree targets for a larger number of key objectives or action programmes. For Strategic Planning companies, profit targets are important, but not the only objectives that matter. When trade-offs must be made between short-term profit and long-term strategy, Strategic Planning companies are frequently willing to favour the long-term strategy. Because Strategic Planning companies tend to deal with a larger number of strategic objectives, profit targets are less prominent than in Strategic Control companies.

In *Strategies and Styles*, the control approach of Strategic Planning companies was described as "flexible strategic control". Our current research suggests that this description is generally appropriate. The strategic control process is important, and there is a need to identify objectives by which strategic progress can be monitored. However, the need for flexibility in interpreting achievements against planned objectives is recognized, and the link between these achievements and personal reward is indirect. The characteristic features of the control processes of Strategic Planning companies are, therefore:

- Identification of strategic targets or milestones to complement annual financial targets for profit and cash flow. Strategic Planning companies are typically willing to deal with a rather larger number of targets (10–15 per business per year) than Strategic Control companies (4–6 per business per year).
- Indirect links between strategic targets and personal rewards.

SUMMARY

Figure A4.2 summarizes the premises behind the control approaches of the four management styles we have discussed. Strategic controls are needed only under the Strategic Planning and Strategic Control management styles. The different ways of implementing strategic controls are fully described in Chapters 2–4 of this book.

In practice, of course, the four management styles are not rigidly distinct categories, but represent ranges along a continuous spectrum. Hence unequivocal classification of individual companies sometimes can be difficult. BP, for example, has some of the features of the Strategic Planning style and some of the Strategic Control style. Although it was once a relatively centralized company, it now delegates a great deal to its business streams (Exploration, Downstream Oil, Chemicals, Nutrition), providing more limited steering and coordination from the centre, and concentrating in the control process on measures of overall strategic performance rather than on more detailed issues. General Electric is another company whose management style has shifted towards the boundary between Strategic Planning and Strategic Control, this time from an initial position that was more decentralized. Moreover, management styles may vary from one level of a company to another (see Appendix

Figure A4.2 **The Control Approaches of the Four Management Styles**

Strategic management style	Responsibility for strategy	Need for measures of overall business performance	Importance of short-term profits in control process	Nature of controls
Centralized	Centrally Directed	Lowest	Important, but mainly as test of implementation effectiveness	Operating controls
Strategic Planning	Shared	Lower	Important, but part of a wider assessment	Strategic controls
Strategic Control	Delegated	High	High, but not paramount	Strategic controls
Financial Control	Highly delegated	Very high	Paramount	Profit controls

2). Our purpose, however, has been to describe the range of practice that exists, not to stick labels on individual companies. The difficulty of classifying companies simply reflects the variety and subtle shades of difference that prevail in practice.

We also found that a higher level of central involvement and influence in planning strategy does not always lead to the establishment of more numerous and detailed strategic control parameters. Most companies, whether they adopt a Strategic Planning or a Strategic Control approach to the formulation of strategy, see the motivational benefits to be gained from focusing on a comparatively small number of key control objectives. This means that, while the management philosophies of Strategic Planning and Strategic Control companies clearly differ in terms of the degree of influence and involvement of the central team in planning, the distinction is more blurred when it comes to strategic control. The most important distinction among companies' approaches to strategic control, we found, has to do with the formality and explicitness of the process they adopt, not their underlying management style.

Reference

1 Michael Goold and Andrew Campbell, *Strategies and Styles,* Basil Blackwell, Oxford, 1987.

Index